Horizons in Theory and American Culture
Bainard Cowan and Joseph G. Kronick, Editors

Facing *the* Other

Ethical Disruption *and the* American Mind

LINDA BOLTON

 Louisiana State University Press

Baton Rouge

Published by Louisiana State University Press
Copyright © 2004 by Louisiana State University Press
All rights reserved
Manufactured in the United States of America
Louisiana Paperback Edition, 2010

Designer: Barbara Neely Bourgoyne
Typeface: Whitman
Typesetter: Coghill Composition Co., Inc.

Library of Congress Cataloging-in-Publication Data

Bolton, Linda 1955–
    Facing the other : ethical disruption and the American mind / Linda Bolton.
        p. cm. — (Horizons in theory and American culture)
    Includes bibliographical references and index.
    ISBN 0-8071-2940-2 (cloth : alk. paper)
    1. United States—Politics and government—1775–1783—Sources.   2. United States—Politics and government—1783–1865—Sources.   3. Ethics—United States—History—Sources.   4. Political ethics—United States—History—Sources.   5. United States—Intellectual life—1783–1865—Sources.   6. Criticism, Textual.   7. Other (Philosophy).   8. Ethics in literature.   9. Liberty in Literature.   10. Justice in literature.   I. Title.   II. Series: Horizons in theory and American culture.
E302.1.B65   2004
172'.0973—dc22

                                                                            2003021388

ISBN-13: 978-0-8071-3646-1 (paper : alk. paper)

The paper in this book meets the guidelines for permanence and durability of the Committee on Production Guidelines for Book Longevity of the Council on Library Resources. ∞

For my first family:

Lorraine Williams Bolton
Dowling Martin Bolton
Reverend Martin E. Bolton
Rita W. Vaughan
John E. Vaughan
and
the magnificent Tipper Pie

Contents

Acknowledgments ix

Abbreviations xi

Introduction
Towards Confronting the "Hatred by the Other Human" 1

1 Facing Alterity
   The Ethics of Conversion in Crèvecoeur's *Letters from an American Farmer* 17

2 In the Name of "Justice and Humanity"
   Thomas Paine's Ethical Envisionings of the American Republic 54

3 Standing in the "Field of Freedom"
   Thomas Jefferson and the Reverberations of that Declaratory Promise 94

4 Fugitive Poseurs
   The Native Eloquence of Frederick Douglass and Sarah Winnemucca 124

5 In the Presence of the Great American Criminal
   John Brown's Triumphant Failure at Harpers Ferry 172

Bibliography 199

Index 205

Acknowledgments

I must first thank my exquisite teachers at the University of Arizona who guided and mentored me as I began this journey into ethics: Charles Sherry, Larry Evers, Susan Aiken, Charles Scruggs, and especially N. Scott Momaday and Joy Harjo, who taught me so well how to become a warrior in the name of justice. Finally, but not least, I want to thank John Kerr at the Kent School, who initially taught me to appreciate the beauty of language and the power of literature. I am grateful to each of you for the gift of your stunning generosity.

I thank my colleagues in the Department of English at the University of Iowa. Their unwavering support has grounded me in the completion of this project. I offer a special thanks to Tom Lutz, Tom Simmons, Kevin Kopelson, Miriam Gilbert, and Garrett Stewart for the inspiration they have given me in the crafting of this work. I am especially grateful to those whose intrinsic faith in me and my work has helped to carry me across the tough bridges along this journey. I am deeply indebted to Brooks Landon, Dee Morris, Alvin Snider, and, most of all, Ed Folsom. In true Levinasian spirit, you have stood beside and behind me in each moment that I needed you. I am also genuinely grateful to Tom Gannon, whose tireless efforts as my research assistant over the past five years have been unbelievably generous and unspeakably valuable.

I want to thank the family of friends who have loved me well through this journey of challenges and the sweet victories of healing: Barbara Meredith, Kate Vandemoer, Barbara Grygutis, Maja-Lisa Von Snydern, Barbara Welch Breder, Margaret Bass, the late Audrey Qualls, Natasa Durovicova, Susie Phillips, Bob Braverman, Marilyn Dispensa, Julie Moffitt, Deb Pearson, and especially Dianne Finnerty and Jill Jack—and not least, Howard I. Weinberg and Sue Fuortes, for walking me home. There is a special debt of gratitude that I owe to Alberta Owens Richardson, Gayle Sand, and Chandra D. Cox, my sisters in heart and spirit. Your love, faith, and embrace have saved me more times than you can know. I love you dearly.

My gratitude also goes to John Easterly, Gerry Anders, and Lee Campbell Sioles of the editorial staff at Louisiana State University Press, and especially to Joseph Kronick of LSU, for his support of this project several years ago and his wise guidance in the later revisions of the manuscript. I also want to thank Alisa Plant for her mindful and meticulous work in the editing of the book.

Finally, I want to honor the many amazing students who have graced my life and inspired me during my tenure at the University of Iowa, especially Dean Williams, Ryan O'Connor, Megan Newell, Paul Aumer-Ryan, and Erin McGee. As Levinas has taught me, I know in my heart that it is you who continue to be my very best teachers. I am forever grateful.

ABBREVIATIONS

ColW   Thomas Paine, *Collected Writings*. Ed. Eric Foner. New York: Library of America, 1995.

CW   Thomas Paine, *The Complete Writings of Thomas Paine*. Comp. Philip S. Foner. New York: Citadel, 1945.

EN   Emmanuel Levinas, *Entre Nous*. Trans. Michael B. Smith and Barbara Harshav. New York: Columbia University Press, 1998.

FP   Gerald Vizenor, *Fugitive Poses*. Lincoln: University of Nebraska Press, 1998.

LAF   J. Hector St. John de Crèvecoeur, *Letters from an American Farmer*. New York: Dutton, 1957.

OG   Emmanuel Levinas, *Of God Who Comes to Mind*. Trans. Bettina Bergo. Stanford: Stanford University Press, 1998.

PLB   Stephen B. Oates, *To Purge This Land with Blood*. Amherst: University of Massachusetts Press, 1984.

TI   Emmanuel Levinas, *Totality and Infinity*. Trans. Alphonso Lingis. Pittsburgh: Duquesne University Press, 1969.

Facing *the* Other

INTRODUCTION
Towards Confronting the "Hatred by the Other Human"

A year before his death, Thomas Jefferson reflected upon the meaning of the Declaration of Independence he had drafted a half-century earlier. The real purpose or "object" of the Declaration, Jefferson stated, was "not to find out new principles, or new arguments, never before thought of, not merely to say things which had never been said before; but to place before mankind the common sense of the subject, in terms as plain and firm as to command their assent, and to justify ourselves in the independent stand we are compelled to take. Neither aiming at originality of principle or sentiment, nor yet copied from any particular and previous writing, it was intended to be an expression of the American mind."[1]

The subtitle of my book, *Ethical Disruption and the American Mind*, is indebted to and echoes Jefferson's prophetic words. In declaring his text an "expression of the American mind," Jefferson was among the first to cast the Declaration as a sacred document in a new territorial landscape: one that had not merely called into being a new era in political existence, but, equally important, one that simultaneously signified the philosophical *weltanschauung* of a newly constituted republic of citizens who were committed to the ideal of freedom.

Yet during the time in which Jefferson was himself a participant in the process of drafting the Declaration, there were 175 human beings of African blood in his legal possession. Here, at the dawn of the American experiment, is the presence of the Other human whose rights to freedom are categorically denied through the laws of enslavement. This Other is already deprived of

---

1. Thomas Jefferson, "Letter to Henry Lee," *The Life and Selected Writings of Thomas Jefferson*, ed. Adrienne Koch and William Peden (New York: Random House, 1972), 719.

the Declaration's explicit promises of freedom. And because the African exists, albeit repressed within the dark recesses of the newly formed republic, the disruptive challenge of ethics lies hidden at the very core of the American commitment to a democracy predicated upon the rights of man. If, as Jefferson proclaimed, the Declaration signified the unqualified existence of an "American mind," that mind would soon commit itself to the constitution of its particular freedom, even as it denied the very same right of liberty to the Other whose presence it refused to recognize. When viewed from an ethical perspective, Jefferson's celebratory veneration of the Declaration of Independence signals the triumph of the "I" purchased at the cost of the Other's persecution. From that perspective, the Declaration is a text that celebrates freedom in the absence of justice. Indeed, it is only when we consider the ethical, as opposed to the political, issues framed by the Declaration that we can understand the importance and implications of this absence.

Jefferson's reflection on the Declaration serves as my point of entry into a series of ethical dialogues that revisit six resonant moments in the historical archive of American letters. These moments center upon the writing and lives of J. Hector St. John de Crèvecoeur, Thomas Paine, Thomas Jefferson, Frederick Douglass, Sarah Winnemucca, and John Brown. Rather than aiming to revise or enlarge the historical record, I will interrogate the existing archive and its body of critical interpretations that continue to inform our cultural understanding of a history that is specifically American. Focusing on six textual and performative moments during the eighteenth and nineteenth centuries, I will revisit and reenvision those historical encounters through the language and from the perspective of ethics. Each of the six events considered here is an inherently disruptive moment—one in which the challenge of ethics in the form of the Other (as the African and Native presence) serves to disrupt the prevailing American discourse on freedom, as well as the ontological, subject-centered bias of its philosophical underpinnings. My book challenges the American valorization of freedom by focusing on moments in our literary and historical past when the ideal of freedom ran headlong into the ideal of justice. What happens when freedom eclipses justice, when freedom breeds injustice?

In its attempt to answer such questions, this study builds on the philosophical legacy of Emmanuel Levinas. Born in 1906 of Lithuanian and Jewish parents, Levinas became the preeminent twentieth-century philosopher of ethics. His work challenges the primacy of the ideal of freedom and asserts the primordial inviolability of the obligation to the Other. A French citizen and a distinguished student and interpreter of Heidegger, in the 1930s Levinas was captured by the Nazis and imprisoned in a Jewish labor camp. While his wife and daughter found refuge in France, Levinas's brothers and parents were murdered during the genocidal reign of Nazi totalitarianism. During Levinas's internment, he began work on his first full-length study, *Existence and Existents* (published in 1947), in which he embarked upon his critique of the ontological foundations of Continental philosophy. He began to achieve recognition as an original thinker in 1951, upon the publication of his essay, "Is Ontology Fundamental?"—a provocative critique of Heidegger that gained the respect of the postwar community of prominent existential philosophers, including Marcel, Sartre, and Camus. But Levinas's philosophical originality gained renown only after the publication of his pivotal *Totality and Infinity* in 1961, which numerous critics have heralded as a "revolutionary" text, citing its bold critique of phenomenology as well as its challenge to the entire history of European philosophy.[2]

One particularly eloquent reader of Levinas's philosophical legacy has been Adriaan Theodoor Peperzak. Peperzak's *To the Other: An Introduction to the Philosophy of Emmanuel Levinas* and *Beyond: The Philosophy of Emmanuel Levinas* are immensely important works that have brought Levinasian thought to the forefront of contemporary philosophical debate. Without dispute, one of Peperzak's greatest strengths has been his ability to investigate and illuminate difficult Levinasian concepts through a language that makes their intrinsic complexity far more accessible to a reader unacquainted with the rigorous and evolutionary nature of Levinas's thought. In order to help clarify some of the key aspects of Levinasian ethics, I draw upon Peperzak's analyses in the sections that follow.[3]

In *Totality and Infinity*, Levinas more fully develops his arguments against a western philosophical tradition ruled by what Peperzak terms a "desire for totalization," a tradition historically persistent in its attempts "to reduce the

---

2. Emmanuel Levinas, *Existence and Existents*, trans. Alphonso Lingis (The Hague: M. Nijhoff, 1978); Levinas, "Is Ontology Fundamental?" in *Basic Philosophical Writings* (Bloomington: Indiana University Press, 1996).

3. Adriaan T. Peperzak, *Beyond: The Philosophy of Emmanuel Levinas* (Evanston, Ill.: Northwestern University Press, 1997); Peperzak, *To the Other* (West Lafayette, Ind.: Purdue University Press, 1993). These works will hereinafter be cited parenthetically by page number in the text as *Other* and *Beyond*.

universe to an originary and ultimate unity by way of panoramic overviews and dialectical syntheses." But *Totality and Infinity*, as Peperzak notes, also announces the priority of Levinas's emphasis upon the Other. In arguing that the "human and the divine Other cannot be reduced to a totality of which they would only be elements" (*Beyond*, 4), Levinas radically challenges the traditional conception of the Subject as the I, for whom the world of experience and encounter constitute a panoramic totality of being. In establishing the transcendent presence of the Other as the face whose presence cannot be contained within the reality of the Subject's totality of experience, Levinas fundamentally redefines the Other as that essential entity in being whose presence cannot be represented through an ontological framework—precisely because that framework neutralizes the Other's otherness. In short, the Levinasian Other asserts the unique being of the individual whose difference validates—not negates—her presence as an existent in the world.

Totality and Infinity ultimately asserts the necessity of an ethical reorientation in Western thought. As Peperzak clarifies, Levinas argues that to "encounter another is to discover that I am under a basic obligation: the human Other's infinity reveals itself as a command: the fact of the Other's 'epiphany' reveals that I am his or her servant" (*Beyond*, 5). In the preface to *Totality and Infinity*, Levinas refutes and rejects the classic Western philosophical perspective through a succinct yet radical reflection upon the nature of violence. Real violence, Levinas proposes, "does not consist so much in injuring and annihilating persons as in interrupting their continuity, making them play roles in which they no longer recognize themselves, making them betray not only commitments but their own substance, making them carry out actions that will destroy every possibility for action" (*TI*, 21). This imposed "betrayal," for Levinas, becomes the basis of war, but its context is ethical rather than ontological or overtly political. And it is precisely in this context that the imperatives of ethical philosophy justify a reconsideration of our distinctly American historical experience.

Throughout this book, I will draw upon the perspective of Levinasian ethics to critique the ideal of freedom as it was constructed in documents of the new republic and as it is popularly (mis)understood today. My critique will reveal the American propensities to subscribe to a philosophy of autonomy and power that "presupposes that freedom itself is sure of its right, is justified without recourse to anything further."[4] The philosophy of freedom, as this study investigates it, is grounded in an ontological orientation through which the Ego, as the I, encounters the Other as an object or obstacle whose very alterity (as her absolute and uniquely foreign otherness) must be "integrated into the identity of the Same." Insofar as the American philosophy of freedom involves the negation of the Other's alterity, it becomes a philosophy of power—one that "makes of [the Other] its theme, and then its property, its booty, its prey, or its victim" (*Other*, 109), as if the Other were not already suffering in the world. But the Other, as Levinas has demonstrated, is already living and breathing in the landscape in which the legitimate American subject seeks the realization of his freedom. The presence of the Other—and most noticeably in the American setting, the African and Native face—can thus initiate the dialogue of critique that "calls into question the exercise of the same" (*TI*, 43).

This Levinasian concept of the "exercise of the same" is a critical one, for it is there that Levinas distinguishes between the relationship with an Other that originates in the desire for knowledge and the relationship that is potentially ethical. Knowledge, Levinas argues, is motivated by the desire for comprehension: other beings (as existents) in the world are approached by the I whose sovereign powers of cognition seek to neutralize that other, to render its foreignness, as an alterity, intelligible. It is as if the Other, revealed as an existent in the world, is suddenly subject to the light of reason, and the I who has encountered this other will not permit itself to be alienated or altered by this other's presence. The Other, however, through its very appearance and its mysterious presence within the horizon of sight, is suddenly categorized: "that is, taking its place in the light—is precisely his reduction to the same," because the Other's alterity is here "somehow betrayed." Now—as if caught by surprise—this other "appears, lays itself open to grasp," and through the intervention of cognition, she becomes, for the investigating I, not an absolute alterity, but rather a "concept" (*TI*, 43). In other words, when the I approaches the Other as an object (or oddity) in the world, it is the Other's difference that the I desires to understand. As long as that fundamental mystery of difference can be explained, then the Other's purpose (or

---

4. Emmanuel Levinas, "Philosophy and the Idea of the Infinite," reproduced in Peperzak, *Other*, 94.

place) in the I's experience of reality is definable. It is this desire for knowledge that turns Native Americans into Indians and thus enables their symbolic construction as an obstacle in the European American's quest for settlement.

But the moment that an existent is constituted as a "concept," its original alterity is negated, for it is now subsumed under the province of the subject's primacy of knowledge. This is the manner of encounter—mediated by reason and subject to the categories of understanding—that Levinas designates as the "exercise of the same." It is the reduction of a full, complex, and distinct being to an idea, a diminished person subdued under the subject's control.

Levinas traces this notion of the "exercise of the same" to the Socratic conceptualization of freedom, which he characterizes as the desire "to receive nothing of the Other but what is in me, as though from all eternity I was in possession of what comes to me from the outside—to receive nothing or to be free." Freedom and cognition are thus inextricably linked—"sovereign reason knows only itself" and "nothing other limits it" (*TI*, 43). This means that the relationship between the I and the Other is constructed through domination, not obligation—for one is ultimately not obligated to objects. Once again, this is the ontological bias towards Being, where the intent of the I is to neutralize the "existent in order to comprehend or grasp it." To "grasp" the Other as an existent open to comprehension is, in the end, "not a relation with the other as such but the reduction of the other to the same" (*TI*, 46).

The ethical relationship, however, is enacted as a critique. It is first a relationship with an existent that "refuses to give itself," to surrender itself under the light of intelligibility. Its presence as Being thus challenges the sovereignty—and hence the freedom—of the I. Through this refusal of surrender, the absolute alterity of the Other is maintained; rather than "question oneself concerning him"—which would require his surrender as an object—"one questions him" (*TI*, 47). This is the encounter with an Other whose presence defies my comprehension, who now faces me in the light of his authority, and "who arises behind the theme in which he is presented." To encounter him is not to encounter or even "to think an object," but to confront an interlocutor. In such a meeting, "I cannot disentangle myself from society with the Other, even when I consider the Being of the existent he is" (*TI*, 47). I cannot "disentangle myself" because the "way in which the other presents himself, *exceeding the idea of the other in me*, we here name face" (*TI*, 50). This concept of the "face"—and the event of "facing"—appears frequently in my study, as it helps to elucidate the originary encounter between human beings, however different their individual identities. Most importantly, the event of facing opens the possibility for an ethical relationship.

In the language of Levinas, this meeting with the face of the Other is the essence of ethics. Only the face of the Other can wholly exceed my powers of comprehension and thereby disrupt my spontaneity in freedom:

> We name this calling into question of my spontaneity by the presence of the Other ethics: The strangeness of the Other, his irreducibility to the I, to my thoughts and my possessions, is precisely accomplished as a calling into question of my spontaneity, as ethics. Metaphysics, transcendence, the welcoming of the other by the same, of the Other by me, is concretely produced as the calling into question of the same by the other, that is, as the ethics that accomplishes the critical essence of knowledge. And as critique precedes dogmatism, metaphysics precedes ontology. (*TI*, 43)

Ultimately, Levinas insists that to face the Other, whose alterity surpasses every idea of his otherness in me, is "to have the idea of infinity." As *Totality and Infinity* argues, it is solely the idea of infinity in which "its *ideatum* surpasses its idea"—meaning that "we could conceivably have accounted for all the ideas," realities, and things, "other than that of Infinity, by ourselves" (*TI*, 49). In this context, if the face of the Other fulfills the possibility of an "*ideatum*" that "surpasses its idea," it would be only the Other who could call into question the "exercise of the same." From a Levinasian perspective, the command of ethics necessarily disrupts the ontological prerogative, for "infinity, overflowing the idea of infinity, puts the spontaneous freedom within us into question" (*TI*, 51).

Not only does the Other face us as "face"; she brings into the world (and into the I's experience in it) a "notion of meaning prior to my *Sinngebung*" (my sense of linguistic expression and representation), and thus she reveals herself as "independent of my initiative and my power" (*TI*, 51). This is the foundation of her power of critique. In the American landscape, in which the identity of the I is conceptually European, it is solely the face of the Indian and African Other that arises to contest the unrestricted privileges of freedom and to demand that freedom answer to justice. My study will focus on six important instances in which the face of the Indian and the African disrupt the discourse on freedom to demand this ethical accountability.

> The hard decision had to be made that this people should be caused to disappear from the earth. . . . Perhaps, at a much later time, we can consider whether we should say something more about this to the German people. I myself believe that it is better for us—us together—to have borne this for our people, that we have taken the responsibility for it on ourselves (the responsibility for an act, not just an idea), and that we should now take this secret with us into the grave. (Heinrich Himmler, secret address to SS officers, Poznan, June 10, 1943)[5]

In the dedication of his second major work, *Otherwise than Being; or, Beyond Essence,* Levinas writes, "To the memory of those who were closest among the six million assassinated by the National Socialists, and of the millions on millions of all confessions and all nations, victims of the same hatred by the other man, the same anti-Semitism."[6] Peperzak argues that Levinas's intention is to establish an equivalence between the genocidal persecution of the Eastern European Jew and the historical record of hatred "which is not limited to a particular nation, race, ideology, practice, or faith; it is hatred of the human, of humanity as such," and it "is the root of any form of antihumanism" (*Beyond,* 74).

Peperzak further insists that the "victims of this hatred, be they Jews, gypsies, blacks, or Vietnamese, symbolize humanity as such: they are hostages, subjected to suffering and persecution, humiliation and death" (*Beyond,* 74). At stake here is the critical relevance of Levinasian philosophy for the rereading of the American archive that I undertake in this study. For Levinas, "hatred of the human" lies at the very origins of evil and injustice. If we are willing to recognize that injustice as it found expression in the Holocaust, then we become obligated to recognize anti-Semitism as emblematic of an antihumanism that has permitted the persecution of the Other in diverse cultural and historical moments. To employ a Levinasian perspective in revisiting the American historical legacy enables us not merely to reengage the facts of that history, but to investigate the philosophical tradition in which it is grounded.

When Levinas dedicates *Otherwise than Being* to the "millions upon mil-

---

5. Quoted in Beryl Lang, *Act and Idea of the Nazi Genocide* (Chicago: University of Chicago Press, 1990), 3.

6. Emmanuel Levinas, *Otherwise than Being; or, Beyond Essence,* trans. Alphonso Lingis (Boston: M. Nijhoff, 1981), n.p.

lions of all confessions and all nations," he compels us, as participants in an evolving history of humankind, to recognize that anti-Semitism is an antihumanism that transcends the Nazi atrocities, one that existed prior to its irruption in Hitler's National Socialist regime. In the American landscape, the enslavement of Africans and the near extermination of Indians constitute an equivalent antihumanism. In Peperzak's terms, this "hatred of the other human" originates in a "specific way of relating to the world, others, society, history, oneself, and Being as such; a way of relating expressed in Western civilization" and its philosophical orientation (*Beyond*, 74).

One of the foundational tenets of Levinasian ethics is its critique of the privilege of freedom, which is evidenced through its refutation of the classical relation between the I and the Other. In the early pages of *Totality and Infinity*, Levinas defines the traditional subject of Western philosophy as an Ego, or I, whose integrity in being is grounded in its sense of self, as identity, as the "content" of its essence. But the I, Levinas qualifies, "is not a being that always remains the same, but is the being whose existing consists in identifying itself, in recovering its identity throughout all that happens to it." In this sense, the I "is the primal identity, the primordial work of identification" (*TI*, 36). Yet, as we know, the I exists in a world of experience and encounter that constantly challenges its integrity of identity; indeed, the world is first experienced as foreign and hostile—as an "other" against which the I must recover its essence of identity. But the foreignness of the world is eventually revealed as discoverable; its otherness lends itself to the possibility of intelligibility and conquest.

Levinas names this process of integration, through which the otherness of the world is mediated and converted into the experience of the subject, the "way of the same." In a world in which the I can exert its powers of possession, the foreignness or otherness of the world is neutralized, and the integrity of the I reemerges in the knowledge of its mastery. This is the essence of the meaning of freedom, Levinas argues: the ability of the subject to maintain its integrity of identity "against the other, despite every relation with the other to ensure the autarchy of an I" (*TI*, 46). This relationship to the other underlies Levinas's critique of ontological philosophy.

Also present in the world that the I engages is an other whose presence in being either resists the possibility of possession or whose otherness exceeds mediation through the mastery of the I. This is a different entity in otherness, however—one best defined through the language of an absolute alterity that defies, in formal terms, the unity of sameness or the totality of meaning in which the subject dwells. This is the Levinasian Other: "The absolutely other is the Other" as Other, she is the "Stranger who disturbs the being at home with oneself" (*TI*, 39). In the language of Levinas, the encounter between the I and the Other is the disruptive intervention of the face: this Other "at each moment destroys and overflows the plastic image it leaves me" (*TI*, 51). Through its very expression, the Other not only resists my powers of possession but calls into question the very essence of privilege that constitutes my reality in freedom. This calling into question of the subject's assumptions of freedom distinguishes Levinasian ethics. In the experience of facing the Other, the I encounters not an object, but a Stranger who is also free, and whose intrusion upon its world interrupts the spontaneity and scope of its powers.

One of the difficulties of a study that rereads American history through the perspective of Levinasian ethics is the necessary inclusion of a terminology unique to that philosophical vision. While my book engages many of the concepts that distinguish Levinasian ethics, it does not seek merely to translate the American past into the often difficult and sometimes cumbersome language that characterizes ethical philosophy. And while it is true, as Peperzak suggests, that some "interpreters think that Levinas's work only translates old convictions into a phenomenological or quasi-phenomenological jargon, without adding anything important to the actual practice of philosophy" (*Beyond*, 17), such a reading tends to minimize the radical intervention that Levinas's ethical vision imposes upon the Western literary and philosophical tradition.

When Levinas critiques the sovereignty of the traditional subject, his work goes against the grain of a philosophical tradition that has historically regarded ethics as a secondary imperative—one dependent upon the volition of the subject, whose encounter with the world is constituted through his construction of a narrative of history that is based upon his experience and his powers of cognition. In that context, Levinasian ethics must be understood as fundamentally disruptive, demanding a rethinking and reinterpretation of the history of Western ontology. Western thought has tended to misrepresent the relationship between its subject and the Other's existence. As Peperzak explains, "If I reduce the Other to an interesting topic for my observation or reflection, I am blind to the claim that is constitutive of the

Other's coming to the fore" (*Beyond*, 34). That "blindness" surrenders justice to the prerogative of the subject.

This is the intrinsic failure that Levinas underscores when he names the ontological tradition as an "egology," for insofar as ontology renders the other an object of reflection, it can also subsume the human Other in the "same," neutralizing her difference and subverting the possibility of an obligation that precedes (and exceeds) the subject's freedom. When Levinas asserts that "*Being* before the *existent,* ontology before metaphysics, is freedom (be it the freedom of theory) before justice" (*TI,* 47), his words highlight the ethical problem that characterizes the traditional relationship between subjectivity and alterity. When the ideal of freedom precedes the notion of an obligation to otherness, it is potentially guilty of sanctioning the other's destruction or murder. As Levinas argues, "Ontology as first philosophy is a philosophy of power"; as such, "Ontology is, as first philosophy which does not call into question the same, a philosophy of injustice" (*TI,* 46). In this respect, power—"by essence murderous of the other"—constitutes freedom precisely as if the Other were yet another entity in the world that is open to possession. And while the desire for possession may affirm and acknowledge the other's presence, it does so "within a negation of its independence: 'I think' comes down to 'I can.'" Freedom, and hence power, are revealed to be an "appropriation of what is, to an exploitation of reality" (*TI,* 46). From the viewpoint of ethics, this is a "movement within the same before obligation to the other" (*TI,* 47).

Here, then, are two of the more radical insights that have influenced my turn to Levinasian ethics as a perspectival foundation for rereading selected texts that illuminate pivotal moments in American history. First, Levinasian ethics prioritizes the existence of the Other, rejecting the possibility that the other human being can be converted into "booty" or dismissed from the landscape in which the ego dwells. When Levinas critiques the ontological tradition, he does so not to invalidate a philosophical history that has made the pursuit of knowledge and freedom achievable ideals, but to command us to confront the fact that freedom is a privilege, not a license to commit murder. Levinasian ethics reminds us that the world is not an uninhabited site for our unfettered enjoyment. Living beside us is the Other, whose right to freedom not only equals ours, but—as Levinas insists—precedes ours. Levinasian ethics does not aspire to negate the subject, the I, nor to impoverish his freedom; rather, it asks that the I be accountable for the ways (and manner) in which his freedom is exercised in a world where Others already exist.

If we return to the words of Heinrich Himmler that opened this section, we bear conscious witness to the extreme violence that unrestricted freedom can permit. For Himmler, as for many people in Hitler's Germany, the Jew existed as an obstacle: one whose very presence was deemed unnecessary, expendable, and, most importantly, conquerable through the exercise of right and force. The atrocities of the Nazi genocide continue to haunt us, and rightfully so. The possibility and reality of the Nazis' crimes were ineluctably tied to a philosophy of freedom that negated the Other's priority, the Other's face. Here, Levinasian ethics powerfully illustrates how the ideal of freedom—in itself, a worthy and rightful human cause—can betray the commands of justice. The command that establishes justice also requires the accountability of a free subject, as the I, for whom the fact and face of the Other interrupts the world of unlimited choice to impose the limits of freedom. The imperative of justice occurs when "power, by essence murderous of the other, becomes, faced with the other and 'against all good sense,'" recognizes the "impossibility of murder" as precisely the "consideration of the other, or justice" (*TI*, 47). The reality of a power that refuses this "consideration of the other" and then negates the "impossibility of [her] murder" is the ethical horror that lingers in our remembrance of the Nazi Holocaust.

When Levinas prioritizes the existence of the Other, his philosophical vision is inclusive: it reveals the Other as a transcendent presence, a presence whose being exceeds her representation through the nomenclature of "slave" and "Indian." Despite its linguistic persistence in the American lexicon, we must remember that "*Indian* is a simulation and loan word of dominance,"[7] and as such, its connotation and denotation mark the absence of the Native face and fail to register its reality as existent. Not only does Levinas assert the presence of the Other, he argues that she exists before my arrival in consciousness, before the I realizes the panorama of possibilities that might constitute the boundaries of my enjoyment. Yet from the moment in which the Other faces me, she exists outside the narrative of history. If only the face of the Other can call the "exercise of the same" into question, as an existent irreducible to the language of ideas, she becomes the disruptive entity to whom and before whom even the narratives of history are accountable. As

---

7. Gerald Vizenor, *Fugitive Poses* (Lincoln: University of Nebraska Press, 1998), 14.

Levinas writes, "To say that the other can remain absolutely other . . . is to say that history itself, an identification of the same, cannot claim to totalize the same and the other" (*TI*, 40).

Thus, the American patriot or the soldier in Hitler's army is not called to question or contest the privileges of his freedom—it is not the "I who resist[s] the system . . . it is the other" (*TI*, 40). Solely the face of the Other, in expression and in speech, can "thereby invite me" into the relationship that is specifically ethical. In the face of the Other resonates the "primordial expression" that is the "first word" of ethics: "You shall not commit murder" in the pursuit of your own rights to freedom (*TI*, 199). In this respect, the face of the other "brings us to a notion of meaning" prior to and independent of my claim to freedom. This ethical relationship "signifies the philosophical priority of the existent over Being"—since to face the Other is to recognize an "exteriority that is not reducible . . . to the interiority of memory" (*TI*, 51), nor to the narrative of history that the subject constructs. Indeed, as Levinas maintains, "When man truly approaches the Other he is uprooted from history" (*TI*, 52).

The second distinctly radical insight that Levinasian ethics imposes upon the Western philosophical tradition resides in its assertion that the privilege of freedom must be mediated by the command for justice. Justice, seen in a Levinasian perspective, is not simply one of the possibilities that exists in the panorama of free choice; it is a responsibility already in place. Since the Levinasian ethical relationship begins in the act of facing, not only is the Other already in the world with me, but it is precisely because she faces me that I am suddenly made accountable in her presence. Because that Other is there, looking back, it is her presence—and the possibility of her death—that calls me to answer to a responsibility beyond my privilege, even if it is one that I have neither anticipated nor specifically chosen. In other words, for Levinas, the command for justice necessarily precedes the enjoyment of freedom. Regardless of the rightful privileges that freedom, as an ideal, ordains and ensures for the human subject, it cannot permit, ignore, or condone the persecution of the Other as a justifiable consequence of one's existence. Here again, Levinasian ethics compels us, as free and conscious agents, to be accountable: not only to concede the Other's presence, but to welcome it (despite the inconvenient, if not disruptive, intrusion of her alterity), and to craft a human community in which her suffering is not permissible.

When the Other looks at me, when she speaks to me, I am compelled to acknowledge her address, and thus her transcendence beyond the realm of objectivity and the economy of objects. This is what Levinas suggests when he argues that the "other qua other is the Other," and that to "'let him be' the relationship of discourse is required" (*TI*, 71). As a social relation founded in language, justice "consists in recognizing in the Other my master." As Levinas argues, "Equality among persons means nothing of itself," for "it has an economic meaning and presupposes money." Justice, however, "begins with the Other." Through my "recognition of his privilege qua Other and his mastery" (*TI*, 72), I begin to imagine a language that might enable me to come to embrace this Other, whose difference first strikes me as threatening. The language linking me to the Other is what opens the possibility for justice: to "speak is to make the world common." Language thus "abolishes the inalienable property of enjoyment" (*TI*, 76).

This Levinasian concept of justice is pivotal to my study. While the possibility of justice always originates in the face-to-face encounter with the Other, in the end justice is not a relation between two human beings, an I who faces an Other. The aspiration towards justice is rooted in a social relationship that includes those whom Levinas names "the third party." The presence of "the third" is essential to the possibility of justice. Only in recognition of "the third" does the responsibility of the I transcend the realm of intimacy to enter into the universal order in which justice might prevail. As Peperzak explains, "The third is the one who, with and already in the primary Other, concerns me like the Other. The fact that I cannot get to know everyone and that most people stay nameless for me cannot degrade them into a secondary species of human beings" (*Beyond*, 127).

Of critical importance here is the fact that justice is not the result (nor the province) of intimacy—despite our relation to Others with whom we choose to respond responsibly or before whom we decide to act with accountability. The third party, as Levinasian ethics reminds us, is the Other to whom I have not chosen to obligate myself. She is the Other who stands invisibly beside and behind the Other whose face I have learned to recognize and whom I may be willing to admit into the narrative of history where the rule of "sameness" prevails.

But the ethics of justice are intrinsically impartial: the "society that arises from the universality of the third is a community of rights and interests where the relations of love and intimacy are submitted to an impartial justice." This, Peperzak contends, is a justice that must impose "limits on the demands and desires of those who would like to dedicate themselves unreservedly to a restricted number of others" (*Beyond*, 128). Here, the turn to a Levinasian perspective greatly impinges upon our comprehension of history and the legacies of responsibility that haunt our collective memory. The anonymous body of the African and the faceless Stranger named "Indian" constitute the third party in an American republic committed to the ideal of freedom. While Frederick Douglass and Sarah Winnemucca succeed—in differing ways—in overcoming their initial subjugation to an economy that regulates property and objects, it is the multitude of all those who stood (and stand) beside and behind them to whom justice must finally answer.

The six literary and performative moments in eighteenth- and nineteenth-century American history that make up this book are instances when the challenge of ethics—brought to the fore through the face of the Other—disrupts the republic's veneration of the ideal of freedom. I read each of these six moments as disruptive events—moments in which the Other's presence achieves a unique distinction. Each of these moments reverberates in the Levinasian challenge, where the "Other imposes himself as an exigency that dominates this freedom" and thereby "invites" the American subject into the discourse that makes justice a real possibility (*TI*, 87).

I will investigate two differing textual modes of interaction: the literary and the performative. The first three chapters explore the promises of freedom, prosperity, and happiness as expressed in classic American texts: J. Hector St. John de Crèvecoeur's *Letters from an American Farmer*, Thomas Paine's *Common Sense* and *Rights of Man*, Thomas Jefferson's *Notes on the State of Virginia*—arguably, as Roy Harvey Pearce suggests, the first articulation of an "American idea of savagism"[8]—and the Declaration of Independence. These works have been exhaustively mined in the annals of literary criticism, but I employ a Levinasian perspective in order to focus upon specific, charged moments in those texts, where an attention to ethical philosophy necessarily complicates their larger meaning. The final two chapters engage three performative legacies—verbal, visual, and violent actions that extend beyond the act of writing—in the late nineteenth century: Frederick Douglass's transnational abolitionist oratory, Native activist Sarah Winne-

---

8. Roy Harvey Pearce, *Savagism and Civilization* (Berkeley: University of California Press, 1988).

mucca's unprecedented emergence in American theater and photography, and John Brown's legendary attack at Harpers Ferry.

Facing the Other crosses traditional boundaries between literary criticism, philosophy, and history. The challenge of ethics as a perspectival foundation for reengaging the past also transcends boundaries, for the presence of the Other is not (and cannot be) contained within a single perspective restricted by history, genre, or discipline. And while *Facing the Other* is a series of studies rooted in the experiences of the past, these studies are invested in the assertion that the "past, even if it is not (or ever will be) 'settled,' weighs continuously on the present, whether as writing or as being written about."[9] Even the Other's death that precedes our time raises important questions about the conception of time itself, as well as about the relationship between the past and the future. If, as Levinas argues, the "Other concerns me as a neighbor," then "in every death is shown the nearness of the neighbor, and the responsibility of the survivor."[10]

Writing as a "survivor" of the unjust persecution of the African and Indian Other, I base *Facing the Other* on the conviction that the "most pressing concerns of ethics originate and conclude in the particularity of historical events and in the particularity of the agents involved in them."[11] It is in the spirit of this possibility—in which ethics is essentially invested—that the discussions that follow are conceived.

9. Lang, *Act and Idea*, xxii.
10. Emmanuel Levinas, *God, Death, and Time*, trans. Bettina Bergo (Stanford: Stanford University Press, 2000), 17.
11. Lang, *Act and Idea*, xxii.

1   FACING ALTERITY
    The Ethics of Conversion in Crèvecoeur's *Letters from an American Farmer*

In September 1759, Michel-Guillaume-Jean de Crèvecoeur, having resigned his commission as a second lieutenant in the French Canadian militia, arrived in New York City. Although born in France, Crèvecoeur had been a resident of England before his initial emigration to Canada. It was in America, however, that he would realize the promise of distinction that had previously eluded him. Upon his arrival in New York, Crèvecoeur reinvented himself as "J. Hector St. John"—surveyor, merchant, farmer, and eventually, as A. W. Plumstead suggests, "one of the most admired literary men of his epoch." Purchasing 120 acres of virgin land near Chester, New York, Crèvecoeur devoted the following six years of his life to the discovery of "what it is to be an American farmer—to be free to enjoy a life he could create himself."[1] This endeavor would prove to be fertile ground for his first and most celebrated book.

In 1780, having endured the strains of war, imprisonment, and a forced departure from his newly adopted homeland, Crèvecoeur returned to the country of his birth to begin reworking and revising the "trunk full of manuscripts" in which he had recorded his travails in the New World. Two years later, under his adopted name, he emerged as the admired author of *Letters from an American Farmer*. Far beyond its popularity among the literate European audience, *Letters* gained Crèvecoeur distinction as an American author. Through its rustic images of a "pure, idyllic life" and "gentle geography of meadowland . . . woods, cattle, hogs, birds, [and] bees," *Letters from an Ameri-*

---

1. A. W. Plumstead, "Hector St. John de Crèvecoeur," in *American Literature, 1764–1789*, ed. Everett Emerson (Madison: University of Wisconsin Press, 1977), 214.

can *Farmer* would serve as a template for a pastoral vision of an America in which freedom, prosperity, and happiness prevailed.[2]

If *Letters from an American Farmer* opened a vista through which the New World could be imagined, its real significance lay in its transformative power. Not only did *Letters* represent the American territories as a promised land in which the European commoner could discover the miracle of personal metamorphosis, but through language and the performative power of text, Crèvecoeur reinvented himself as the literary first farmer of the American landscape. In 1784, only two years after publication of *Letters*, Benjamin Franklin would signal the national importance of Crèvecoeur's book, turning to it as an exemplary representation of the social and physical landscapes that characterized the interior regions of the New World's enterprise in freedom. Over the next two hundred years, *Letters* has continued to be read as a representative text of the early American experience—perhaps eclipsed only by Franklin's subsequent *Autobiography*—and it has become famous for its particular enunciation of American identity.

More traditional interpretations of *Letters* have read it in three ways: as an initially celebratory presentation of the New World as an Edenic garden, full of the possibility of an unparalleled experience in freedom; as an "impassioned, unqualified defense of American agrarianism"; and as a work that attempts a "straightforward natural and social history of young America" through the experiential eye of its prototypical American narrator, the farmer James.[3] At the heart of *Letters*, and of tremendous import in its classification as an authoritative text, is Farmer James, who comes to embody the myth of the American self through his claim to an individuality that is both unique and symbolic. What is unique about Farmer James is his natural innocence. As the simple farmer, James must rely primarily upon his natural "perspicuity," as well as a "warmth of imagination" through which his encounters with the world can be mediated. As James's minister suggests in the introductory letter, part of what qualifies him for this literary undertaking is not his stature as a man of letters and philosophy, but rather his singular capacity for original reflection. James is the untainted I/eye, a *"Tabula rasa*, where spontaneous and strong impressions are delineated with facility" (*LAF*, 11). This untainted innocence makes James a credible individual through whom the "truth" of the American experience can be rendered in print.

---

2. Ibid., 215.
3. Ibid., 213.

But James is not a "tabula rasa" of pure impression, and his conclusions quickly supersede the parameters of mere individual perception to become both exemplary and emblematic. In this regard, several forces collude to transform *Letters* from the purely subjective musings of a curious, adventurous individual into representative literature. As Thomas Philbrick argues, Crèvecoeur composed *Letters* "at a time when interest in agriculture, both in England and on the Continent, was at its peak." Thus, far from constituting an originary contribution to eighteenth-century literary culture, *Letters* takes its cue from an increasing interest in agriculture as a redemptive and honorable vocation, one in which the simple farmer emerges as the "'natural man,' man uncorrupted by the perversions and artificialities of civilization . . . ennobled by close and essential contact with the wisdom and beauty of nature."[4] Given the correlation Philbrick asserts between the "exaltation of farming and the promise of the New World," evident in several late eighteenth-century texts (Abbé Raynal's 1770 *Histoire philosophique* in particular), Crèvecoeur's Farmer James can be seen as a representative voice of the American self whose virtue is demonstrated through his simple but rigorous dedication to the land and, in certain respects, through his very "sameness" of person and purpose.[5]

Equally influential in establishing *Letters* as a representative text is its reliance upon and incorporation of an Enlightenment rationality that makes possible the elevation of the senses—Farmer James's "spontaneous impressions"—into an evidentiary ground upon which material reality can be unveiled. On the one hand, Crèvecoeur creates in James a narrator who appeals to readers through what at least one critic has described as a "logic of association": it is not simply that James reports what he sees, but that his narrative asks his readers "to feel with James, to engage with him imaginatively as he engages his world," thus enabling the construction of a text in which Americanness is made a "product of the personal," and therefore one that solidifies

---

4. Thomas Philbrick, *St. John de Crèvecoeur* (New York: Twayne, 1970), 56.

5. In attributing a quality of "sameness" to James's "person and purpose," I want to suggest the way in which his desire is endemically characteristic of the American, beyond the space of individuality. Within the text, that desire is echoed in the story of "Andrew, The Hebridean," where James's intentions are representative rather than individualistic. The idea of a rule of sameness in which American identity is constituted in the text will be discussed at length later in the chapter.

a "new way of defining national identity."[6] On the other hand, James's concluding observations and their rise to "representative" status also engage the problematic notion of correspondence that troubles Enlightenment reason. Insofar as *Letters* reveals its Enlightenment bias, it presumes an uncontested faith in the materiality of the world that makes possible the "conflation of sense with reason," as if the world could be rendered empirically intelligible. Here, "sense and reason, materiality and reality would all be strung together into a series of equivalencies: symmetrical, airtight, mutually entailed, mutually reflexive."[7] The difficulty with reading *Letters* solely in terms of its representative stature involves this ideology of equivalence. By its very nature, such a reading precludes the disruptive potential of the Other.

If Crèvecoeur's *Letters* is a representative text, it is also a text that continues to resonate with the disruptive and troublesome face of Otherness, which bears no such representable equivalence. I am interested in reading *Letters* in terms of its excess—its moments of dissonance and diachrony, in which the presence of the Other pierces that particular free American identity. Indeed, it is the face and presence of the Other that persists and contests all ideals of phenomenological symmetry. In *Letters,* the face of alterity has not yet relinquished its gaze—it stares back from beyond the parameters of narrative, unsettling the conclusiveness of historical discourse.

In the most famous of the letters, "What is an American?" Crèvecoeur provides a definition of Americanness in which the national identity of the new republic is projected through personal experience and imagination. At the same time, the essay supersedes *Letters*' purely historical context to "foreshadow with striking completeness and precision the characteristics and values that in the nineteenth and twentieth centuries were to be enshrined as national ideals."[8] If *Letters* anticipates the articulation of the ideals at the heart of a future American identity, it also anticipates the move in Western philosophy towards the valorization of freedom as the ultimate end of human existence. *Letters* might then be read as a text that opens onto yet another

---

6. Christine Holbo, "Imagination, Commerce, and the Politics of Associationism in Crèvecoeur's *Letters from an American Farmer*," *Early American Literature* 32 (1997): 33.

7. Wai-chee Dimock, *Residues of Justice: Literature, Law, Philosophy* (Berkeley: University of California Press, 1996), 67–8.

8. Philbrick, *Crèvecoeur,* 70.

moment in the historical evolution of Western thought. Its essential equation for the forging of individual identity participates in what will later distinguish metaphysical philosophy.

When Crèvecoeur represents the essence of the American through the figure of the farmer, he celebrates the possibility of an individual freedom that is inherent in a New World society characterized by the ideal of democracy. This notion of democracy is predicated upon the representation of an America in which the political and social hierarchies of the European past are dismantled, leaving the individual, suddenly released from the burden of history, free to pursue and define the parameters of his own self-worth. "By what invisible power has this surprising metamorphosis been performed?" James asks his readers. His answer is twofold: first, through the protective agency of a system of "indulgent laws" that safeguard the rights of the individual, and second, through the "accumulated rewards" of land that confer the "title of freemen," to which "every benefit is affixed which men can possibly acquire" (*LAF*, 38).

In Crèvecoeur's admiration for laws that "stamp" upon the dispossessed European the "symbol of [his] adoption," one is reminded of the voice of John Adams, who twenty-three years earlier had argued that a unique aspect of the American experiment would be the constitution of laws in which the rights of the general populace—rights "undoubtedly, antecedent to all earthly government" and "derived from the great Legislator of the Universe"—would achieve recognition.[9] But it is Crèvecoeur's James through whom the acquisition of rights is eloquently articulated through the paradigm of property. In the Crèvecoeurian model, individual identity is achieved through the acquisition of land. Above all, the "rewards" of property enable the metamorphosis from invisibility into subjectivity, according the rights of citizenship and the entitlement to freedom.

Numerous critics have pointed out that Crèvecoeur's concept of property is indebted to a Lockean philosophy of natural right in which the right of property is both a moral imperative and a necessary element in the transition from natural life into civil society. Yet this concept overflows the specificity of its historical origins. Crèvecoeur's understanding of property to some extent foreshadows that of Hegel. In *Letters*, James's acquisition of land estab-

---

9. John Adams, "On the Feudal and the Canon Law," in *The Rising Glory of America, 1760–1820*, ed. Gordon S. Wood (Boston: Northeastern University Press, 1990), 26.

lishes the foundation of his freedom. The prospective American first learns how to sustain his own existence—one carved, as it were, from the ground of nature and thus self-interest. That labor lays the foundation for acquisition, and soon thereafter he purchases land: "His good name procures him credit. He is now possessed of the deed, conveying to him and his posterity the fee simple and absolute property of two hundred acres of land. . . . He is become a freeholder, from perhaps a German boor—he is now an American" (*LAF*, 55). James's scenario describes the process through which the dispossessed move from invisibility, as the "slave of some despotic prince," into the domain of visibility—"from nothing to start into being"—where it is possible "to become a free man, invested with lands" (*LAF*, 55–6). For Crèvecoeur, property becomes the sign of the self: the validation of personal existence by the investment of individual will into that which enables its external recognition.

In the language of Hegelian philosophy, particularly in *The Philosophy of Right*, it is the function of property to effect the translation of personal freedom into the external world so that it can achieve existence as an Idea. The abstract personality, as the nascent presence of self-knowledge, aspires towards its certainty as a reality in the public sphere of the tangible. In Hegel's words, the personality struggles "to give itself reality, or in other words to claim that external world as its own." To achieve that claim, which is imperative to the articulation of self-certainty, a "person must translate his freedom into an external sphere in order to exist as Idea." Here is the miraculous metamorphosis that property effects: as the site of the individual will, the external proof of an inherent subjectivity, property enables the representation of the self through its translation into the visible. Hegel asserts that "from the stand of freedom"—where one becomes an entity discernible even to the self—"property is the first embodiment of freedom and so is in itself a substantive end."[10]

The importance of the acquisition of property as a "substantive end" in Crèvecoeur's narrative needs little elaboration. That property constitutes the "stand of freedom" is similarly evident. Property bestows upon James the right of membership in the social realm; moreover, it is the site of freedom, through which an otherwise unknown individual gains visibility. When James

---

10. Georg Hegel, *Phenomenology of Spirit*, trans. A. V. Miller (Oxford, U.K.: Oxford University Press, 1976), 38–42.

proclaims in Letter II that "the instant I enter on my own land, the bright idea of property, of exclusive right, of independence exalt my mind" (*LAF*, 20), his words perpetuate an "idyll of domestic felicity"[11] and thus participate in the Romantic mythology of agrarianism.

But it is also true, as James subsequently proposes, that the acquisition of land becomes the ground upon which his freedom is constituted as an objective fact; it effects the translation of selfhood from the realm of potentiality into the sphere of materiality, where what is "first only a possibility" is constituted as a manifest Idea. This is the equation that informs James's assertion that the farm he has inherited from his father "has established all our rights; on it is founded our rank, our freedom, our power as citizens, our importance as inhabitants of such a district" (*LAF*, 20–1). James's language here is significant, since it is property—as the sign of individual freedom—that comes to constitute "what may be called the true and the only philosophy of an American farmer" (*LAF*, 21).

If property forms the foundation of the philosophy of the American farmer, it does so through a process of translation through which the self comprehends the actuality of its own freedom and converts it into an incontrovertible presence, visually readable in the external world. James's farm is suggestive of the Hegelian ground in which freedom is invested, because it is through the farm that James emerges into the world as a person both capable and worthy of recognition. For Hegel, recognition is an essential component in the struggle that self-consciousness undergoes in its pursuit and claim for certainty. The claim that the farm enables James's emergence as "person" relies upon a distinction like Hegel's between a notion of "subject" and "person." In this context, the term *subject* represents a state of incompleteness: "every living thing of any sort is a subject." To become a person, however, is to be a "subject aware of [its] subjectivity." In other words, "A person is a unit of freedom aware of its sheer independence. As *this* person, I know myself to be free in myself." Here, property becomes the means of that transformation because of its unique capacity for the "supersession of the pure subjectivity of personality."[12] Once we recognize that Crèvecoeur constructs property as Hegel would, rather than as Locke had, we must also recognize that Lockean interpretations of Crèvecoeur tend to underempha-

---

11. Philbrick, *Crèvecoeur*, 60.
12. Hegel, *Phenomenology*, 235.

size the pivotal relationship between property and the embodiment of freedom.

Eric Cheyfitz has written compellingly on the process of translation that inheres in the concept of property. He makes the argument that the histories of both self and property are inseparably interwoven into the historical discourse of Western cultures.[13] Although Cheyfitz's immediate intent in his chapter "Translating Property" is on the intranslatability of the term *property* in the initial meetings between the English colonists and the Native American peoples, his remarks concerning the signification and function of property within the cultural landscape of European thought are particularly relevant to this study. Cheyfitz writes, "Property is not essence, which is the very heart of identity in Western metaphysics; yet it is the sign of essence," that which bears the weight of signification through which a "perpetually transcendent identity" is glimpsed. He continues:

> Paradoxically, property is the language of an always silent essence, its figure in the world. In the metaphysical realm, property is the shadow of substance. But as we translate property across the frontier into the physical realm, it becomes substance itself. And those who own it and who in this system of property must inevitably ground their identities on it become its shadow. In the West's system of things, we are the shadows of property; and if we own nothing, then even this obscure visibility is denied to us. In the West, property, in that tangled space where the physical and the metaphysical mix, is the very mark of identity, of that which is identical to itself: what we typically call a "self" or an "individual," indicating the absolute boundaries that are predicated of this entity.[14]

Cheyfitz's analysis of the place of property in Western logic points explicitly to the connection between self and sign, abstract potentiality and material embodiment, that is so fully resonant in Crèvecoeur's *Letters*. My intent here is to suggest the ways in which *Letters* anticipates the move in nineteenth-century philosophy that articulates identity through the embodiment of property precisely because it establishes the ground of freedom. In Letter II, James confesses a "happiness" that is directly tied to his "new situation" as the American farmer "possessing freedom of action, freedom of thoughts" (*LAF*, 18). All of these things are conferred upon him by the material reality

---

13. Eric Cheyfitz, *The Poetics of Imperialism* (Oxford, U.K.: Oxford University Press, 1991).
14. Ibid., 49–50.

signified in his farm, his house, his barn. One might say that James's notion of happiness is conceived in the evidentiary ground of place, not only as the sign of his freedom but as the originary site of his dwelling in the world.

This logic of identity, characteristic of Western ontological philosophy, constructs the self through a fundamental opposition to the external world. The way of the I, as subject, is rooted in a process of translation through which it discovers that it exists—the "I am"—as a recognizably definable presence. But the relationship between the self (as I) and the world is one of concrete signification. It is not enough to know merely that one exists; rather, it is incumbent upon the I to establish the domain of its superiority. As the quotation from Farmer James suggests, the experience of freedom reveals itself not only in the awakening to being, but in thoughts and actions, whereby the initial and formal hostility of the world is converted into that space in which the self constitutes its home. Property functions in this specific context—not as the essence of self, but as the sign and site of a recognizably identifiable individual.

This process of conversion is often represented through the metaphor of negation: the I uncovers its own powers through the use and possession of the world that opposes it. But we can better understand the process of conversion as the perpetuation of sameness. As Levinas argues in *Totality and Infinity*, in a world that is characterized primarily by its hostility and foreignness, the "way of the I against the 'other' of the world consists in *sojourning*, in *identifying oneself* by existing here *at home with oneself* [*chez soi*]." The activity of domestication comes as an existential imperative: "Dwelling is the very mode of *maintaining oneself* [*se tenir*], not as the famous serpent grasping itself by biting onto its tail, but as the body that, on the earth exterior to it, holds *itself* up [*se tient*] and *can*. The 'at home' [*Le 'chez soi'*] is not a container but a site where *I can*, where, dependent on a reality that is other, I am, despite this dependence or thanks to it, free" (*TI*, 37).

Levinas is describing that essential component of Western identity which necessitates the conversion of alterity—indeed, its suspension—so that the I maintains its cohesion and reconfigures its presence in the world as the one who possesses and sojourns. "The possibility of possessing, that is, of suspending the very alterity of what is only at first other . . . is the *way of the same*. I am at home with myself in the world because it offers itself to or resists possession" (*TI*, 38). Levinas designates this process of conversion as the imperialism of ontology. As he argues, the relationship with "Being that is enacted as ontology consists in neutralizing the existent in order to comprehend or grasp it," which results in the negation of the other's independence: "'I think' comes down to 'I can'—to an appropriation of what is, to an exploitation of reality" (*TI*, 46).

We can witness this ideology of progression in Farmer James's description of the conversion of the landscape from the frontier of a "great woods" into the site of domestic dwelling: "He who would wish to see America in its proper light, and have a true idea of its feeble beginnings and barbarous rudiments, must visit our extended line of frontiers where the last settlers dwell, and where he may see the first labours of settlement, the mode of clearing the earth, in all their different appearances" (*LAF*, 42–3). In James's depiction, the frontier is characterized by its "barbarous" hostility, its inherent potential for corruption—for it is not yet rendered neutral by the activities of conversion that will ensure its receptivity to the real American, who will turn it into the site of home. The frontier is first and foremost the place of alterity, of the presence of difference that resides both in the physical character of the land and in its quasi inhabitation by the frontiersman, or "back settler," whose presence constitutes a similar threat to the autarchy of the farmer.

Farmer James's representation of the back settlers is interesting on several counts. As a people "who have suddenly passed from oppression, dread of government, and fear of laws, into the unlimited freedom of the woods," their presence on the frontier is both necessary and threatening. As the ones who come first, whose labor paves the way for "more industrious people, who will finish their improvements," they are a necessary evil; their settlements are an essential step in the transformation of a "hitherto barbarous country into a fine fertile, well regulated district" (*LAF*, 43). Redeemed by their performance as "precursors or pioneers," the back settlers are nevertheless positioned beyond the authentic parameters of the republic. As such, their necessary persistence is a threat to the integrity of sameness, which is embodied in the rule of the freeholder-farmer. One can argue that the sin of the frontiersman is his seduction by the presence of an absolute alterity, and therefore something that is utterly nonnegotiable within the sphere of a civilized totality. Because the back settlers choose to reject the rewards of property to remain in the "unlimited freedom of the woods," they are necessarily excluded from the settlement of the republic.

It is no accident that James represents the frontier-settler through a language that, at least in its historical application, had first inscribed the figure of the Indian, in order to signify his essential Otherness to the European arriving on the American shore. Like the back settler's, the Indian's lack of desire to translate the landscape into parcels of property first distinguished his "difference." From the beginning, as Roy Harvey Pearce compellingly demonstrates, the Indian entered the European mind as the symbol of an alterity so absolute that the very fact of his presence could only be understood through the logic of a nonnegotiable opposition: "The Indian became important for the English mind, not for what he was in and of himself, but rather for what he showed civilized men they were not and must not be."[15]

Pearce begins his study, *Savagism and Civilization*, by asserting that it is a "book about a belief"—an "idea of order"—that inspired the settlement of colonial America. This idea was so compelling that it revealed itself as an "eternal and immutable principle which guaranteed the intelligibility" of the relationships between the European self and the otherness of the New World. For Pearce, that principle privileged the imposition of order upon the chaos of the natural frontier: "It was a principle to be expressed in the progress and elevation of civilized men who, striving to imitate their God, would bring order to chaos. America was such a chaos, a new-found chaos. Her natural wealth was there for the taking because it was there for the ordering."[16]

This notion of the supremacy of a particular kind of order, as the perpetuation of an "immutable principle" of sameness, transformed the Indian from mere difference—a Stranger to the European sensibility—into the emblem of all that stood "fiercely and grimly in the path of civilization."[17] The ideology of "civilization," which Pearce astutely identifies here, finds its origin in the imperialism of ontology, for it is based upon a thematization and conceptualization through which the independence of the Other is suspended and neutralized.

Ontology concerns itself with the truth of existence. The ontological imperative works to differentiate between "real existence" and the realm of appearance. In other words, its intent is inherently investigative. Ontology interrogates the nature of reality, or Being itself, in order to discover how entities belonging to various logical categories may be said to exist. Its over-

---

15. Pearce, *Savagism and Civilization*, 5.
16. Ibid., 3.
17. Ibid., 11.

arching desire is grounded in an ideal of totality; it aims to characterize the truth of existence in order to establish the foundational principles upon which all subsequent knowledge can be built. And here it is important to remember that the "philosophy" of Farmer James is specifically tied to the recognition of a "system of rational laws founded on freedom" (*LAF*, 86).

Yet to posit the possibility of a totality of meaning in which the truth of existence—and hence any given existent—can be known is also to assert the primacy of theory as the indubitable principle through which the essential alterity of the world can be made comprehensible. Ontology acknowledges alterity through an epistemology in which the otherness of the Other can be apprehended and ultimately suspended in order to permit its foundational comprehension. More simply, the ontological relationship is one predicated upon the translation of difference into the language of cognition. As such, it enacts a relationship with alterity that solicits its comprehension and compliance, seeking the reduction of the Other's alterity under and within the rule of the same. The imperialistic desire, Levinas argues, resides through the sovereignty of reason: "The neutralization of the other which becomes theme or object—appearing, that is, taking its place in the light—is precisely its reduction to the same. To know ontologically is to surprise in the existent confronted that by which it is not this existent, this stranger, that by which it is somehow betrayed, surrenders, is given in the horizon in which it loses itself and appears, lays itself open to grasp, becomes a concept" (*TI*, 43–4).

The imperialism inherent in this perspective, in which the Other comes to presence, defines itself as the imposition of unity, such that the Other, situated within a given horizon, is contained within the circle of meaning that reason, as logos, constructs. To situate alterity within a horizon where the totality of meaning—the coincidence of existent and idea—prevails is to enact an imperialism that denies alterity its very otherness. This insistence upon the correlation of existent and logos ultimately results in what Drucilla Cornell terms a "philosophy of reflection," where the "'I' sees itself reflected in the other but does not see the other looking back. The other is reduced to a mirror for oneself."[18]

Thus Farmer James can lay upon the American landscape a hierarchical grid through which alterity is rendered comprehensible without assaulting the integrity of the idealized American self. The back settlers are guilty of

---

18. Drucilla Cornell, *The Philosophy of the Limit* (New York: Routledge, 1992), 22.

violating the rules of order: their proximity to the woods makes them vulnerable to that once-demonic sphere of puritan savagism and all its powers of corruption. Indeed, the frontiersman, seduced by the wildness of his environment and its illusion of an unlimited freedom, commits the first violation of European integrity: he becomes a hunter. By doing so, he positions himself beyond the boundaries of civilized society. But the real transgression of the frontiersman is his alignment with the absolute alterity of the Indian. In his adoption of Indian ways, the back settler violates the logic of identity through which the new American has been forged. If the Indian, as Pearce suggests, is the sign of everything the European "is not and must not be," then the Indian is a disruptive presence which contests both the law of order and the reign of sameness by which the free subject maintains its autarchy.

Nevertheless, the frontier-settler is a recoverable entity within the totality of meaning that ontology permits. Despite his alleged "lawless profligacy" and mongrel breeding, the frontier-settler is not Indian but European; he is not the savage upon the horizon. Rather, his existence is still characterized by the imperative of choice. Like James's father, who initially belonged to that rank of "offcasts," the frontier-settler can choose to purge himself of the influence of the woods; by adopting the "honest principles" of the farmer, he can reintegrate himself within the bounds of the republic. Even those who choose to remain frontiersmen persist as progressive agents. Although their presence may threaten the home-site of the freeholder, it is still negotiable and purposeful. Because "Americans are the western pilgrims, who are carrying along with them that great mass of arts, sciences, vigour, and industry" (LAF, 39), the frontiersman has a place in the teleological progression of history as the one who pushes the boundary. His industry clears the land, not only of its unwanted forestry, but also of its problematic and contestatory inhabitants whose difference is beyond recoverability. The critical difference between the frontiersman and the Indian is one of ontological privilege: the settler retains a claim to place through the agency of purposiveness, while the Indian does not.

Letters is an anticipatory work that gestures towards the primacy of ethics as the ground upon which justice must be forged. I want to turn to the ethical implications and disruptive force of Crèvecoeur's text, for it is in the presence of the Other that Crèvecoeur's celebration of freedom finds its as-yet-unanswered critique.

There are three faces of alterity in James's representation of the American landscape: the landscape itself, the Indian, and the African. As we have seen, one of the primary themes that motivates *Letters* is the activity of conversion, through which the New World landscape is translated from wilderness to farm, frontier to home-site. The landscape is converted from its original alterity through an imagined community of providentiality and entitlement. Richard Slotkin engages this argument when he suggests that from the very beginning, the New World was cast in terms that emphasized its magicality, its promise as a newfound Garden of Eden: "The magic of the discovery of a New World proved anything was possible; it followed that in exploiting that discovery, everything was permitted."[19] Crèvecoeur's frontier occupies that site of discovery and possibility, and its conversion into the place of home involved an ideology of entitlement through which the colonist made manifest his providential role as the American, a "new man, who acts upon new principles" and "new ideas," and whose labor is "rewarded by ample subsistence" (*LAF*, 40).

Given that the American landscape was initially a hostile and alien territory, the mythology of the frontier enabled its theoretical conversion. As Slotkin demonstrates, that mythology well served to mask its inherent alterity. Similarly, the ideology of myth permitted the colonists to reconstruct themselves in the language of the heroic, for the "errand into the wilderness" became one of sacred proportions. Thus Crèvecoeur's farmer, like the puritan fathers who preceded him, participates in a providential mission in which the implicit violence of conversion is subsumed in a valorization of agrarianism that "substitutes the cultivation of the land, the interaction of man with pure and inanimate nature, for the human conflict of Indian dispossession."[20] The confrontation with alterity that *Letters* dramatizes involves not merely the conversion of landscape as a physical site, but the inclusion of its Native inhabitants, whose alterity is equally suspended and whose freedom is rendered obsolete.

For the most part, the Indians who appear in *Letters* have already undergone the conversion from Stranger to savage. Inseparable from the landscape in which they dwell, their presence is neutralized through the logic of catego-

---

19. Richard Slotkin, *Regeneration through Violence: The Mythology of the American Frontier, 1600–1860* (Middletown, Conn.: Wesleyan University Press, 1973), 44.

20. Ibid., 52.

rization. As both Pearce and Slotkin have argued, since the Indian is first a thematic element in the puritan drama of providential entitlement, they quickly become an impediment to the triumph of democratic freedom. Once Indians are made into "savages," their potential erasure is entirely explicable and, as a result, conceptually ordained.

James draws upon this mythology in his presentation of the Indian most clearly in Letter IV. While a few Nantucket Indians remain, James informs his reader, "They are hastening towards a total annihilation, and this may be perhaps the last compliment that will ever be paid them by any traveller" (*LAF*, 98). But James is careful to assert the natural cause of their imminent disappearance: "If their numbers are now so decreased, it must not be attributed either to tyranny or violence, but to some of those causes, which have uninterruptedly produced the same effects from one end of the continent to the other, wherever both nations have mixed" (*LAF*, 99). James equates the Indian's disappearance with "annihilation"—a term explicitly connoting the unnaturalness of violence—even as he effaces the burden of responsibility for that disappearance from European consciousness. The Indian is depicted as the almost accidental product of historical misfortune.

Farmer James acknowledges that the Indian's misfortune coincides with the arrival of the European, but he ascribes no fault to the consequences of that arrival: "When the Europeans came [the Indians] caught the smallpox, and their improper treatment of that disorder swept away great numbers: this calamity was succeeded by the use of rum; and these are the two principal causes which so much diminished their numbers, not only here but all over the continent" (*LAF*, 101). Slotkin's notion of the role of myth is relevant here, for James's account implicates the improprieties of the Indian—not the actions of the Europeans—as being responsible for his own demise. Indeed, moments later James suggests that the Indian's "physical antipathy" or inferior constitution prefigures his doom. If the Indian is a victim of New World expansion, which James is reluctantly willing to grant, he is also an agent in his fate. In this sense, James's narrative supports Slotkin's thesis. The mythology of the frontier permits James to read the disappearance of the Indian as if it were merely the inevitable product of history, as if there were no human accountability. His remarks thus stand as a latent justification for the Indian's extermination, placing the "moral responsibility for that outcome on the enemy, which is to say, on its predicted victims."[21]

21. Ibid., 61.

But the ramifications of *Letters'* acceptance of the Indian's disappearance are more philosophically severe. Once the alterity of the Indian is subsumed under the concept of the savage, his existence is relegated to the domain of the ahistorical. The Indian exists prior to the commencement of American history, yet "less than two hundred years" after the arrival of the European, James can conclude that "they appear to be a race doomed to recede and disappear before the superior genius of the Europeans" (*LAF*, 102). James's assertion, steeped in a notion of history in which the difference of the Indian can play no part, reveals its ontological bias. The conversion of the Indian's Otherness into the ahistoricity of savagism removes him from the ontological playing field, for it effectively divests the Native face of its capacity for critique. The Indian appears on the horizon, or comes to light, as a vestige, as what Jacques Derrida calls "the remains."[22] As James points out, there were "numerous tribes which formerly inhabited the extensive shores of the great bay of Massachusetts. . . . They are gone, and every memorial of them is lost; no vestiges whatever are left of those swarms which once inhabited this country" (*LAF*, 103). The tribal peoples who still persist in the landscape do so only as "the remains"—the scattered and dispersed remnants of an ancient time and race, whose unwillingness and "unapt[ness] to imitate, or to follow any of our trades" (*LAF*, 104) necessarily precludes the possibility of their recovery within the totality of meaning that ontology constructs.

Even as Derrida and Cornell hold open the possibility that through "the remains" we may be reminded of the excess that would call us to responsibility, the Indian's presence as "the remains" operates in the reverse. In the world of Crèvecoeur's text, the disruptive potential of the Indian's demise is not counted. It is not an occasion for mourning; instead, it attains an appointed intelligibility, one through which its contestatory meaning—and its ethical content—is denied. The Indian is quite literally the antithesis of those qualities that distinguish the free subject. As such, the Indian becomes the other "whose existence does not and cannot count. This refusal reinstates the subject-centered system that fails to heed the call of otherness."[23] The relega-

---

22. For further discussion of the concept of "the remains," as that presence which through memory and mourning bears within it the possibility of an ethical call to responsibility, see Jacques Derrida, *Memoires for Paul de Man*, trans. Cecile Lindsay, Jonathan Culler, and Eduardo Cadava (New York: Columbia University Press, 1986); Cornell, *Philosophy of the Limit*.

23. Cornell, *Philosophy of Limit*, 72.

tion of the Indian to the province of death, as "the remains," divests his presence of its inherently ethical capacity for critique—that is, as the Other who interrupts the spontaneous freedom of the I, pursuing his enjoyment and legitimacy of identity. In *Letters*, it is therefore the African who most fully fulfills the promise of disruption, and whose presence is founded in a resistance that not only interrupts James's sojourn in the world, but intervenes in such a way as to shatter his illusion of self-certain sovereignty.

Letter IX, "Description of Charles-Town," is, as many critics have noted, the arrestingly symbolic moment in Crèvecoeur's text. Its gruesome and horrific scene of the "African in the tree" resonates still, transcending its contextual meaning and its containment in the historical drama of American identity and freedom. The encounter between Farmer James and the African in the tree is a literary moment that exceeds its representational "truth," which has yet to exhaust its cultural significance, and so continues to resound with meanings that betray its assignation "as a piece of cultural work that has already served its purpose, that has meaning only in reference to the past."[24] In this particular moment of symbolic artistry, *Letters* transcends the categories of its representative status to become one of those texts that disrupts the discourse on freedom in American letters. In so doing, *Letters* begins to assert the ethical as the means through which a notion of justice can emerge to challenge an American mythos constructed from uninterrogated ideals of freedom.

Letter IX begins in the aftermath of James's encounter with the African, disrupting even the stylistic and chronological devices of the narrative. In his journey to Charleston, unlike his visit to Massachusetts, James's experience with the materiality of American freedom is disjunctive, contradictory, and nearly apocalyptic. Charleston is a reality entirely removed from the innocence of the interior farmland or the romantic potentiality of the frontier. Instead, Charleston appears as a pinnacle of achievement in which elegance, sumptuousness, and magnificence attest to the unparalleled success of the American experiment in freedom and settlement. If the demise of the Indian is somehow explicable in James's order of consciousness, the persecution of the African is not. The difference may lie in James's accountability as observer. Since the conversion of the Indian has almost been completed, James can only note his absences. For him, the Indian persists in the imagination as the sign of a history to which he is an inheritor, not an author.

24. Dimock, *Residues of Justice*, 78.

Yet even the Indian's persistence in the memory is doubtful, for its most discernible trace lies in "one extraordinary monument, and even this they owe to the industry and religious zeal of the Europeans." What James refers to here is the "Bible translated into the Nattick tongue" (*LAF*, 103), a "monument" that is the sign and evidentiary proof of the singularity of European culture as superior, the standard by which alterity is relegated to inessentiality. But, as we have already seen, to be "the remains" is to be removed from the plane of facticity and relegated to the realm of representation, where the violence of conquest has already been performed.

In Charleston, however, the violence of conquest is not lodged in a narrative of history that presents itself as an unalterable past or as the inevitability of a providential outcome. Instead, James encounters a specificity of violence revealed in the present, a perpetuation of a peculiar manifestation of freedom in excess, before which he is called to become an unwilling witness. This is a pivotal difference between his experiences in Massachusetts and in Charleston. In Massachusetts, James is primarily an observer, a traveler. Whatever injustice has been committed against the Indian belongs to a previous era, one already subsumed in a logical and sayable history, for which there no longer remains an identifiably accountable author.

By the time James reaches the Massachusetts shore, the face of the Indian has already passed into the sphere of obscurity—perhaps still recognizable in a rhetoric of nostalgia and nobility, but nonetheless divested of its ethical content and its power to effect the command of justice. In Charleston, quite the opposite is true; James is brought face to face with the African in the tree. Because of this, Letter IX emerges as a supremely disruptive moment, a "hellish vision of chaos and violence [that] marks the crisis of the book."[25] Here, the prevailing discourse on freedom is called to account.

Although Western ontology is the "way of the same," ethics is founded upon the encounter that disrupts, making possible the "calling into question of the same." The rule of Levinasian ethics is to disrupt the spontaneity of that Self, which is grounded in the certainty of its own freedom, in order to submit it to question. As Levinas has argued, "We name this calling into question of my spontaneity by the presence of the Other ethics. The strangeness of the Other, his irreducibility to the I, to my thoughts and my possessions, is precisely accomplished as a calling into question of my spontaneity, as ethics" (*TI*, 43).

25. Philbrick, *Crèvecoeur*, 82.

At stake in the ethical encounter is the experience of the face. Only in the face-to-face meeting does the Other—always subject to competing versions of narrative—break free and present herself as the one who contests. This is the irreducible moment of encounter to which James is unwillingly subject. It is a "facing" in its most absolute sense: after the narrative idyll of domestication that pervades the previous letters, James is suddenly and arrestingly called by the face of the Other to be accountable. He will be a witness to this Other's murder, and that exacts a burden of responsibility that he would rather resist.

Significantly, James's encounter with the African occurs during his traversing the landscape, which, while foreign in its southernness, is nevertheless a site of invitation and engagement: "In order to avoid the heat of the sun, I resolved to go on foot, sheltered in a small path, leading through a pleasant wood." At the inception of his journey, the "wood" through which James saunters appears familiar, safe—an extension of the space of home—and he enters its bounds "leisurely," uninterrupted in the activity and privilege of his sojourn in the world. In the penultimate moment of his encounter with the African, James is actively engaged with the landscape around him; he recounts, "I was leisurely travelling along, attentively examining some peculiar plants which I had collected." Seemingly, the landscape is already subdued and pliable. But then "all at once I felt the air strongly agitated, though the day was perfectly calm and sultry" (LAF, 166). This descriptive detail—the movement of the air—is almost Whitmanesque in its hinting at that correlation between the affairs of men and the designs of heaven. It memorializes the moment, as if the motion of the air itself contains an image through which the "internal ideological meaning of the event itself" could be made discoverable.[26]

But in the next moment, a "sound resembling a deep rough voice, uttered, as I thought, a few inarticulate monosyllables," and the reader, like James, is stunned by the intrusion of a presence both sinister and indigenously foreign. Alarmed, James narrates, "I perceived at about six rods distance something resembling a cage, suspended to the limbs of a tree, all the branches of which appeared covered with large birds of prey." James fires

---

26. I am grateful here to the words and insight of Wynn Thomas's remarks regarding the connections between Whitman and weather that informed his lecture at the University of Iowa, February 24, 1998.

on the birds, and as he uncovers the reason for their convergence, we as readers—and therefore as "commanded partners" in the challenge this text imposes upon us[27]—are made to bear witness to a moment in American letters nearly unequaled in its visual horror and unadulterated violence:

> Horrid to think, and painful to repeat, I perceived a negro, suspended in the cage, and left there to expire! I shudder when I recollect that the birds had already picked out his eyes, his cheek bones were bare; his arms had been attacked in several places, and his body seemed covered with a multitude of wounds. From the edges of the hollow sockets and from the lacerations with which he was disfigured, the blood slowly dripped and tinged the ground beneath. No sooner were the birds flown, than swarms of insects covered the whole body of this unfortunate wretch, eager to feed on his mangled flesh and to drink his blood. (LAF, 167)

The African is, even in James's own account, abruptly intrusive; he represents an encounter with an alterity whose freedom has not yet been neutralized but remains brutally suspended—in a very literal sense. The caged African signifies the existential violence perpetrated against those whose blood bears the stain of African origin. More importantly, the discovery of the African in the tree disrupts James's sojourn in the world: without warning, he is called to bear witness to the excessive rule of freedom, which grounds its justification in the insatiable imperialistic desire for its own "joy, festivity, and happiness" (LAF, 155).

The African disrupts James's experience in the American landscape that he deems home—and in that sense, the face of the African has not yet been fully thematized in the emerging story of American settlement. While the freedom of the African has been violently suspended, that suspension, both literally and philosophically, is more an infliction of war than the imposition of a rhetoric of history. When James later tells us that "by virtue of . . . gold, wars, murders, and devastation are committed in some harmless, peaceable African neighborhood, where dwelt innocent people, who even knew not but that all men were black" (LAF, 156), his words signify a recognition of a native freedom, autochthonous in its own world of experience.

---

27. I draw here upon my dialogue with Eric Neel on the issue of obligation and the ethical responsibility of the reader of literary "texts." The idea that the reader is a "commanded partner" originates in Neel's dissertation, and I want to acknowledge my debt to his critical thinking, as well as his influence upon my own formulations in this particular area.

For James, the Indian is a presence whose face is displaced in the narrative representation of the American experiment in freedom, whereas the African is a crudely disruptive presence whose face signifies the excesses of that freedom, as well as its corruption in the hands of that "chosen race [who] eat, drink, and live happy . . . without labour, without fatigue, hardly subjected to the trouble of wishing" (LAF, 155). But the southerner's disposition towards enjoyment does not solely account for his violence. That arc extends even further, since to exist in the "enjoyment" that the violence of slavery makes possible is to exist via an ontological violence towards the Other. It is to exist and live as if one were alone in the world. It is an existence steeped in the violence of violation, and thus blatantly egoistic and unredeemably guilty.

"I found myself suddenly arrested by the power of affright and terror; my nerves were convulsed; I trembled, I stood motionless, involuntarily contemplating the fate of this negro, in all its dismal latitude" (LAF, 167). The African's power actively to interrupt James's sojourn, to "arrest" him in the experience of a seemingly innocent and spontaneous enjoyment of his uncontested freedom, represents the disruptive potential of ethics, embodied in the face and speech of the Stranger. That James accidentally stumbles upon this encounter is secondary; what is important is that he does so. Once he does, he is irrevocably altered. Had James journeyed this path in the aftermath of the African's death, the ethical efficacy of the encounter would have been diminished, if not altogether erased. In that case, the African, reduced to the essentiality of the body, would belong to the objectifiable past, as the "already happened" (TI, 65). He would become translatable as an historical item open to interpretation (via the "idea of order"). But the fact that the African still lives and speaks in the midst of the violence so brutally imposed against him is incontrovertible proof of his reality and being, as the absolute Other whose very existence introduces into the world a resistance before whom James has no power. In the context of Crèvecoeur's predominantly celebratory narrative, this scene commands our attention: it calls for critical reading and reinterpretation, and its real sublimity lies in its repressed ethical ambiguity.

Situating this scene within the context of Edmund Burke's theory of the sympathetic imagination, Christine Holbo provocatively argues that the representation of James's response to the African "literalizes the argument—implicit in Burke's psychology and in the work of moral theorists such as Adam Smith—that self-interest is the ultimate ground of sympathy. When Burke argued in purely psychological terms, he concluded that sympathy arises from imaginative extension of the instinct of self-preservation. The best example of this function . . . was the relationship between the spectator at a torture and its victim. Because of man's ability to generalize from his own condition, the imaginative identification of the spectator with the victim transmits the agony between them. A peculiar community is thus formed by the sympathetic transmission of suffering."[28] Holbo subsequently delineates the "strange community of feeling" that arises between James and the African, arguing that "James's sensations parallel those of the Negro" to such an extent that ultimately James's own "loss of self-control in astonishment imitates the real annihilation occurring in the slave."[29]

Holbo contends that James's "experiences parody—and grotesquely accomplish—a move from the sublime to the beautiful," which could potentially "produce a localized ethics, a bond between people that is also a shared understanding of moral boundaries." Despite James's sympathetic response, there is an implicit failure that undermines his moral agency. Citing the fact that in the aftermath of his encounter, James remains willing to dine in the house of those individuals responsible for the African's tortuous murder, Holbo argues that in a very real sense, the "moral effect of James's participation in the scene is indifference." This failure of ethics is revealed in James's seeming inability or unwillingness to refute the arguments of the slaveholders, who justify the African's murder as one rendered "necessary" by the "laws of self-preservation" (LAF, 168). Holbo is led to conclude, "Though the spectacle of torture appeals to sympathy, . . . it fails to produce an active, ethical sympathy."[30]

Holbo's reading is provocative because it raises the question of the relationship between sympathy and ethics and the possibilities of the associative imagination as conducive to the emergence of ethical consciousness. Her reading holds open the possibility that sympathy can become the basis for ethical action. In the Burkean scheme, James's apparent indifference to the African's plight is a failure of the sympathetic imagination: specifically, the failure "to produce an active, ethical sympathy." But if sympathy is an "imaginative extension of the instinct of self-preservation," as Holbo argues, then its relation to ethics is necessarily problematic. Given that Holbo's interpreta-

---

28. Holbo, "Imagination, Commerce and the Politics of Associationism," 46.
29. Ibid., 47.
30. Ibid.

tion is grounded in Burke, I want to examine the theoretical ideal of sympathy in its relation to ethical agency. The distinction between ethics and sympathy is important to a consideration of James's response to the African.

Burke defines sympathy as that specific passion through which "we enter into the concerns of others . . . are moved as they are moved, and are never suffered to be indifferent spectators of almost any thing which men can do or suffer." In this sense, sympathy appears to echo the call of ethics; it is constituted as a movement beyond the self, towards the suffering of the other. In fact, Burke's language echoes that of Levinasian ethics. Burke asserts that "sympathy must be considered as a sort of *substitution*, by which we are put into the place of another man, and affected in many respects as he is affected."[31] In the Burkean context, however, sympathy must be understood as an affective capacity grounded in the imaginary. It is an activity of the imagination enabling the self ostensibly to escape the confines of its own experience, "to identify with other people, to perceive things in a new way, and to develop an aesthetic appreciation of the world that coalesces both the subjective self and the objective other."[32] The sympathetic imagination is that faculty of the self that enables a fusion between the isolate Ego and the external world, as experienced through Nature and the suffering of the Other. Through the sympathetic imagination, the predicament of the Other becomes conceivable to the Self who approaches the Other as spectator or observer. Upon discovering the African in the tree, James "trembled," and "stood motionless, involuntarily contemplating the fate of this negro, in all its dismal latitude" (*LAF*, 167). He is purely a spectator. The African's suffering presents itself as entirely isolate from James's own experience and knowledge of suffering. As his words reveal, his ability to "contemplate" the African's predicament suggests the distance that sympathy entails.

Burke's definition of sympathy presupposes a certain experience of "delight" for the one who observes the Other's suffering. As Burke states, "The delight we have in such things, hinders us from shunning scenes of misery; and the pain we feel, prompts us to relieve ourselves in relieving those who suffer; and all this antecedent to any reasoning, by an instinct that works us

---

31. Edmund Burke, *A Philosophical Enquiry into the Origin of Our Ideas of the Sublime and Beautiful*, ed. James T. Boulton (Notre Dame, Ind.: University of Notre Dame Press, 1986), 44.

32. James Engell, *The Creative Imagination* (Cambridge, Mass.: Harvard University Press, 1981), 144.

to its own purposes, without our concurrence."[33] Burke's conception of the sympathetic imagination is thus potentially ethical—particularly as it implies that the call to response, in the presence of the Other's suffering, is antecedent to reason and prior to the motivation of conscious self-interest. This element of ethical possibility informs Holbo's argument. As James Engell suggests, it would seem that sympathy can become the basis for ethical action, particularly as the sympathetic response works to both "override our selfish impulses and . . . give pleasure to ourselves. As it prompts actions that alleviate the sorrows of others, it also increases our own joy."[34]

Yet sympathy is a self-reflexive experience. It relies upon an activity of egological translation, in which the encounter with the Other's suffering is assimilated into the imaginative experience of the Self. While sympathy may be one of the ways in which the Self is able to dissolve the boundaries between its experience and that of the Other, the necessity for assimilation both restricts and undermines its ethical potential. As Engell points out, the danger of interpretation, of translation, is at work: "However much we sympathize with another, we can never be sure that our imagination is accurately reproducing what he feels. We may misconstrue his experience. This may then not be sympathy but a form of empathy, projecting how we imagine a person feels and then identifying with that (false) projection."[35] Engell's insight reveals the inherent egoism through which the sympathetic imagination must operate. While sympathy may make possible the movement from the interiority of the Self towards the suffering of the Other, it is predicated upon the self-reflexive experience of the I's autonomy. This is why James first responds to the African by desiring to perform "so kind an office" as to be able to "have dispatched him." James's reaction is grounded in his own sense of autonomy—as the one not persecuted unto death. The alterity of the Other's experience is made comprehensible only through its translation into the cognitive and emotional experience of the I. Even as the sympathetic imagination gestures outward, beyond the ego, its ultimate movement is one of return: sympathy recuperates the experience of the Other into the totality in which the autonomous Self resides. In terms of Levinasian ethics, sympathy fails in such moments, for in its recovery of the Other's experience, it be-

---

33. Burke, *A Philosophical Enquiry*, 46.
34. Engell, *Creative Imagination*, 150.
35. Ibid., 158.

comes a kind of emotional appropriation—and as such, a mode of relationship constituted through comprehension. As a response generated in the desire for knowledge, even as a desire for emotional commiseration, sympathy returns the Other to the experiential province of the Self(-Same). As Adriaan Peperzak explains, "Knowledge is a form of appropriation and domination and thus of autonomy. The dimension of knowing is the dimension of a solitary I trying to subdue everything to the mastery of its thought."[36]

Indeed, one might argue that the sympathetic response is predicated upon the Self's granting of an equivalence to the Other who suffers. In the experience of encounter, the "solitary I" grants the Other an equivalence of identity—as an Other like me. Sympathy thus originates in the I's own notion of mastery and freedom. Situated in the imagination, sympathy emerges as an act of will or choice, through which the relationship between the Self and the Other is represented as being between equal subjectivities. The spectator chooses to recognize the suffering of the Other, but his choice is already grounded in an ideal of freedom and autonomy, because the suffering of the Other is imaginatively represented through the experiential history of an independent ego. In this sense, it becomes possible to consider sympathy as a response prior to the ethical, in that the spectator-self has not yet discovered the already existent obligation owed to the Other confronting him.

If we read James's response to the African as issuing from sympathy, the extent of its ethical insufficiency, as Holbo argues, becomes apparent. Although James offers water to the African and sympathetically muses, "Had I had a ball in my gun, I certainly should have dispatched him" (*LAF*, 167), his response is necessarily temporal and situational. It is premised upon the desire to end the immediate suffering of an Other like himself—an Other who, he imagines, would wish to be put out of his misery, thus ending James's own sympathetic suffering. Since James cannot relieve the African's torture, he is free to walk away, to disengage himself from the disruptive intervention of the encounter. His decision to dine in the house of the slaveholders appears to reinscribe the extent of his indifference. This is precisely the manner in which sympathy falters in the presence of the Other's suffering, for it is situated in the momentary, almost accidental, experience of encounter.

Both Burke and Levinas utilize the term *substitution* to name the experi-

---

36. Peperzak, *To the Other*, 71.

ence of response that occurs in the subject upon whom the Other intervenes. If we return to the Burkean definition of sympathy, James's sympathetic response is based upon a kind of substitution, both circumstantial and temporal, in which the suffering of the Other may be said to occur as an acute intervention, but one from which the subject can subsequently flee. Because the sympathetic identification is symmetrical, the arc of its command is tied to a given present, a distinct moment in time in which the subject is immediately confronted. As James's response to the African demonstrates, when the arrested subject engages the Other, that engagement is transient and contingent. It is a being-with-the-Other, an act of identification in which the Other is brought into the experiential world of the Self, but it is also an encounter in which the subject remains wholly intact and wholly free. The subject, initially free to sympathize, is equally free to dissolve the bonds of entanglement, and so to return to the province of his autonomy. Burkean substitution returns the subject to the realm of self-interest, thereby preserving the possibility of his disengagement, his abdication of responsibility. This is what James appears to effect in his return to the world of reason, where the "laws of self-preservation" render the African's death reasonably justifiable. In other words, through his sympathetic response, James suffers with the African as Other; he does not suffer for the African as well.

In Burkean terms, substitution implies the possibility of sympathy's movement towards the realm of ethics. Both sympathy and ethics are dependent upon an encounter with the Other, through which the face of the Other intervenes upon the subject's experience of his autonomy and freedom. But as Levinas utilizes the concept of substitution to describe the position of the self in reference to the Other she encounters, substitution overwhelms and transcends the limits of the sympathetic imagination. This distinction between Levinas and Burke might best be understood in terms of the symmetry of selves and the issue of temporality.

Sympathy emerges through an activity of identification, a being-with-the-Other; it is located in the temporal present. Because the response to the Other is occasioned by circumstance, sympathy (like ethics, to an extent) depends upon a kind of proximity through which the suffering of the Other is made visible to the I. But the sympathetic subject is a mere observer, a subject "called to play the role of a perceiver that reflects or welcomes."[37]

---

37. Emmanuel Levinas, *Otherwise than Being*, 82.

This activity of reflection—whether it manifests itself as knowledge or as emotional collaboration—nullifies the Other's alterity and recuperates her suffering into the experiential territory of the self. The proximity of sympathy is thus a closeness expressed through reciprocity. In that sense, it is a relationship founded upon a kind of elemental symmetry. And as a relationship characterized by the projected symmetry of subjectivities, the sympathetic experience as manifested in actual time is really synchronic. The suffering of the Other belongs to a distinct atemporal present, which is not yet implicated in the historical experience of the autonomous self.

The sympathetic response tends towards the ethical as an act called forth from the subject's freedom. In other words, the sympathetic subject may choose to act morally towards the Other who suffers, but such a choice arises from a return to the totality of consciousness, where the subject stands in the awareness of his own freedom and absence of suffering. As such, he is the spectator-self, whose morality emerges from a consciousness of self "as the identity of an ego endowed with knowledge or (what amounts to the same thing) with powers."[38] Cognizant of his own power—even to relieve the Other's suffering—he is not yet responsible, not yet awakened to the guilt he bears. In this sense, sympathy fails to discover the command through which the ethical self is born. This is James's initial stance. His desire to relieve the African's suffering is reflected in his offer of water, but he remains a sympathetic spectator. Only after the encounter does James begin to confront his own guilt and awaken to his responsibility in the politics of race that permit the African's unjust persecution.

When Levinas names the response to the Other as one predicated upon substitution, we must understand "substitution" beyond the notions of imaginary representation, intentionality, or the play of an "auto-affection as an auto-revelation," where the Self "is in the end affected only by itself, freely."[39] This is exactly the discourse that sympathy invites. Whereas sympathetic substitution enables a being-with-the-Other, the Levinasian concept of substitution entails a being-for-the-Other: it is not the posture of a subject freely contemplating the plethora of his possibilities of action, but the posture of a subject who is brought to discover that he is guilty, accused, and already responsible for the Other who confronts him. "A subject is a hostage," Levinas

---

38. Ibid., 83.
39. Ibid., 111.

argues; in so doing, he constructs subjectivity as "*sub-jectum*," where the self, called by the face of the Other, awakens to discover that he is neither alone nor autonomously free, but already "under the weight of the universe, responsible for everything."[40]

To postulate such a concept of subjectivity is to displace the subject in his notion of an historical identity. If sympathy originates in the sphere of the temporal, ethics points to and postulates the existence of a responsibility, a being-for-the-Other, that precedes conscious choice. The Self born into the world is already implicated in the existential plight of the Other, and the conditions of that implication are beyond deniability. The encounter with the Other intervenes upon the conscious comprehension of my freedom; it calls me to the awakening of my guilt and my realization of the inescapable exigency of my responsibility. In the presence of the Other who suffers, Peperzak clarifies, the I is not a spectator or an interpreter. In the ethical substitution, I encounter the Other who suffers, and in that confrontation I discover the "obligation that is imposed on me in responsibility [and] makes me guilty—a debtor—without my having made any choice." In other words, "I stand under an accusation that I have not earned."[41]

According to Levinas, if the ethical self is already guilty, its history is neither temporal nor linear, but primordial and transcendent. Ethical responsibility is neither circumstantial nor accidental. It is not incurred in the moment of encounter, when the Other appears suddenly to intervene upon the perimeters of one's freedom; as Levinas writes, "Responsibility for another is not an accident that happens to a subject, but precedes essence in it, has not awaited freedom, in which a commitment to another would have been made. I have not done anything and I have always been under accusation—persecuted."[42] Here, the ethical explicitly and sharply distinguishes itself from the possibilities that sympathy postulates. Ethical responsibility is not a choosing, but an answering. It is the posture of the self as hostage, in which "the word *I* means *here I am*, answering for everything and for everyone. Responsibility for the others has not been a return to oneself, but an exasperated contracting, which the limits of identity cannot retain."[43] In this con-

40. Ibid., 116.
41. Peperzak, *To the Other*, 222.
42. Levinas, *Otherwise than Being*, 114.
43. Ibid.

text, James's encounter with the African appears as more than accidental. Its inclusion in Crèvecoeur's previously celebratory narrative signifies the radical reverberations of its import.

Yet even as one is tempted to name the ethical desire as that of an answering subject, it is not merely an issue of the vocative, or the experience of being addressed. Although ethics is predicated upon the event of being addressed, of encountering the call that issues from the face of the Other, the notion of "answering" cannot be understood as mere reciprocity. The act of being addressed, Levinas asserts, is not sufficient—nor is an answering that presents itself as a resolution, as the return of a "*reciprocal hello* [that] maintains me in my 'for oneself.'" As Levinas emphatically concludes, "The vocative is not enough!" (*OG*, 99). Ethics is the "exasperated contracting" of the self, not the congratulatory expansion of self-aggrandizement that mutuality fosters.

In Levinasian terms, the ethical frustrates the satisfactory conclusiveness of the traditional moral experience as well. While morality signifies the actions of a subject who answers, those actions are expressed by a subject who "first of all, *is* and who, at a certain moment, has a moral experience" (*OG*, 90). Having satisfied the demands of an experiential immediacy, the subject returns to the province of its own history—enlarged, perhaps, through the pleasure of its good deed. In sum, the ethical response is an answering in the form of an accusation from which it is impossible to flee. This is the experience of "exasperation" and "contraction," of a particular kind of assignation: rather than addressing a subject who acts intentionally (for-oneself), morally or otherwise, ethics is the answering of a subject who discovers that he is now and forevermore the object of the other's intentionality (for-the-other). The subject has been put in question, beyond the possibility of thematizing or reducing to comprehension the extent of his responsibility. To say that ethics is an answering is also to say that it is a discovery: "Ethics is when I not only do not thematize another; it is when another *obsesses* me or puts me in question. This putting in question does not expect that I respond; it is not a question of giving a response, but of finding oneself responsible" (*OG*, 99).

Let us return to Farmer James, whose encounter with the African in the tree presents itself in terms both sympathetic and ethical. I concur with Holbo that James's response to the African, in the immediacy through which sympathy is generated, fails—for its impetus as desire neither establishes a "psychologically universalized aesthetics" that could potentially "produce a localized ethics," nor results in a "bond between people that is also a shared understanding of moral boundaries." As the sympathetic observer, James is sympathetically challenged. Given that this incident is narrated at the end of the letter, with no qualifying words of objection or agency, Holbo seems right to conclude that this scene of abject horror is a "passage [which] exemplifies an aesthetics detached from ethics."[44]

But to read this scene through the language of the ethical is to open up the possibilities of its meaning. If James fails as the sympathetic spectator whose interpretive translation necessarily originates in his own auto-affective powers of revelation, perhaps he partially succeeds in awakening to a recognition that is potentially ethical. Once the African speaks and turns his face to James, he initiates and invokes a relationship rooted in discourse. In the act of speech, the African is revealed in his alterity—not as an object reducible to whatever idea James may wish to impose upon him, but as a presence exceeding James's imaginative representation of him. In this context, it is significant that James names the African as "negro," and not "slave." From the moment of his speaking, the African necessarily disrupts and shatters the falsity of his categorization as "slave" to reveal himself as an inherently foreign autonomy, whose freedom exceeds any rational classification. This is what Levinas means when he argues that the "work of language" is not reducible to a relationship characterized by object cognition, but that language itself presumes the existence of a plurality, a relationship between interlocutors. Its "work" therefore "consists in entering into relationship with a nudity disengaged from every form, but having meaning by itself" (TI, 74).

The validity of speaking of the African in the tree as a "nudity disengaged" and simultaneously as "having meaning by itself" is borne out by James's immediate situation: he is apprehended in the midst of his own freedom, and he finds himself suddenly obligated to respond to that voice, that face, calling him towards responsibility. The African's nudity is more than philosophical symbolism: it is real and horrific beyond words. This Other's skin and flesh have been picked from his bones; even while he appears as Other, he is disappearing between (or beyond) the modalities of life and death. The African is an Other whose very being-in-otherness is beyond

---

44. Holbo, "Imagination, Commerce, and the Politics of Associationism," 47.

imagination or conceptualization. In this sense, the encounter begins to exceed thematic representation.

What is critically important is the fact that James, as surprised and terrified as he is, responds to and recognizes the address of this Other. This recognition is less an issue of James's immediate response than that of a response occasioned in trauma, which will ultimately emerge as responsibility. In the immediacy of the moment, there is little James can do to lessen the African's suffering. As we have seen, James's efforts in the temporal present are ineffective and futile. But in the end, the temporal does not distinguish this narrative event or the site in which its ethical power is housed. James's encounter with the African opens into a dimension of time that is atemporal and therefore disruptive far beyond his solitary retreat from the forest.

When the African turns his mangled and sightless face towards James, he initiates a moment of engagement—of absolute and unadulterated "facing"—seldom equaled in American literature. While numerous critics have noted the singularity of this moment in Crèvecoeur's text, its stunningly ethical reverberations have been largely effaced in more traditional readings. Considered from the perspective of ethics, however, this moment illuminates the validity of Levinas's claim that only in the act of facing does the Other transcend the categories of his objectivity. Because of—and in spite of—the unutterable horror and abject violation imposed upon the African, James is thrown into a situational proximity that neither lends itself to the powers of abstraction nor permits the exigency of flight. The event of the African's appearing constitutes a proximity that signifies far beyond the accident of nearness or the imaginary unity of fusion. "Humanity herself would have recoiled back with horror" (*LAF*, 167), James says, and his words reveal the practical impossibility of fusion. This is an existential nightmare—indeed, one genuinely unimaginable in James's projections even of his own death. Because the encounter with the African precludes this sympathetic leap of fusion, it becomes an event marked by trauma, one that precipitates a certain irretrievable fissure of the self. And here is where its ethical content begins to emerge.

Despite the ineffectuality of his temporal attempts at redress, James's encounter with the African is not "finished" in his decision to walk away. The letter ends as if James had returned to the world of his peers without much difficulty; but taken as a whole, the letter defies such conclusiveness. James's encounter with the African disrupts the celebratory valorization of freedom, which is the ontological imperative that underpins the internal logic of *Letters from an American Farmer*. Ethics resides in the proximity that achieves both fissure and fraternity, and this "proximity is not a configuration produced in the soul. It is an immediacy older than the abstractness of nature. Nor is it fusion: it is contact with the other. To be in contact is neither to invest the other and annul his alterity, nor to suppress myself in the other."[45]

If James's encounter with the African in the tree occasions a peculiar kind of fraternity, one beyond the sympathetic, its real meaning and resonance lies in its dissonance and diachrony. Rather than fusion, there is fissure—a kind of temporal reversal—in the subversive chronology of Crèvecoeur's narrative strategy. Indeed, the effect of James's encounter with the African is shown in the opening words of the letter and its preliminary paragraphs. In the prolegomena of this letter, James rises above the parameters of his subjectivity, as ego, to discover a realm in which he is guilty, even though he has not been the agent of such a horrendous and tortuous death. In the face of the African in the tree, James discovers the murderous potential of freedom in its most extreme imaginable expression, as a philosophy of power, privilege, and birth; it would permit the death of the Other in order to maintain and perpetuate the rule and sovereignty of the Same. The epiphany of the face that this African turns upon James is a Levinasian *otherwise*: "You shall not commit murder." This is its epiphany, its enunciation as a saying before which James is called to answer. This is the command of the face that shatters the immediacy of the sympathetic response to reveal a responsibility and guilt "anterior to all the logical deliberation summoned by reasoned decision" (*TI*, 111), which opens into that space where "proximity" becomes something other than reciprocity and leans towards ethics.

In the aftermath of his encounter with the African, James comes to discover that freedom is potentially a philosophy of power, dependent upon the surrender of difference to the rule of individual freedom. In this instance, the privilege that is freedom begins to be unmasked as appropriation and power. The epiphany of the face that the African turns towards James is elemental and disruptive. Its expression bears the first words of Levinasian ethics: "You shall not commit murder" (*TI*, 199). The African's speaking is a resistance that contests every effort on the part of his persecutors to render

---

45. Levinas, *Otherwise than Being*, 86.

his death explicable. In fact, the African resists all such ideological distinctions—his is the disruptive face of alterity, the face that is its own epiphany, and its command is that freedom must answer to ethics, that justice must mediate freedom.

And yet the African is essentially faceless: his is, in effect, the faceless face. But rather than negating his power as interlocutor, his facelessness raises it to the level of symbolic signification. The opposition of the African in the tree transcends the purely personal, for he becomes the sign of all persons of African blood whose destiny he potentializes. Here again is where ethics exceeds the possibility of sympathy, for the relation to the Other must radiate beyond the proximity of closeness or the restricted response to the neighbor. The fact that James can effectively do nothing for the African does not release him from accountability. Instead, his encounter with the African is an invitation towards the plane of responsibility that both precedes and exceeds the African's appearance and death. The essential facelessness of the African in the tree initiates a proximity that escapes pure representation, and thus ushers James into relationship with all Others who are African, whose lives are marked by the brutality of persecution that is slavery.

Here, too, is a particular opposing freedom, this dying African, whose intervention is urgently specific; in this respect, the force of his disruptive capacity is immediate in its call upon James, and prophetic for the republic as a whole. To the extent that we can read James's encounter with the African as a representation of the problem of difference persistent within the American landscape, the African's presence exceeds the bounds of James's experience, as well as Crèvecoeur's narrative. The African in the tree continues to resonate as that unanswered call in the face of the Other, which by its very being resists the tyranny that the uncontested rule of freedom makes possible, insisting upon the primacy of justice.

Yet despite James's failure toward the African—his willingness to resume his place at the slaveholders' table—if we think of ethics as an optics, as a way of seeing, then James's participation in the experience of community he shares with the African is implicitly disruptive. The African is the one who breaks up the totality of perspective in which the valorization of freedom has reigned without question. In consequence of that face-to-face meeting, James is brought to a recognition in which the essential freedom of the African as Other has been rendered visible. Indeed, James's recognition of the African's alterity implicates the entire structure of the totality. It calls into question the ideal of freedom as the ground upon which reason, and its imposition of order, instantiates itself.

Even as James resumes his sojourn in the landscape, his consciousness has been altered. This is the voice that comes to presence at the very beginning of Letter IX, in the recognition that enslavement of the Other is an act of war that is premised upon power and violence. James admits that the forced labor of the African is an indefensible violation perpetuated by "persons they know not, and who have no other power over them than that of violence." The commerce of slavery is the commission of a fraud "surpassing in enormity everything which a common mind can possibly conceive" (*LAF*, 156–7), for its real intent has been revealed as the permission to commit murder. From the perspective of Levinasian ethics, even the desire to murder attests to the "native freedom," as James calls it, of the African as Other.

If "murder exercises a power over what escapes power," then "I can wish to kill only an existent absolutely independent, which exceeds my powers infinitely, and therefore does not oppose them but paralyzes the very power of power. The Other is the sole being I can wish to kill" (*TI*, 198). This recognition of the African's absolute Otherness, before which James has no power, not even the possibility of any real comprehension, is precisely what commands him to critique the ideal of freedom and to recognize its false constitution as truth—as if freedom bore no obligation or responsibility to the Other against whom its violence is waged. "Whence this astonishing right, or rather this barbarous custom, for most certainly we have no kind of right beyond that of force?" (*LAF*, 161).

Whereas in Letter III, James was moved to ask, "What is an American?" and cast his answer in terms that valorized the American's unique legacy of freedom and entitlement, by Letter IX, the question has become: "What then is man; this being who boasts so much of the excellence and dignity of his nature, among that variety of inscrutable mysteries, of unsolvable problems, with which he is surrounded?" (*LAF*, 158). It is a question made possible only by the intervention of the Other's presence, and it is ultimately a question motivated by the discovery of guilt and shame. James's recognition that the "history of the earth" is one steeped in "avarice, rapine, and murder" calls into question the very foundation of power by which freedom asserts its unqualified rule (*LAF*, 162).

The encounter with the African marks the critical ethical awakening in James's narrative journey, and its ramifications resonate through the remainder of the text. In Letter XII, "Distresses of a Frontier Man," the experience of fissure reaches the full force of its expression. By this last letter, the voice that predominates is one of fear, floundering, and flight: "I wish for a change of place; the hour is come at last, that I must fly from my house and abandon my farm! But what course shall I steer, inclosed as I am?" (*LAF*, 192). This final letter is glaring in its pessimism, its slide away from the pastoral visions of the republic that dominated earlier letters, and its nearly frantic projections of enclosure, death, and persecution. While the earlier letters resounded with the unified voice of certainty and place, the final letter moves towards the dissolution of self-certainty and the impending abandonment of place—an abandonment that cuts to the heart of James's previous paradigm of identity.

In contrast to Letter IX, the final letter is a return to the primacy of self. Whereas in the aftermath of his Charleston visit, James is brought to question the laws of "self-preservation" as they imperil the life of the Other, here, in the onslaught of revolution, "self-preservation" surfaces as the "rule of nature" and the "best rule of conduct" (*LAF*, 198). In this case, however, James has now become the persecuted Other. Holbo rightly argues, "Even as the letter returns to James's situation . . . it actualizes the alienation from community and from particular identity that was imaginatively enacted in the previous letters: in moving to the frontier, James proposes to abandon the propertied stability and community membership which earlier formed the foundations of his identity."[46] While Letter XII appears to enact a return to the primacy of subjectivity, it simultaneously undoes the certainty of James as autonomous subject. In order to save himself and his family, he must accept and confront the breakup of a totality in which his consciousness of self has been invested.

But the solution is not simply that James will move further into the frontier, and thus into the province of the backwoodsmen that he had previously denigrated. He schemes to take flight and to seek refuge among the Indians, those Others whose alterity had previously been relegated to an ahistorical past. Arguably, the dissolution of identity that erupts in the final letter is not restricted to James, but reflects a dissolution of the cultural totality itself: a dissolution precipitated by the imposition of trauma, which essentially disrupts the very categories through which the identities of the subject (as I)

---

46. Holbo, "Imagination, Commerce, and the Politics of Associationism," 53.

and the Other (as woodsman and Indian) have been formulated. This is part of the experience of fissure that James undergoes. In the flight to the Indian, James's previous and prevailing notion of an unerring telos, of a foundational progression in which history proceeds, is dismantled. In this final letter, one might argue that James questions the very ideal of history. The flight to the Indian becomes both a (re)turn to the past—a time antecedent to the republican reign of freedom—and a thrust forward, beyond the oppositional boundaries against which American identity has been cast.

The final letter complicates James's earlier reading of the Indian face and presence. Even as he fears the potentially corruptive influence of Indian culture upon his children and laments the vicissitudes of change in language, custom, and habit that such a transition will entail, he now possesses a quasi respect, a willingness to question the assumptions of knowledge he once held dear. Reflecting upon the incidence of European captives who, in freedom, choose against all logical reason to remain with their Native captors, James is forced to comment, "It cannot be, therefore, so bad as we generally conceive it to be; there must be in their social bond something singularly captivating, and far superior to anything to be boasted of among us." Here, Native culture is recovered as one more imaginatively universal, one "more congenial" to the human spirit and "disposition . . . than the fictitious society in which we live" (*LAF*, 209). That the world of the once fully autonomous American has become "fictitious" clearly demonstrates the shattering of the totality of meaning, reason, and the subject itself.

As numerous critics have noted, the tone of the final letter is dark and apocalyptic. James seems nearly mad, flitting between poles of contradiction, suffering from "wild . . . and trifling reflections," even on the edge of "dangerous extremes of violence" (*LAF*, 210). Yet despite its darkness of vision, the final letter bears within it the seed of hope, of possibilities not yet known or charted. In the midst of its chaotic flights of fear and fantasy, there is promise. That James must relinquish his homestead, let go of the stability of self first promised in the dream of the American farmer, reveals that the sojourn is over. For both James and the emergent republic he reveres, freedom is in question. This is precisely what Levinas identifies as the aporia of possibility. As he writes, "Freedom consists in knowing that freedom is in peril" (*TI*, 35).

If *Letters* ultimately fails to achieve the unity of self and society, its failure is nevertheless genuinely anticipatory and liberating. It is only in the experience of fissure, of knowing that freedom is in peril, that there is an opening for justice to emerge. Whatever else James may learn from his life among the Indians, in his flight he will be brought face to face with the indigenous Other whose freedom has been violently disrupted from the beginning. Here is the space of ethical possibility, of a radical disruption and alteration, where history might begin again in the potential of an as-yet-undiscovered justice.

Crèvecoeur's *Letters*, then, exceeds the bounds of its purely "fictional" representation. I have approached *Letters* as a text of opening and anticipation, one which articulates a distinctly American ideology, but which also resonates with the possibility of disruption. That disruption becomes the inception of the American revolution, rooted in the twin ideals of freedom and justice. While *Letters from an American Farmer* made its print debut six years after the publication of Thomas Paine's *Common Sense*, it nevertheless might be considered as its literary precursor. The originary images of Crèvecoeur's agrarian and pastoral America, pre-1776, are representative images emanating out of the nonfictional experience of this emigrant author. If J. Hector St. John de Crèvecoeur would become the first farmer of the American experiment in freedom, there is yet another emigrant, an orphaned Englishman, who would become her catalytic and radical first statesman. That individual is Thomas Paine.

2 In the Name of "Justice and Humanity"
Thomas Paine's Ethical Envisionings of the American Republic

On January 10, 1776, when Thomas Paine's *Common Sense* first appeared in print, its intent was revolutionary, its effects dramatic and disruptive. Almost immediately, Paine's insurgent pamphlet achieved unprecedented sales, surpassing "those of any of the other 400 pamphlets of the pre-Revolutionary debate: in twenty-five American editions some 120,000 copies were sold in the first three months alone and perhaps half a million in the first year."[1] As one eighteenth-century observer noted, *Common Sense* "burst 'forth like a mighty conqueror, bearing down all opposition.' "[2] Throughout the colonies, in varying circles of influence and station, the praise for Paine was nearly unanimous: "Nothing could have been better timed than this performance. . . . It has produced most astonishing effects; and been received with vast applause; read by almost every American; and recommended as a work replete with truth." Paine's contemporary Benjamin Rush asserted the pivotal importance of Paine's incendiary text in terms that bear directly upon the themes of this study: "Its effects were sudden and extensive upon the American mind. It was read by public men, repeated in clubs, spouted in Schools, and in one instance, delivered from the pulpit instead of a sermon by a clergyman in Connecticut."[3]

That Paine's *Common Sense* captured the American imagination is certain. Its arguments in the name of independence and its fearless condemnation of the tyranny of government were stunning elements of its radicalism

---

1. Gregory Claeys, *Thomas Paine: Social and Political Thought* (Boston: Unwin Hyman, 1989), 51.
2. Quoted ibid.
3. Quoted in John Keane, *Tom Paine: A Political Life* (Boston: Little, Brown, 1995), 112.

and popular appeal. But Paine was hardly the first to call for American independence, and it is not merely his revolutionary rhetoric that distinguishes his emergence in American consciousness. Thomas Paine is that presence in the American mind and landscape who is called forward in the pre-Revolutionary moments of potential chaos to speak and to answer for the destitute, unknown, Levinasian Others whose voices have yet to be heard. In his charged and accusatory words, a new language surfaces, and an originary political possibility is envisioned. Neither an American farmer nor a Founding Father, Paine's investment in the American landscape is one of vision and possibility rather than of property or conquest. In Paine's fervently idealistic vision, America is the "only spot in the political world where the principles of universal reformation could begin," and where, echoing Crèvecoeur, "Man becomes what he ought to be" (*ColW*, 548).

"It was the cause of America that made me an author," Paine asserted seven years after the publication of *Common Sense*. These words suggest his difference from the Crèvecoeurian farmer who is forced into flight as the prospect of war impinges upon his horizon. In the latter moments of *Letters*, Crèvecoeur's representation of the American situation is marked by uncertainty and the terrifying trauma of fissure. Farmer James, in the forced departure from his farm and the threatened invasion of his home, undergoes a kind of symbolic death that is revelatory of the chaos that war and revolution entail. The implication of death, as the process through which the existing totality of meaning must perish or be transformed, applies not only to James (whose life is irreparably altered), but to the republic as a whole. Implicit in the advent of war is the shattering of a national identity previously articulated through the paradigm of property and the self-certain identity of the farmer, whose privilege is suddenly subject to question. At the end of *Letters*, Farmer James runs to the safety of the Indian; yet this safety is housed in a Romantic possibility. The Indian towards whom James flees is the Other whose very being has been relegated to another historical time. When James takes refuge in the culture of Native peoples, he does so to escape the threat of discontinuity, the brutal experience and dislocation of revolution. In other words, he takes refuge out of time, in an ahistorical past prior to the disruptive threat of revolutionary war.

In that breach of meaning and historical uncertainty, Thomas Paine comes to voice. Unlike Crèvecoeur, Tom Paine has no desire to be an American farmer. Unlike Jefferson or John Adams—who regarded Paine's words and work as a "poor, ignorant, malicious, short-sighted crapulous mass"—Tom Paine is not particularly invested in the territorial prospect that America might offer.[4] Where Crèvecoeur finds propertied prosperity and Jefferson envisions territorial sovereignty, Paine discovers a site of sterling possibility, one in which the yet-to-come of a just republic might be genuinely imagined. For him, the uncertainty and chaos of revolution is not terrifying, but the site of an aporia. He finds opportunity rather than fear in the prospect of the American Revolution. His perspective engages a particular *anschauung*, or optics, that looks forward to change and challenge—towards the space of remaking and renaming the world around him. As he would comment in the years between the writing of *Common Sense* and *Rights of Man*, "The present condition of the world, differing so exceedingly from what it formerly was, has given a new cast to the mind of man. . . . Our style and manner of thinking have undergone a revolution more extraordinary than the political revolution of the country. We see with other eyes; we hear with other ears; and think with other thoughts than those we formerly used." ("Letter to the Abbé Raynal," *CW*, 243). The passionate, extraordinary legacy of Thomas Paine is birthed in the ideal of an equity that might evolve towards justice, an ideal that is firmly rooted in an ethical notion of time and responsibility. To postulate an alternative optics, as another way of seeing, is itself a critique of the "American mind" that Jefferson will deem as committed to the ideal of freedom; one is already invested in the privilege that property and place signify.

"My principle is universal," Tom Paine said in defense of his own unprecedented celebrity. "My attachment is to all the world, and not to any particular part." Paine's America is the starting point, the space of inception, where revolution is welcomed as the event through which human beings are asked to recall a primordial past, one initially biblical, through which human identity can be reenvisioned. In the rupture that is revolution, Paine responds in a language both historically radical and performatively prophetic. His words are a challenge to the people—the ordinary, the poor, and the dispossessed orphans of the world, like Paine himself. His specific challenge to the people is that they become authentic citizens and active participants in a new and revolutionary ideal of government, where they direct and own government rather than being owned by it. Both in *Common Sense* and in *Rights of Man* (1791), Paine sounds the call "for a revolution in consciousness,

---

4. Quoted in Bernard Bailyn, *Faces of Revolution* (New York: Knopf, 1990), 71.

in the interiority of mankind." It is a challenge inherently disruptive and explicitly ethical, for its goal is to "make imaginable, to bring into being a new world and a new sense of human possibility in that world."[5]

In the introductory words of *Common Sense*, Paine declares that the "cause of America is in a great measure the cause of all mankind." For historian Bernard Bailyn, Paine's greatest contribution to the struggle for American identity resides in this passionate effort to challenge and dismantle the prevailing assumptions of European and Anglo-American notions of government. Bailyn argues that underlying the proliferation of political and social arguments for an independent American republic, there remained "unspoken, even unconceptualized presuppositions, attitudes, and habits of thought that made it extremely difficult for the colonists to break with Britain."[6] With the publication of *Common Sense*, those unspoken and yet deeply held assumptions—in the wisdom of nobility, the justifiable constitution of government through monarchy, and the natural inequity of birth and circumstance—were not simply challenged, but subverted.

Although Paine's ideas were not directly implemented or fully embraced, Bailyn writes, they "forced thoughtful readers to consider . . . a wholly new way of looking at the entire range of problems involved." Unlike many of his New World colleagues, Paine sought not reformation but revolution. According to Bailyn, "The aim of almost every other notable pamphlet of the revolution . . . was to probe difficult, urgent and controversial questions and make appropriate recommendations." Bailyn insists that "Paine's aim was to tear the world apart—the world as it was known and as it was constituted."[7] As such, the language of *Common Sense* is neither timid nor diplomatic; it comes to voice as a text that eschews mere politics for the higher ground of moral certitude and ethical challenge.

"We have it in our power to begin the world over again," Paine states in *Common Sense* (*ColW*, 52). His words announce the universal import of the American opportunity for revolution. At stake for Paine is neither the personally transformative "admission" possible through Crèvecoeur's "great asylum," in which the dispossessed European finds "place" through the paradigm of property, nor the potentially public recognition offered in the

---

5. D. A. Beale, "Language, Poetry, and the Rights of Man," *Theoria* 75 (1990): 39.
6. Bailyn, *Faces of Revolution*, 76.
7. Ibid., 75–6, 82.

Jeffersonian promise that "every man is a sharer in the direction of his . . . republic . . . and is a participator in the government of affairs."[8] The Jeffersonian promise, as Gordon Wood points out, is founded in the notion of a natural aristocracy, based on birth, name, and cultural clout. For Paine, in contrast, at stake in the American enterprise is a biblical notion of human redemption whereby all human beings will rediscover the truth of an originary kinship, lacking in any intrinsic inequity. Paine's America becomes the practical opportunity to determine the external restraints upon people's natural freedom—restraints made necessary by immorality and greed.

Among the radical aspects of Paine's argument in *Common Sense* are its assertions of the "evil" of government and the original equality of human beings. Government, Paine argues, "even in its best state is but a necessary evil," for "government, like dress, is the badge of lost innocence. . . . For were the impulses of conscience clear, uniform, and irresistibly obeyed, man would need no other lawgiver" (*ColW*, 7). This assertion sounds distinctly Rousseauian. Paine embraces the ideal of a natural, initially moral society, prior to the imposition of government. While he classifies that earlier existence as the "state of natural liberty"—as opposed to Rousseau's "natural society"—in both constructs, want and necessity disrupt the initial state of liberty and sever the I's original relation to Others. As Rousseau explains, "As soon as one man needed the help of another, as soon as one man realized that it was useful for a single individual to have provisions for two, equality disappeared, property came into existence, labor became necessary."[9]

In Paine's construction, it is government, more than property, through which human beings suffer the loss of equality. Government, for Paine, is the explicit sign of "man's fall"—the "badge of lost innocence"—for its necessary emergence marks a specifically moral failure: "Here then is the origin and rise of government; namely, a mode rendered necessary by the inability of moral virtue to govern the world" (*ColW*, 8). Paine, like Rousseau, believes in the originary goodness and fraternity of human beings. Yet whereas Rousseau's "natural man" is solitary and areligious, Paine's "natural man" is inherently Christian, existing in a spiritual and therefore a more ethical relationship to others.

---

8. Jefferson, *Life and Selected Writings*, 661.

9. Jean-Jacques Rousseau, "Discourse on the Origin and Foundation of Inequality among Mankind," in *The Social Contract and Discourse on the Origin of Inequality*, ed. Lester G. Crocker (New York: Simon and Schuster, 1967), 220.

Common Sense is Paine's critique of the evolution of government as an increasingly immoral agency, through which human being itself is falsely differentiated. As evidence, Paine cites the imposed distinction between "kings and subjects"—a distinction, he reminds us, "for which no truly natural or religious reason can be assigned." He argues, "Male and female are the distinctions of nature, good and bad are distinctions of heaven; but how a race of men came into the world so exalted above the rest, and distinguished like some new species, is worth inquiring into, and whether they are the means of happiness or misery to mankind" (*ColW*, 12). The conclusion, Paine asserts, is simple, specific, and obvious to common sense: the construction of government through monarchy constitutes a violation of both the natural and moral orders. If the establishment of government—particularly a monarchy—disrupts human equality as the original order of creation, it represents an unequivocal sin against the scriptural command of God, since "it is the pride of kings which throws mankind into confusion" (*ColW*, 12). Added to that initial sin is the notion of hereditary succession—"an insult and an imposition on posterity"—that perpetuates a social and political reality that "nature" itself abhors:

> For all men being originally equals, no *one* by *birth* could have a right to set up his own family in perpetual preference to all others for ever, and though himself might deserve *some* decent degree of honors of his contemporaries, yet his descendants might be far too unworthy to inherit them. One of the strongest *natural* proofs of the folly of hereditary right in kings, is, that nature disapproves it, otherwise she would not so frequently turn it into ridicule by giving mankind an *Ass for a Lion.* (*ColW*, 16)

For Bailyn, *Common Sense* is a revolutionary document because Paine's critique of the structure of British government overturned the prevailing assumption, one particularly operative in the thirteen colonies, that the "liberties Americans sought were British in their nature: they had been achieved by Britain over the centuries and had been embedded in a constitution whose wonderfully contrived balance between the needs of the state and the rights of the individual was thought throughout the Western world to be one of the finest human achievements."[10] It was not simply that Paine blatantly attacked the historical and immediate failings of the British monarchy and its "farci-

---

10. Bailyn, *Faces of Revolution*, 69.

cal" constitution (as he termed it), but that he simultaneously rejected the philosophical foundations upon which the very concept of government had been erected. At its heart, *Common Sense* could be nothing less than revolutionary. Beneath its rhetorical maneuvers "was the flaming conviction, not simply that Britain was corrupt and that America should declare its independence, but that the whole of organized society and government was stupid and cruel and that it survived only because the atrocities it systematically imposed on humanity had been papered over with a veneer of mythology and superstition that numbed the mind and kept people from rising against the evils that oppressed them."[11]

The revolutionary effect of Paine's conviction in *Common Sense* is not solely the result of his attacks upon the political legacy of British government. Paine's vision in *Common Sense*, and even more directly in *Rights of Man*, exceeds the realm of politics to engage and encompass a notion of the ethical. This is one of the issues that A. Owen Aldridge takes up in his study *Thomas Paine's American Ideology*, in which he argues that Paine's literary motives were far more "moralistic than political," and that *Common Sense* "must be interpreted as embodying an ideological structure, the essence of which was fundamentally ethical." For Aldridge, what distinguishes Paine's contribution to the literature of the American Revolution is its emphasis on the moral justification for American independence. Whereas most of the literature of the period focused upon the economic rationale for the colonists to achieve independence, Aldridge argues, "Paine clearly believed that considerations of ethics overbalanced those of self-interest in the behavior and thinking of the American people. . . . Paine in *Common Sense* had sought to justify independence as a legitimate moral enterprise before proposing it as either desirable or feasible. Only after undertaking this moral justification as a preliminary step, did he proceed with his efforts to convince his readers that independence was also the most expedient solution to their problems and to demonstrate that they possessed the military and economic resources necessary to gain it."[12]

Without question, Paine's orientation is both political and ethical. One of the first places in which that union achieves presence is in Paine's notion

---

11. Ibid., 82.

12. A. Owen Aldridge, *Thomas Paine's American Ideology* (Newark: University of Delaware Press, 1984), 17, 25.

of time and history, where something akin to the Levinasian idea of an "immemorial past" emerges as a conceptual ideal through which human beings must reenvision the original nature of their relationship to one another. In the concluding words of *Common Sense,* Paine asserts that the independence of America is still up for grabs: its authority could come from military power, through a "mob," or through the "legal voice of the people." It is the last of these choices that will enable the possible construction of the "noblest purest constitution on the face of the earth," where human beings recall an original fraternity in which "a race of men . . . are to receive their portion of freedom" (*ColW,* 52). Paine's argument demands a particular notion of memory, one antecedent to the "remembered past," which is, in Paine's terms, a return to the rule and reason of "antiquity."

On the question of human rights, Paine responds definitively in terms of a history before law: authority resides in the prior signification of "antiquity." As he says in *Rights of Man,* there is "authority against authority all the way till we come to the divine origin of the rights of man at the creation. Here our inquiries find a resting-place, and our reason finds a home" (*ColW,* 462). What Paine envisions here is close to the Levinasian "immemorial past"—a past not wholly recoverable or documentable, but still one in which the responsibility to the Other comes first. In its way, it is a rightful obeisance before the word and command of God.

When Aldridge speaks of the morality of Paine's vision, he gestures towards this element of divine authority. But there is another path of interpretation that opens here, having to do with what Levinas names "ethical anteriority" (*TI,* 111) or, in Paine's language, "begin[ning] the world over again" (*ColW,* 52). As D. A. Beale suggests, "Paine is not only recovering a voice: he is evolving and discovering another voice . . . one capable of revealing the inhuman reality behind the 'decent drapery of life.'" What Paine would accomplish is nothing short of absolute rebellion and revolution. Much like Martin Buber, Beale asserts that Paine would make a "new house in the cosmos," in which the previously unheard and unseen—"the dispossessed, the 'voiceless,' and the voteless"—are given a "mode with which to understand their world and the tricks of verbal hegemony that underpin it, so that they might come to withstand its blandishments."[13]

When Paine refers his readers to the original fraternity of human beings

---

13. Beale, "Language, Poetry, and the Rights of Man," 40.

at the creation of the world, his words suggest the existence of a historical past in which the ethical truth of human relationship is discoverable. In *Rights of Man*, Paine argues for the return to antiquity, as the essential and elemental authority through which human identity must be understood. The problem, he suggests, is that "those who reason by precedents drawn from antiquity, respecting the rights of man . . . do not go far enough into antiquity. They do not go the whole way" (*ColW*, 461). To "go the whole way," he argues, would be to uncover a history that precedes remembered history, one that "has its origin from the maker of man," and one in which individual identity is marked by an originary sense of obligation—"whether to his creator, or the creation of which he is a part" (*ColW*, 464). In Paine's version of antiquity, human existence may be characterized by a vision of natural liberty, yet his vision is not one in which "everything is possible and everything is permitted."[14] Indeed, Paine is quite clear that while human beings possess intrinsic natural rights, including "those rights of acting as an individual for his own comfort and happiness," those rights are mediated by the obligation one bears in terms of one's "duty to God," and "with respect to his neighbor." More precisely, one is not free to act in ways that "are injurious to the rights of others" (*ColW*, 464). The lesson of antiquity is that freedom must bow before the duty of human beings to honor the obligation emanating from the word of God, and to honor the existence of the Other.

Insofar as Paine turns towards the rule of antiquity as a model for human identity and relationship, it becomes possible to think about his argument as one in which the trace of Levinasian ethics resonates. In *Time and the Other*, Levinas designates a notion of the "immemorial past," as that which "articulates itself—or 'thinks itself'—without recourse to the memory, without a return to 'living presents,'" but rather as a past that "signifies starting from an irrecusable responsibility." While Paine locates "irrecusable responsibility" in the biblical creation, Levinas posits a past "where everything must have begun," one that "has the signification of an inveterate obligation, older than any engagement, taking the whole of its meaning in the imperative that commands the ego by way of the Other's face." If the "immemorial past" is a past that we cannot recover through memory or representation, it is nevertheless a conceptualization of time "where obedience is the proper mode of

---

14. Emmanuel Levinas, *Time and the Other*, trans. Richard A. Cohen (Pittsburgh: Duquesne University Press, 1987), 124.

attending to the commandment" that issues from the presence and face of the Other.[15]

My intent here is not to try to establish an absolute equivalence between Paine's ideal of the creation and Levinas's "immemorial past." Rather, I am arguing that the way Paine thinks about the time of creation is implicitly ethical and bears a distinct resemblance to the Levinasian "time before time." Paine's construction is an ideal in which human relation is conceived through an originary obligation; Levinas agrees that the very "notion of creation . . . implies that" (*OG*, 97). Even if one reads Paine's time of creation as a literal moment in the history of human existence, its reality as a site of origin remains beyond, or imaginatively "before," the span of memory. Its meaning is essentially mythological. Paine's return to the order of creation might be understood as a return to the biblical commandment, where, as Levinas argues, "There is always a priority of the other in relation to me" (*OG*, 91). In that sense, Paine's return to the ideal of creation in order to discover—or recover—the originary rights of human beings before the corruptive imposition of government can be read in the Levinasian sense of a "time before time [when] something takes on a sense, starting from the ethical, and this sense is not a simple repetition of the present; for it is something that is not re-presentable" (*OG*, 97). In other words, it is possible to read Paine's ideal of the creation as one marked by an ethical *anschauung*, in which the obligation to others exists as an inherited duty that precedes the imposition and creation of government.

What is most important about Paine's assertion of the original and natural rights of human beings (evidenced in the model of creation) is that it reveals his commitment to an ideal of justice based on ethical responsibility. One of the most radical texts Paine authors is "African Slavery in America," written in late 1774 and first published in March 1775. Paine's essay is not merely a denunciation of African enslavement; it is, in no uncertain terms, an argument on behalf of the African Stranger, before whom the American free self is both guilty and obligated. In its opening lines, Paine asserts the reality of slavery as "violence and murder for gain" and condemns it as a "savage practice" that is absolutely "contrary to the light of nature, to every principle of justice and humanity" (*CW*, 16). His arguments are not especially original, particularly given that even Jefferson had argued in 1769 before the Virginia Assembly for the cessation of the slave trade.

---

15. Ibid., 111, 113.

What distinguishes Paine's essay is its refusal to question the essential integrity of the African's difference, as well as its fundamental accusation that the American practice of enslavement persists as a crime against human beings and God, as the "height of outrage against humanity and justice" (*CW*, 18). At no point does Paine question the essential freedom or full humanity of the African. Unlike Jefferson, who asserts in *Notes on the State of Virginia* an inherent "inferiority" in the very being of the African, Paine argues the "natural, perfect right" of the African's claim to freedom—a claim, most importantly, that the African has not agreed to forfeit. Paine insists that despite the violence of slavery, the enslaved African remains the "proper owner of his freedom" and "has a right to reclaim it, however often" he or she is "sold" (*CW*, 17). This is where Paine's notion of an originary right supersedes the rule of authority grounded in law.

In its essence, Paine's argument is ethical: the American and the European who perpetuate and attempt to justify slavery are explicitly guilty. The defense of slavery is a blatant argument in defense of murder: "Certainly one may, with as much reason and decency, plead for murder, robbery, lewdness, and barbarity, as for this practice. They are not more contrary to the natural dictates of conscience, and feelings of humanity; nay, they are all comprehended in it" (*CW*, 18). Writing in the name of "Justice and Humanity," Paine's essay anticipates the importance of the Levinasian concept of "the third party," the unknown Other for whom justice must be rendered. "African Slavery in America" is addressed "To Americans," but its focus is not the compact between Paine and his audience as free subjects and speakers; rather, it sounds a call in the name of "the third party" whose freedom has been wrongfully and violently usurped. The fact that Paine speaks in the name of "Justice and Humanity" suggests that he speaks for the fate of the African; the command for justice is accordingly sounded in terms of what Levinas would name the African's "useless suffering." As Levinas explains, "Thus the very phenomenon of suffering in its uselessness is, in principle, the pain of the other. For an ethical sensibility, confirming, in the inhumanity of our time, its opposition to this inhumanity, the justification of the neighbor's pain is certainly the source of all immorality" (*EN*, 98–9).

One of Paine's key arguments in "African Slavery in America" is his attack upon the flagrant immorality of the American Christian's willingness to allege that the "sacred scriptures . . . favor this practice." Here Paine anticipates his later arguments in *Rights of Man*, for it is clear that the model of creation is to be understood in terms of the commandment it imposes upon human beings: "Christians are taught *to account all men their neighbors; and love their neighbors as themselves; and do to all men as they would be done by; to do good to all men; and man-stealing is ranked with enormous crimes.* Is the barbarous enslaving our inoffensive neighbors, and treating them like wild beasts subdued by force, reconcilable with all these *divine precepts*?" (*CW,* 17). The ethical impetus of Paine's argument raises the question of whether one's relationship to God, expressed through "divine precepts" that command the love of one's neighbor, is not simultaneously a relation to the Other, and thus a relationship originating in the ethical. Paine's answer comes amazingly close to that of Levinas. Levinasian ethics is neither dependent nor predicated upon the biblical image of creation—for when Levinas names an "immemorial past," he says, "This is the past in which I also never return to a creator God either, but rather toward a past more ancient than any rememberable past, and one where time is described in its diachrony" (*OG,* 96). The "diachrony" of that past resonates in Paine's vision of a new beginning, forged in a past essentially unrecoverable, unrememberable, yet still ethically binding. Levinas similarly reveres the sacred bond between word and obligation. As he asserts, "There is no separation between the Father and the Word; it is in the form of speech, in the form of an ethical order, an order to love, that the descent of God takes place. It is in the Face of the Other [*Autre*] that the commandment comes which interrupts the progress of the world" (*EN,* 110).

One might argue that the entire corpus of Thomas Paine is intended to "interrupt the progress of the world." In "African Slavery in America," Paine desires not only to interrupt the criminal practice and justification of slavery, but to insist upon the obligation towards justice that commands the American, and particularly the New World Christian, to act upon a responsibility that is specifically ethical. This requires a responsibility that demands not only the abolition of slavery, but also acknowledges the historical burden of an injustice already waged against an innocent and "inoffensive people": "The gain of that trade has been pursued in opposition to the Redeemer's cause, and the happiness of men. Are we not, therefore, bound in duty to him and to them to repair these injuries, as far as possible?" (*CW,* 19). This responsibility bears the weight of what Levinas names an "irrecusable obligation" before the face of the Other that one does not have the right to murder.

In the case of the African, Paine asserts the fundamental obligation of the American self to obey a specifically ethical order, through which justice becomes possible. For Levinas, this is an "order to love," through which the "descent of God takes Place." Paine thus emerges as an accusatory interlocutor, who in the name of the African reveals the "wicked and inhuman ways" of the violence in slavery and asserts that an ethical imperative—a challenge yet to be answered—exists for the future of a just America. At the end of "African Slavery in America," Paine reiterates the issue of scriptural obligation and duty when he laments, "But what singular obligations are we under to these injured people!" (*CW*, 19).

Thomas Paine may not deserve the "'honor' bestowed upon him by Moncure Daniel Conway 'of being the first American abolitionist'"[16] (quoted in *CW*, 15); his antislavery rhetoric is not entirely original. Yet his impassioned appeal on behalf of the African is one in which the command of ethics rings most clear. In the name of "Justice and Humanity," Paine stands as one of the first American statesmen to insist that the relationship between the free and legitimate American colonist and the African, as the Stranger against whom injustice continues to be perpetrated, is one of asymmetrical proportion. In this respect, Paine's arguments are uniquely radical in a specifically ethical context. In other words, Paine constructs the relationship between the free American subject and the enslaved African as one that is asymmetrical in its essence. The fact that Paine writes under the sign(ature) of "Justice" suggests that his argument intends to assert the priority of the enslaved, as the Other for whom justice is lacking. In Paine's formulation, justice would seem to be predicated upon the admission of an essential belonging to humanity that is denied the African under the legal sanction of slavery. Thus from the very beginning of his literary career, Paine aligns himself with the Other—in this case, the African who is forcefully subjected to enslavement, commodification, and murder—in order to argue the ethical obligation incumbent upon free citizens as protectors and guarantors of the Other's fundamental right to "Humanity and Justice."

From an ethical perspective, Paine's notion of justice postulates an asym-

---

16. As Foner points out, Paine was not the first or only American of his era to advocate the abolition of slavery. Jefferson argued for the eradication of slavery in 1769, well before the publication of Paine's essay. It is significant, however, that Paine's essay makes a different argument than Jefferson's, and that it was published on March 8, 1775, less than a month before the first antislavery society (of which Paine was a founding member) was organized in Philadelphia.

metry of relation in which the burden of obligation falls upon those who enjoy the rights of privilege. He argues that the possibility of justice is predicated upon an unequal burden of responsibility. In Paine's essay, the African comes first, whose lived experience persists as an indictment against those who claim the right to freedom. The presence of those destitute and persecuted human beings reveals the false humanity of the American, even in the precursory moments before his freedom has been officially ordained.

Perhaps the most ethically radical aspect of "African Slavery in America" is its temporal dynamics. Not only does Paine anticipate the Levinasian "third party," but he holds up the intrinsic freedom and natural rights of this wronged *being*—as that particular freedom against whom the war of uncontested racism is waged—above and before the legal rights of potentially full-fledged American patriots. It is possible to read Paine's early essay as privileging the alterity of the Other as that which comes not just before, but from "on high," from the beyond—in the "dimension of height," as Levinas might say. In this sense, Paine can be read as one of the first American ethicists, for whom the experiential history of the Other reverberates, altering the interiority and gaze of the legitimate American self.

In "African Slavery in America," Paine assumes the original and hereditary rights of the African, but he does not engage with the philosophical foundations of that assumption. It is in his later work, specifically *Rights of Man* and *Age of Reason*, where he develops the ideational ground of his argument, and where the force of his ethical vision becomes most apparent. Although *Rights of Man* first fully articulates an ideal of government "founded on a *moral theory, on a system of universal peace, [and] on the indefeasible, hereditary rights of man*" (*ColW*, 130), the concept of an "immemorial past" is best elucidated in *Age of Reason*. Here, in one of his most controversial works, Paine's language and vision are focused and fearlessly disruptive. If *Age of Reason* cost Paine his celebrity and cultural currency on both sides of the Atlantic (at least in part), it is nevertheless an extraordinary text, and one in which the ethical ideal of creation is boldly presented.

"Are we to have no word of God—No revelation? I answer yes. There is a word of God; there is a revelation. THE WORD OF GOD IS THE CREATION WE BEHOLD: And it is in *this word*, which no human invention can counterfeit or alter, that God speaketh universally to man" (*ColW*, 686). In this quotation, the connection between Paine and Levinas is distinctively resonant. When Paine argues the revelatory power of the "word of God," he asserts its originary presence in terms of a linguistic command, not unlike the Levinasian "first word" that speaks through the Other's face, which one is called to acknowledge and answer. As Paine argues, there is a *"first cause"* that one cannot help but recognize in the "immensity of creation," in the "unchangeable order by which the incomprehensible Whole is governed," and in the "mercy" of a God "not withholding that abundance even from the unthankful" (*ColW*, 687). Like Levinas, Paine postulates a notion of the creation that is conceived in a universal language, one that is multiplicitous in its resonance.

In *Age of Reason*, the model of creation is no longer merely metaphorical or mythological, as in *Rights of Man*. In *Age of Reason*, Paine writes of a creation that "speaketh," the language of which, while universal, is antecedent to reason, to law, and to government. The language of the creation, Paine argues, is independent of human activity and comprehension, absolute and separate from "human speech or human language." The language of creation is the "word of God" making its descent and appearance. In Paine's radical vision, it reverberates as an "ever existing original, which every man can read" (*ColW*, 687). If one wanted to doubt its efficacy as an ethical contract, binding upon the individual whether she agrees or not, Paine has a clear answer. The "word of God," made manifest in the immemorial precedent of the creation, is real, authentic, and inviolable: "It cannot be forged; it cannot be counterfeited; it cannot be lost; it cannot be altered; [and] it cannot be suppressed" (*ColW*, 687). Paine, like Levinas, argues the "irrecusability" of this "word" as one that exceeds the privilege of person or nation, suggesting that here is the initial command that demands and binds us to the building of a world in which the Other is made welcome.

Paine insists that the "word of God" exists in the historically transcendent present, as the "ever existing original, which every man can read." This returns us to one of the pivotal themes in Paine's political vision, for it signals the primacy of the individual prior to the convention of entitlement. As Paine expresses it, the "word of God" is an undeniable commandment, one through which the difference in human *being* is potentially overcome: "It preaches to all nations and to all worlds; and this word of God reveals to man all that is necessary for man to know of God" (*ColW*, 687).

For Paine, the "word of God" not only "reveals . . . all that is necessary for man to know of God," but also all that is necessary for human beings to know of government. Paine's words in *Age of Reason* lend clarity and substance to his pronouncements on government in *Rights of Man*, where he initiates a vision of political revolution that "promises a new era to the human race" (*ColW*, 130). At the core of his idealism is a political vision of society originating in this ancient "word of God," which would topple all recent and remembered history and its lawful regimes devoted to "aristocracy," as well as "family tyranny and injustice" (*ColW*, 479). When Paine posits the "indefeasible, hereditary rights of man" as the foundation upon which authentic government should be built, his words invoke the reality of the bond, and the inescapable truth, of the creation, where even—and perhaps especially—the poor, the despised, the disenfranchised, and the destitute are returned to the "whole" of creation. Less fervently, but no less sincerely, *Rights of Man* argues the possibility of an ideal in which government might become a means of restoration, an activity of "renovation" in which the "natural order of things" would be reinstated as a "system of principles as universal as truth and the existence of man, and combining moral with political happiness and national prosperity" (*ColW*, 537).

On one hand, Paine's political vision in *Rights of Man* is preoccupied with the future. In this text, Paine strives to imagine a future—both social and political—that would signal the kind of unprecedented achievement worthy of his designation of a "new era to the human race." On the other hand, that "new era" belongs necessarily to the realm of what is essentially the unrepresentable. As Levinas contends, it is a future signified only through "anticipation," because the "future is blocked from the outset; it is unknown from the outset and, consequently, time is always diachrony" (*OG*, 96). If Paine's intent in *Rights of Man*, as well as in *Common Sense*, is to pave the way for a political future not yet achieved, then both texts are anticipatory in the Levinasian sense, for the real efficacy of their vision hinges upon an unknown reality, signified only as a yet-to-come potentiality.

For Paine, the possibility of a just society emerges through his concept of the republic, as the "*res publica*," the "whole and sole object" of good government (*ColW*, 565). But his arguments in praise of republican government are predicated upon his critique of a past and recorded history in which monarchy and convention have ruled. Thus one of the pivotal tenets underpinning Paine's political thought is his rejection of the model of entitlement and the critique of natural-rights theory as it had been practiced in governments founded upon aristocratic rule. In order to understand Paine's faith in republicanism as a more ethical model for government, it is necessary to look at the natural-rights theory against which he rebels.

Historically, natural-rights doctrine has grounded itself in the fundamental supposition of individual inequality. In its classical formulation, what characterizes human reality is an inherent inequity. As Aristotle writes in the *Politics*, "Some are marked out to be ruled, but others to rule." The source of that distinction lies in the individual capacity for thought, for he who "can foresee by *thought* is by nature a ruler," and he who cannot "foresee by thought" but "can carry out the orders with the body is by nature a subject or a slave."[17] As political theorist Leo Strauss has written, Aristotle's doctrine of natural right contends that "some men are by nature superior to others, and therefore, the rulers of others." Strauss concludes that "equal rights for all appeared to the classics as most unjust."[18] If human existence is comprehended as naturally hierarchical, then the greatest possibility for the realization of human liberty or "excellence," as Aristotle deems it, lies with the rule of the wise, through whose rule can be realized the classical ideal of the "best regime."

But the classical ideal of a "best regime" is not exclusively political; it also postulates a particular ontological and ethical *weltanschauung*. As Strauss argues, "The character, or tone, of a society depends on what society regards as most respectable or most worthy of admiration. But by regarding certain habits or attitudes as most respectable, a society admits the superiority, the superior dignity, of those human beings who most perfectly embody the habits or attitudes in question."[19] Strauss contends that classical thought envisioned the best society as a "*politeia*," a term that encompasses the makeup and life of the community as a whole. The *politeia* refers less to the articulation of law than to the entitlement of human beings in a given community and their arrangement within that community with respect to the access and administration of political power.

The prevailing political assumption in Aristotle's *Politics*, and classical theory in general, is that civil society precedes the individual. In other words, to be human is to exist within a political community characterized by specific relationships that define the fundamental reality of all political existence: the

---

17. Aristotle, *The Politics*, trans. Ernest Barker (Oxford: Oxford University Press, 1958), 21, 17.
18. Leo Strauss, *Natural Right and History* (Chicago: University of Chicago Press, 1953), 135.
19. Ibid., 137.

relationships of master and slave, male and female, parent and child. Aristotle recognizes an essential interdependence in human existence, for the "natural" slaves are as crucial to the well-being of the state as the "natural" rulers. But in the logic of classical theory, one is either master or slave, both of whom are bound by an ontological destiny whereby natural law fulfills its telos. Eventually, this results in the attainment of the Aristotelian "supreme good," since "every association is formed for the sake of some good (for all men always act in order to attain what they think to be good)."[20] And it is this ontological bias in Aristotle's notion of the "supreme good" against which Paine rebels in his assertion of an originary human equity.

Aristotle subsequently concludes that the state "exists by nature and is prior to each [of its parts]." If human essence and identity are "fixed," as it were, by nature, and if the prerequisite for self-conscious existence—as the definitive sign of being human—resides in one's position in a system of ontological oppositions, then there can be no human "being" prior to the state. As Aristotle explains, "The state comes into being for the sake of bare existence."[21] Being human achieves its definition through a model of subservience: one is either invested with the responsibility of ruling the state or existing in obeisance to those who rule. Thus, what is by nature "right," and therefore "just," is not rooted in the will or the consent of the people (whose inferior constitution prevents their capacity for decision-making and knowledge of justice), but is ordained by nature. It is the rule of the lower by the higher forms, as logos rules emotion, as the male rules the female, as the soul rules the body, and as the parent rules the child—all towards the service of a supreme end in which "excellence" becomes possible.

In classical natural-rights doctrine, the supreme end is understood not as freedom, but as one's acquiescence to a higher authority that constructs itself as the rule of natural law and hierarchical difference. In Aristotelian thought, the supreme end of human association is an existence defined through the state, in which every relation is contained and authenticated; only through the state is the essence of what it means to be human discoverable. Hegel objects to this position in *The Philosophy of History*, writing that the "consciousness of freedom first arose among the Greeks, and therefore they were free; but they, and the Romans likewise, knew only that *some* are

---

20. Aristotle, *Politics*, 16.
21. Ibid., 19.

free—not man as such. Even Plato and Aristotle did not know this. The Greeks, therefore, had slaves; and their whole life and the maintenance of their splendid liberty, was implicated with the institution of slavery: a fact moreover, which made that liberty on the one hand only an accidental, transient and limited growth; on the other hand, constituted it a rigorous thralldom of our common nature—of the Human."[22]

Hegel's critique reveals the extent to which classical natural-rights theory subjugates human essence to an ontological servitude before the law and rule of nature. Classical natural-rights theory ordains the rule of the majority by the few, whose duty it is to legislate and craft the conditions of a political and public reality. But as Hegel suggests, the classical concept of freedom is constituted through contingency and place. In that respect, Hegel's insight echoes Paine's—for freedom, Paine contends, must not and cannot be determined through the rule of a minority over the will and presence of the majority.

In *The Human Condition*, Hannah Arendt contends that the notion of freedom in classical thought must be understood as coeval with the realm of the polis. Citing the pivotal distinction between the public and private in classical philosophy, Arendt argues that Aristotle's assertion that human beings are by nature first and foremost political beings marks the distinction between the realm of necessity—as the basis for inherently natural human association—and the political, as the realm of action (*praxis*) and speech (*lexis*), "out of which rises the realm of human affairs . . . from which everything merely necessary or useful is strictly excluded." Arendt argues that natural society, as prepolitical association, is characterized by violence. As such, it belongs to the realm of the private, or the household, where the head "ruled with uncontested, despotic powers."[23] The intrinsic violence of natural society is overcome only through the construction of the polis, where speech and persuasion replace the rule of force. Freedom then exists as the exclusive domain of the political, where one is released from the inherent violence and inequality of the household. Arendt concludes, "To be free meant both not to be subject to the necessity of life or to the command of another and not to be in command oneself. It meant neither to rule nor to be ruled. Thus

22. Georg Hegel, *The Philosophy of History*, trans. J. Sibree (New York: Dover, 1956), 18.
23. Hannah Arendt, *The Human Condition* (Chicago: University of Chicago Press, 1958), 25, 26.

within the realm of the household, freedom did not exist, for the household head, its ruler, was considered to be free only in so far as he had the power to leave the household and enter the political realm, where all were equals."[24] But this construction of equality and freedom is contradictory and problematic. If the polis is the sphere of freedom, it is a sphere from which the majority of the populace are excluded. Classical equality inheres in the supposition that the majority are not and cannot be free to rise above the necessity of the biological or the familial to enter the political realm in which individual autonomy and identity are discoverable.

Arendt also makes a connection between the poetics of freedom and the politics of space. Slaves and women, who exist exclusively within the household (and hence within the sphere of privacy), are necessarily denied participation in the larger realm of social reality where speech and action are possible. Arendt explains:

> To live an entirely private life means above all to be deprived of things essential to a truly human life: to be deprived of the reality that comes from being seen and heard by others, to be deprived of an "objective" relationship with them that comes from being related to and separated from them through the intermediary of a common world of things, to be deprived of the possibility of achieving something more permanent than life itself. The privation of privacy lies in the absence of others; as far as they are concerned, private man does not appear, and therefore, it is as though he did not exist.[25]

If the slave and the woman can exist only within the private sphere, their existence is constructed in and through silence; they do not participate in the space of the polis, the sphere of real human affairs, which is distinguished and created through action and speech. To be deprived of speech is thus to be denied genuine identity, for neither the slave nor the woman is allowed appearance in that space constituted as authentic, where freedom is possible, and in which full personhood achieves recognition. In Paine's construction, however, it is not merely the slave and the female who are excluded from the polis. The poor, the disenfranchised, and the uneducated are similarly denied speech and thus are barred from authentic recognition and participation in the objective reality in which relationship—and obligation—occurs.

24. Ibid., 25, 30–1.
25. Ibid., 53–4.

Leo Strauss has argued that the idea of natural right can be understood as an inquiry into the origin of human existence. In its classical interpretation, human nature is distinguished by a hierarchical order, reflected in the capacity for reason and speech. The "good life" consists in "living thoughtfully, in understanding, and in thoughtful action"; in Aristotelian terms, it is a "life of activity governed by reason."[26] When the concept of natural right emerges as a pivotal construct in the articulation of American democracy, its interpretation has changed dramatically from the classical emphasis on duty and privilege. Central to the modern tradition is a rejection of the a priori existence of the state, as well as the postulation of a human existence that precedes political association. The primary characteristic of human identity is no longer conceived as a privilege, but as the intrinsic right of the individual to self-preservation. Political association is understood to emerge through agreement, not through nature, as the conscious activity of human will and reason. Once the right to self-preservation becomes the essential fact characterizing human experience, the ideal of justice must be adjusted: right replaces duty, and consent replaces the authority of tradition and its acceptance of an innate human hierarchy. In other words, modern natural right is predicated upon the priority of consent and the construction of justice through contract.

Thus when Paine argues that "*individuals themselves,* each in his own personal and sovereign right, *entered into a compact with each other* to produce a government," and that such a premise is the "only principle" upon which governments "have a right to be established" (*ColW*, 467), he argues against the historical convention through which natural right has been conceived. While classical theory presupposed the priority of political association, Paine contends that "man must have existed before governments existed," and that "there necessarily was a time when governments did not exist" (*ColW*, 467). At issue here are questions of rights, entitlement, and the relationship between individual freedom(s) and the conceptual crafting of justice. The precedent of antiquity has been a sanction for the rule of the many by the few and, more importantly, a rule the majority has not consented to honor or obey. For Paine, the classical construct of natural right is not merely erroneous, but unjust: it envisions government as a supreme entity that arises "over the people" and not "out of the people" (*ColW*, 467). In terms of ethics, Paine

---

26. Strauss, *Natural Right*, 127.

objects to the classical vision of politics on the grounds that the asymmetry through which the dispossessed person appears must ultimately displace rather than invite her original claim to representation. While the ethical relationship to politics involves a certain asymmetry, it emerges as one in which the Other comes first—from the position of "height," as Levinas has argued. And Paine's ideal of the republic is one in which such an existential possibility is actually envisioned.

Soon after the publication of *Rights of Man*, Paine's political reputation came under attack. Particularly in Britain, the book was denounced as "coarse and rustic"; the greatest criticism centered upon the text and its author's "vulgarity." As biographer John Keane suggests, Paine's treatise was intentionally "vulgar" in the sense of "vulgus, meaning 'common people.'" Keane points out that Paine's very title referred to an earlier poem by Thomas Spence, written in defense of an anonymous British commoner nicknamed "Jack the Blaster," whose protest against the unjust policies of his landlords led him to take up residence in a cave on Marsden Bay. Spence, a later associate of Paine, was among the visitors to the cave; he was sufficiently struck by the tenant farmer's defiance that he penned these lines above the fireplace in the cave:

> Ye landlords vile, whose man's peace mar,
> Come levy rents here if you can;
> Your stewards and lawyers I defy,
> And live with all the RIGHTS OF MAN.[27]

Paine's subsequent decision to name his treatise *Rights of Man* suggests his commitment to all the unpropertied, nameless individuals whose originary natural rights might find protection in a government crafted upon the ideal of republicanism.

While *Rights of Man* generated a major storm of reaction and controversy, Paine most clearly elucidates his vision of the principles of republicanism in an earlier text. In "Dissertations on Government," written in February 1786, Paine speaks in a language that is decidedly ethical, particularly given the tract's emphasis upon the relationship between politics and justice. Drawing upon the American example, Paine defines the republic as that "sov-

---

27. Quoted in Keane, *Tom Paine*, 306.

ereign power, or the power over which there is no control, and which controls all others, [that] remains where nature placed it—in the people; for the people in America are the fountain of power" (*CW*, 369). His vision for republican government invests sovereign authority in the people, whose elected representatives "act for the whole" and who remain absolutely accountable to that unnamed and faceless populace—the forgotten and potentially exploited "Jack the Blasters" of the new world territories—who in turn retain the power to displace those representatives whose actions betray the wishes and welfare of the people.

What is more arresting in this document, however, is the indisputable link that Paine constructs between the constitution of the republic and "certain fundamental principles of right and justice" (*CW*, 372). Right and justice are unequivocally at the center of Paine's republican system, and he argues that "there cannot, because there ought not to, be any deviation" from these principles. Whereas in *Rights of Man* Paine clearly designates the republic as the "*res publica*," defining it literally as the "*public thing*," in "Dissertations on Government" he delves deeper into the issue of the public good that is the object of republican administration. Here Paine writes that the "public good is not a term opposed to the good of individuals; on the contrary, it is the good of every individual collected. It is the good of all, because it is the good of everyone: for as the public body is every individual collected, so the public good is the collected good of those individuals" (*CW*, 372).

But Paine's revolutionary language is not as radical as it first sounds. Its revolutionary quality lies in its participation in the "utopian vision," as Gordon Wood writes, that came to mark the "Americans' conception of the way their society and politics should be structured and operated." What was truly revolutionary, as Wood suggests, is that despite its distance "from the realities of American society," and "contrary to the previous century of American experience," the ideal of a republican government and its vision of a "corporate society, in which the common good would be the only objective of government" represented a radical rejection of historical precedent, experience, and ideology. The reverence for government devoted to the public good became the "central tenet of the Whig faith, shared not only by Hamilton and Paine at opposite ends of the Whig spectrum, but by any American bitterly opposed to a system which held 'that a Part is greater than its whole,'" or that a few should reap the benefits of governmental rule at the expense and to the detriment of the majority. In that sense, Paine's language is far more symptomatic than radical. As Wood writes, "No phrase except 'liberty' was invoked more often by the Revolutionaries than 'the public good.' It expressed the colonists' deepest hatreds of the old order and their most visionary hopes for the new."[28]

Yet there is an aspect of Paine's arguments for the "public good" that exceeds his participation in this fervor of the zeitgeist. To uncover this element, one must read Paine's words in "Dissertations on Government" with an eye towards his larger project, through which his concern for ethics persists. It is thus necessary to examine more precisely Paine's delineation of a republic committed to the "public good" as one founded (and grounded) in the contractual signature of an American people, acting in the name of "Humanity" towards the accomplishment of "Justice."

When Paine defines the "public good" as the ground upon which the republic must stand, he means more than the general notion of a common or corporate welfare. As he writes, "The foundation of the public good is *justice,* and wherever justice is impartially administered, the public good is promoted; for as it is to the good of every man that no injustice be done to him, so likewise it is to his good that the principle which secures him should not be violated in the person of another, because such a violation weakens his security and leaves to chance what ought to be to him a rock to stand on" (CW, 372). At the heart of Paine's representation of justice is its insistence upon the eradication of injustice, here housed in a language that recognizes the intended and willful violation of the "person of another" as implicitly unjust. No doubt many of Paine's political adversaries would also agree to such a claim. Yet Paine veers dramatically from the spirited rhetoric of his peers in the breach that he opens in regard to the "who" of personhood.

As we have seen, Paine's earlier text in defense of the African—the 1774 "African Slavery in America"—constructs an argument through which the African emerges as the persecuted Other, whose natural right to freedom is violated through the American participation in the slave trade. The essay is distinguished by its staunch refusal to question the essential humanity of the African. If we read "Dissertations on Government" in light of his earlier arguments, the very notion of justice becomes vulnerable to critique. In a very literal sense, Paine writes about justice in terms that depend upon the fundamental sanctity of personhood. He has already argued for the native person-

---

28. Gordon S. Wood, *The Creation of the American Republic, 1776–1787* (Chapel Hill: University of North Carolina Press, 1969), 54, 55.

hood of the African, against whom the perpetuation of slavery constitutes a violation "proved contrary to the light of nature, to every principle of *justice* and humanity" (*CW*, 16), and one equal in the severity of its offense—as the brutally insistent practice of injustice—to blatant, intentional murder.

I want to anticipate the objection that this interpretation of Paine's idea of justice might occasion in more traditional Paine scholars. As I suggested in chapter 1, the African is neither a member nor a citizen of the republic towards whom Paine's words are intended and directed. The African, in kinship with the Indian as Other, exists repressed within the territorial parameters of the new republic. One might thus argue that Paine's remarks on justice do not encompass those existents outside the boundaries of authentic American identity. But Paine himself disrupts such a reading.

In its address to the legitimate American subject, who by definition is neither African nor Indian, "Dissertations on Government" nevertheless accounts for the presence of the invisible Other lodged within the republic's contractual boundaries. In Paine's articulation of the republican compact, as the agreement pledged by its legitimate and recognized citizens, members of a republic renounce not only the "despotic principle . . . of being governed by mere will and power"; they also "renounce, as detestable, the power of exercising, at any future time any species of despotism over each other, or doing a thing not right in itself, because a majority of them may have strength of numbers sufficient to accomplish it" (*CW*, 373).

It is no stretch to assert the applicability of Paine's words to the cause of slavery. Paine himself has already initiated this path. If we read his words in concert with his frequent and fervent denunciations of American slavery, his uncompromising commitment to a principle of justice that is extensive rather than selective—inclusive rather than privileged—is beyond question. The terms of justice, Paine asserts, extend beyond the spheres of privilege; otherwise, a potentially natural aristocracy might breed and rule according to the power of number, the power of money, and the corruptive power of will. If Paine is guilty of romanticizing the virtues of republican government, he is also uniquely ethical in his vision of a justice beyond the power of privilege, and perhaps even beyond the compact of a republicanism answerable only to its legitimately named citizenry.

Given that the terms of politics engage the issues of sovereignty, the terms of ethics engage the envisioning of justice. Paine speaks in a language that fuses the two, that offers an opening through which the political leans towards that which is ultimately ethical. Paine writes that the sovereignty of the ideal republic is "exercised to keep right and wrong in their proper and distinct places, and never suffer the one to usurp the place of the other." But even more important, for him, is this essential virtue through which republicanism might aspire towards an unparalleled and potentially ethical vision of being human in the world. "A republic, properly understood," Paine dares to assert, "is a sovereignty of justice, in contradistinction to a sovereignty of will" (*CW*, 375). The difficulty, as Paine himself would discover, is that there are no ideal republics, and that the American enterprise would prove to be no exception in this regard.

In part, the waning of Paine's public reputation was the result of his own personal choices. His unrelenting critique of Silas Deane and his personally charged "Letter to George Washington" worked to undermine his political credibility, as well as to "raise questions about his fitness for public office and allegiance to the principles of republicanism and democracy."[29] Despite the fact that Paine correctly alleged that Deane had embezzled considerable funds from the United States government, the manner of his attack cost him his position as Secretary of Foreign Affairs and substantially damaged his persona in the public sphere. But it was his "Letter to George Washington" that most severely damaged his political reputation and reinforced doubts about his mental and political fitness. The "Letter to George Washington" would ultimately mark Paine's disillusionment with the evolution of the republic in the aftermath of the celebrated events of 1776.

Paine's "Letter to George Washington" was clearly motivated by personal circumstances. His accusations against Washington are based on his personal experience of imprisonment in Luxembourg and his acute sense of betrayal that Washington had not intervened on his behalf. There is considerable speculation about whether Washington was even aware of Paine's situation, but Paine nevertheless held him responsible for the length of his imprisonment. When Paine decided to make his letter to Washington public in the aftermath of his release from prison, he was deemed guilty of introducing his personal affairs into the public and political discourse. Paine qualified and justified his recourse to personal politics by asserting that there is a critical link—one far too important to be overlooked or silenced—between the pri-

---

29. Edward Larkin, "'Could the Wolf Bleat Like the Lamb': Thomas Paine's Critique and the Early American Sphere," *Arizona Quarterly* 55 (1999): 14.

vate character of the individual and his public actions. To Washington, he says without apology, "If I have any resentment you must acknowledge that I have not been hasty in declaring it; neither would it now be declared (for what are private resentments to the public) if the cause of it did not unite itself as well with your public as well as your private character, and with the motives of your political conduct" (*CW*, 695).

It is possible to argue that the real motivation behind this letter is specific to Paine's experience, and that his experience during his ten-month imprisonment in a Luxembourg prison is atypical in terms of the grievances of the majority of American citizens. Yet it could also be argued that in making the personal relevant to political discourse, Paine once again asserts the accountability of government, even republican government, to "the people." The charges of corruption that Paine hurls against Washington hinge upon this accountability, and Paine's arguments reveal the extent to which, in his view, the people are not reducible to the status of an undifferentiated mass, but exist as a citizenry comprised of separate and individual beings, as existents, whose uniquely specific freedoms must be protected.

In that sense, the "Letter to George Washington" serves to raise the question of who is the American citizen to whom government and its elected officials are accountable. Edward Larkin makes this point in asserting that Paine's letter "illustrates the polarizing divisions surrounding who constitutes 'the people' that had arisen in the early years of the republic. While Paine realized that the definition of what America might represent was at stake in this debate, he also realized that his identity as an American was in question." Paine's status as an American citizen had been directly contested at the time of his imprisonment, and his relationship to the republic remained dubious even after his release. Larkin rightfully argues that it was exactly these kinds of complicated questions of private and national identity that "would haunt Paine for the rest of his life" and inform the core of his "Letter to George Washington": "Was Paine really an American? What did it mean to be an American? And, who was more representative of the principles of 'America,' Paine or Washington?"[30]

While Paine's "Letter to George Washington" ultimately served further to alienate Paine from the graces of the republic, it nonetheless exhibited a particular form of rebellious bravery. For Paine to dare to question the ethical

---

30. Ibid., 24.

conduct of his president and administration is an almost perfect dramatization of his notion of the explicit right of "the people" to hold its government accountable. And his letter raises another difficult question. If Thomas Paine's claim to representation could be thrown open to debate, despite the political influence and credibility that he had achieved with *Common Sense*, what then of the anonymous citizen without the reputation of a recognized name? What of those individuals who lacked the benefit of a clearly delineated place in the historical narrative of the republic? If read from this perspective, Paine's "Letter to George Washington" revitalizes his contestatory role in the republic he helped to create.

From the beginning, Paine performed the critical role of instigator. In both *Common Sense* and *Rights of Man*, he labored diligently and fearlessly to awaken the citizenry to the possibilities inherent in the actualization of a republic founded in freedom. But he also insisted upon a fundamental accountability from the people and their elected representatives in government. The "Letter to George Washington" remains true to those ideals, making it possible to reimagine Paine, not so much as an instigator, but rather as the embodiment of the Levinasian interlocutor—the One who comes forward to demand accountability. The accounting that Paine demands is specifically ethical. His "Letter to George Washington" can be read as an anticipation of the fundamental strife between ethics and politics in American culture.

But Paine's disenchantment with the political affairs of the young republic can also be understood as his confrontation with the essence of the ideal of the republic, and that ideal's translation into the politics of representation. In Paine's earlier treatises, the republic emerges as a near utopia: the potential reconstruction of the public sphere in which the rights of all, and especially those previously and historically dispossessed commoners, would find voice, protection, and the power of sovereign rule. As Larkin has noted, "Paine's aim throughout his career was to undermine the authority of any particular institution or stratum of society and to open political participation to 'the people,'" whereby "such citizens could participate in the public sphere and, *de facto*, reform it by asserting their right to shape 'public opinion.'"[31] But the American enterprise was not a perfect republic, and Paine was forced to confront the measurable gap between an idealized theory of

---

31. Ibid., 32.

government, answerable to the voice of the people, and the disparity in virtue and equity between "the people" and their appointed representatives.

The problem of virtue was a concern for many Americans in the eighteenth century. The men active within the public sphere keenly recognized that the idea of the republic depended upon the willingness of the individual to "sacrifice . . . private interests for the good of the country." As Gordon Wood has argued, "A republic was such a delicate polity precisely because it demanded an extraordinary moral character in the people. Every state in which the people participated needed a degree of virtue; but a republic which rested solely on the people absolutely required it."[32] As Wood's study further demonstrates, the American debate over virtue ultimately led to the creation of a cultural and political aristocracy, a natural aristocracy based on merit and experience, through which the difficult issues of equity and virtue could, at least theoretically, be mediated. But access to the public realm was entwined in the politics of property. As numerous scholars, including Larkin, have argued, the emergence of a natural aristocracy ultimately served to nurture the "power base of a stratum of prosperous men who came to see themselves as a 'universal class' and prepared to assert their fitness to govern."[33]

If the "Letter to George Washington" is read in terms of the issues of representation that it raises, then one might argue that Paine's disillusionment is an inevitable consequence of republican politics. In questioning Washington's "fitness to govern," Paine is also questioning the ideal of a natural aristocracy best suited to serve and realize the interests of the American people. As with the Silas Deane affair, Paine interrogates not simply Washington's politics but his character and privilege, as they are directly linked to his use or abuse of political power. Again, there is a personal element in play here. What Paine does not do, despite his popularity and political prominence, is to "reinvent himself as a member of the political or cultural aristocracy."[34] Notwithstanding the fact that he held public office and that the Pennsylvania Assembly had made him a gift of a New Rochelle farm (thereby inducting him into the propertied class), Paine never relinquished his place among the disenfranchised, the common people of the republic. Thus when he publicly questions Washington's person and character, he speaks as one

---

32. Wood, *Creation of the American Republic*, 68.
33. Larkin, "'Could the Wolf Bleat Like the Lamb,'" 32.
34. Ibid., 33.

of the represented, and his inquiry reveals one of the schisms that plagues republican politics.

In certain respects, this is the problem of representation that F. R. Ankersmit addresses in his work on the relationship between ethics, aesthetics, and politics. Ankersmit identifies two opposing theories of representation, the mimetic and the aesthetic, arguing that the American model of representation was initially intended as mimetic, insofar as it claimed that the "representation of the people should reflect the people represented as accurately as possible." In other words, mimetic representation aspires towards an exact equivalence between the people and their representatives, in which the "identity of the representative and the person represented is . . . the ideal of all political representation."[35] The problem that inheres in mimetic representation, Ankersmit suggests, is its metaphorical nature: first, the people to be represented are "never represented *in toto*," and second, given that political representation is premised on the idea of making present (as the will or voice of the people), through a process of substitution (the representatives), what is actually absent, there is necessarily an "unbridgeable gap" between the two. In short, Ankersmit implies that mimetic representation is almost inevitably bound towards failure, because there cannot be a singular or complete correspondence between the collective voices (or will of the people) and those designated to represent them.

Ankersmit's analysis uncovers one of the pragmatic problems that has plagued the American republic since its beginnings. Recalling the fervent idealism that informs Paine's earlier writings on the republic in general and the American embarkation upon republican government in particular, one might conclude, in line with Ankersmit, that Paine's expectations for the republic are essentially naive. Not only can there be no representation that accomplishes a precise and mimetic representation of "the people," but the realms of politics and ethics must remain separate. If there are resonances of an ethical judgment in Paine's critique of Washington, as I have suggested, then Paine may be guilty of confusing the two realms, of imposing ethics where it does not belong. The political, Ankersmit argues, must be conceived as an autonomous realm; politics cannot be reduced to ethical claims or stipulations, which have far more to do with individual actions and choices. As Ankersmit contends, "Ethics attempts to answer the question of how I ought to

---

35. F. R. Ankersmit, *Aesthetic Politics* (Stanford: Stanford University Press, 1996), 28.

act under certain circumstances. Because of this way of putting the ethical question, ethics could never transcend the sphere of what the individual could and would do."[36]

Although I do not agree with either Ankersmit's limited definition of ethics or with his insistence that ethics has no viable role in the political workings of the republic, the problem that his study invites us to consider is immensely important. What is the relationship between the necessarily autonomous sphere of political activity and the commands of ethics? Although all political action cannot be legislated in terms of ethics, the ways in which visions of the political may be informed by an ethical *anschauung* are certainly worthy of investigation. In some respects, these are the hidden issues that resonate in Paine's "Letter to George Washington." Whatever else Paine may be, he is not a pragmatist. His is an inspired vision, in which the presence of the ethical reverberates unapologetically.

I want to offer another way of thinking about Paine's political legacy—one in which the connection between politics and ethics is brought to the fore. In Paine's visionary perspective, there is the Levinasian resonance of a heroic consciousness and conscience, which is devoted and committed to the ideal of an American republic founded in freedom, but which is also forever mindful of the restraints, the mediation, that the higher ground of justice must impose upon that freedom.

When Thomas Paine sets forth his ideal of the *"res publica"* in *Rights of Man*, he envisions the potential of a republican government to realize not only freedom, but a particular ideal of justice. It is no accident that Paine's performative signature in his earliest texts is one proffered through the "sentiments of . . . Justice and Humanity." "Justice," Paine suggests, is a relationship marked by obligation; it is measured by an obligation to that specific "Humanity," constituted in the here and now as "the people." In asserting such a clear connection between the needs, predicaments, and experiences of a given sector of "Humanity" and the potential for a justice realized through and dependent upon government, Paine employs an optics that is more—that is *otherwise*—than mere Romantic idealism. His is an optics specifically ethical, for it leans towards the evocation of a utopian desire. In this sense, Paine's formulation of the republic imagines justice as a higher

---

36. Ibid., 10.

goal than freedom, one through which the specific freedom of the individual is realized and protected.

Perusing the various texts of Thomas Paine, one is confronted with his insistence—or faith—in the capacity of the people, and the republic itself, to act justly. But for Paine, justice is definitively linked to an uncompromising notion of accountability, and to a people who are not permitted to become an undifferentiated mass. "The people" are not an existent reducible to the rhetoric of political persuasion or opportunity. Just as the title for *Rights of Man* evolves out of the particular experience of "Jack the Blaster," Paine's legacy is often centered in the real experiences and stories of "the people" as individuals. What he will not do—and this is clearly a conscious choice—is to become of the government. Nor will he join the class of privileged men whose business it is to see that politics and government work. In a very real sense, Paine takes a stand on the other side of government: as an advocate of the people and, in his best moments, as a messianic voice insistent upon the sole authority of the people as the "ultimate source of signification in both law and language."[37]

In order effectively to assess the legacy of Paine's contribution to the founding order of the new republic, one must acknowledge that his radical ideas for republicanism are entwined in the notion that an authentic community is as much a linguistic accomplishment as it is a political one. From the moment he took up his pen to author *Common Sense*, Paine was engaged in the task of undermining the language of power that he believed had falsely constituted and named the political relationships between the American colonies and the English government. As Thomas Gustafson has argued, one of Paine's most influential accomplishments was his success in making the "language of politics and the politics of language one and the same." Gustafson rightly suggests that Paine's ideals for the republic were contingent upon the discovery of a language through which the claims of an old order could be broken. As he writes, "Paine understood that if America was to begin government at the right end—if it was to build that asylum in the springtime of a new age, if it was to make glorious the American promise and begin the world over again—it had to abandon its old, familiar mother tongue and learn a new language."[38]

37. Thomas Gustafson, *Representative Words: Politics, Literature, and the American Language* (New York: Cambridge University Press, 1992), 269.

38. Ibid., 242.

Gustafson's study returns us to the vision that informs Paine's oeuvre. Not only did Paine replace "sovereign words with representative ideas," Gustafson asserts, but he invested "the people" with the "divine right to name and give meaning" to the political enterprise: "In the beginning is the word of We, the people."[39] To a significant degree, Paine's vision of the republic is constructed through language. And insofar as Paine's republicanism envisions the creation of a political community through the "linguistic communication [and participation] of those who otherwise would be separated," it also invokes an invitation to those who may exist outside that language.[40] This invitation for linguistic participation has the power to disrupt the structures of systemization (as the enforcement of the totality) to hold that very community, as polity, accountable. Here, again, the dimension of ethics intrudes upon the arena of politics. In order to uncover the ethical dimension in Paine's potentially utopian *anschauung* of the American republic, it is valuable to think through the relationship of ethics to politics as it is posited in Levinasian philosophy.

In the concluding pages of *Totality and Infinity,* Levinas meditates on the relationships between the subject (the I), the Other, and the realm of political life: "Metaphysics, or the relation with the other, is accomplished as service and as hospitality. In the measure that the face of the Other relates us with the third party, the metaphysical relation of the I with the Other moves into the form of the We, aspires to a State, institutions, laws, which are the source of universality. But politics left to itself bears a tyranny within itself; it deforms the I and the other who have given rise to it, for it judges them according to universal rules, and thus as in absentia" (TI, 300). Levinas's remarks point towards two separate realms of human interaction: the sphere of sociality, distinguished by "relation," "service," and "hospitality," and that of politics, which, in its insistence upon the laws of "universality," runs the risk of performing an essential "deformity" upon both Self and Other, through which the face of each is potentially erased. It is not the move towards the "We" that threatens the relational or social possibility; it is rather the move towards "the state"—as a totalizing reality before which the individual is asked to sacrifice herself—in which the potential violence of politics is

---

39. Ibid., 269.

40. Harold A. Durfee, "War, Politics, and Radical Pluralism," *Philosophy and Phenomenological Research* 35 (1975): 551.

located. As Harold Durfee points out in his essay on politics and pluralism in Levinasian thought, the entrance to the realm of sociality, and therefore the possibility of ethical community, is marked by communication and language, not by systemization: "Totalization, from which communication is anxious to part company, is the historical foundation for systems of power, for in totalization the group is of primary importance and the self is to serve the system."[41] The difficulty is that in "serving the system," the individual is rendered both faceless and voiceless. Not only is she subsumed in an undifferentiated mass of sacrificial selves, but her very existence becomes replaceable, interchangeable with the countless and equally faceless others who could serve in her place.

Levinas further states that in "political life, taken unrebuked, humanity is understood from its works—a humanity of interchangeable men, of reciprocal relations" (*TI*, 298), where one is reduced to what one does, and where the space for dialogue necessarily ceases to exist. If dialogue is the entrance to genuine sociality, it demands the unique presence and specific accountability of the individual. Since political life makes justifiable the "substitution of men for one another, the primal disrespect, [it] makes possible exploitation itself" (*TI*, 298). Here is the potential site of tyranny—that same tyranny of rule against which Paine steps forward to wage war. The sanctity of the human face is fully displaced in a system of laws and political practice that exerts its rule over "the people" as if they were in absentia. This is Durfee's point when he argues that "any community of the state will simply provide the oppression of totality rather than morality. The inner integrity of the self is constantly violated by the power of the state, and by evaluating one's status in terms of one's works, one is divorced from one's works."[42] But the potential tyranny and violation of the political extends even further. If it results in a state in which the uniqueness of the individual must disappear—predicated upon the notion of substitution and interchangeability—then it also runs the risk of erasing the responsibility of the One (as the I) before the Other.

This is an element of the argument Paine makes against the legality of slavery. The fact that the state sanctions the brutal exploitation and enslavement of the African does not exempt the citizen, as an individual, from the obligation to the Other that precedes the legalization of slavery. Such a con-

---

41. Ibid.
42. Ibid., 555.

ception of the political would demand the silence of the individual and would permit the "useless suffering" of the African Other as if it were justifiable. As Paine demonstrates, the rule of the political without the mediation of the ethical results not only in tyranny, but in an injustice that would permit murder.

Levinas asserts that "justice consists in again making possible expression, in which in non-reciprocity the person presents himself as unique. Justice is a right to speak" (*TI*, 298). We can begin to appreciate the emphasis on language, on the voice of the people—"in the beginning is the word of We, the people"—that informs Paine's vision of the republic. In affirming the essential right of "the people" to speak, Paine proposes the republic as a political community accomplished through the poetics of conversation, so that, as Durfee suggests, "language is the major mode of relationship between the same and the other." To insist upon the primacy of linguistic participation in the crafting of political reality is to invite the Other's presence. At the same time, however, such an invitation constitutes a risk, "for the other's speech may ask one to justify oneself."[43] But through this invitation to speech, the originary unicity of the individual is preserved, so that justice can emerge in all its possibility.

Here we can return to the larger issue of the relationship between ethics and politics as it is raised in Ankersmit's study. My intent is not to collapse politics into some simplistic ethical command. Levinas is absolutely clear that "justice requires and establishes the state." Given the historical necessity of the state, it is also true that in the constitution of the relationship between the people and the state, there is the "indispensable reduction of human uniqueness to the particularity of an individual of the human genus, to the condition of citizen" (*EN*, 196). To make the case for the necessity of ethics as an intervening force of mediation upon the practical work and ongoing revision of the political entity "is in no way a repudiation of politics" (*TI*, 195).

Rather, ethical philosophy recognizes and concedes that political authority, despite its inescapable ways of objectification and reductionism, is the required entity that must arbitrate, judge, and thematize justice—that must, in fact, translate the possibility for justice into the institution of law. "But," Levinas argues, political "justice itself cannot make us forget the origin of the

---

43. Ibid., 551.

right or uniqueness of the other." Neither can we "abandon that uniqueness to political history," where, as history has demonstrated, the "uniqueness of the other" runs the risk of becoming "deformed" or "covered over by the . . . generality of the human" (*EN*, 196).

In at least one sense, ethics is absolutely critical to the realization of a just political reality, for it performs the work of memory. The imperative of the ethical recovers the Other's face, acknowledges and preserves her uniqueness, and recalls the I, as citizen, to its prepolitical obligations to an originary human fraternity. Ethics articulates the "humanity of consciousness," which is not revealed through the acts or privileges of power, but in the call of an antecedent responsibility that will not permit the individual—in spite of his place in the reciprocal relations of citizenship—a stance of indifference before the suffering, pain, or exploitation of the Other. Ethics summons the return of the I to the fraternal obligations of an interhuman community, where the singular and unique I awakens to discover that the responsibility for the Other is "something like an older involvement than any rememberable deliberation constitutive of the human" (*EN*, 114)—or, in this case, constitutive of the political.

When Paine proposes that an authentic republic is one founded upon the "rights of man," his vision is already invested in an ethical ideal. To assert that the rights of man resonate at the heart of republican government, and must therefore dictate its practical policies, is to postulate those rights as originary ones—that is, as rights existent a priori and binding before any idea of merit, virtue, or privilege of entitlement. This is why Paine returns to the "time immemorial" of the creation as his model and evidence. His argument proposes that the "rights of man are more legitimate than any legislation, more just than any justification." As Levinas subsequently argues, the rights of man, "however complex their application to legal phenomena may be, [are] the measure of all law and, no doubt, of its ethics."[44]

I have suggested that there are striking connections between Paine's idealistic articulations of the American republic and the ethical perspective of Levinasian philosophy. But there is yet another synchronistic resonance that enhances my reading of Paine's legacy in the terms of Levinas's ethical project. Significantly, in a lesser-known 1985 essay, "The Rights of Man and the

---

44. Emmanuel Levinas, "The Rights of Man and the Rights of the Other," trans. Michael B. Smith, in *Outside the Subject* (Stanford: Stanford University Press, 1994),116.

Rights of the Other," Levinas himself takes up this particular subject and argues for not merely the originary status of those rights, but for their absolute and ineluctable authority. Here is a direct and specific instance where the eighteenth-century words of Tom Paine bear an uncanny resemblance to the contemporary thought of Emmanuel Levinas.

In "The Rights of Man and the Rights of the Other," Levinas reflects upon the historic and linguistic significance of the "rights of man" and argues that these are a priori rights, due every human being. These originary rights—the "right to respect for the human dignity of the individual, the rights to life, liberty, and equality before the law"—Levinas argues, "do not need to be conferred," because they are rights equally "irrevocable and inalienable." The significance and sanctity of these rights is their confirmation of the "alterity or absolute of every person," an alterity so absolute that it precedes and exceeds all points of reference and is not, in any respect, "conferrable." Levinas further insists that these same "rights of man," so central to Paine's envisioning of the American republic, become—if honored in their originary signification—a disruptive force, a "violent tearing loose from the determining order of nature and the social structure in which each of us is obviously involved."[45]

Thus, when Paine recovers the rights of man as the sole legitimate authority through which the political realm can be constructed, his ideal of the republic is revealed as an ethical imperative. In Paine's vision of the republic, the uniqueness and alterity of the individual is rendered visible, and therefore indisputably authoritative and real. This uniqueness becomes the distinguishing sign of a given alterity, "that is, of the non-interchangeable, incomparable and unique" face of the Other, before whom one is bound and called to recognize and respect a claim to freedom "beyond the individuality of multiple individuals within their kind." What both Paine and Levinas—albeit in differing moments of time and through differing strategies of textual intent—hold forth as an indisputable and inherently disruptive "truth" is the idea that into the prevailing narrative of a historical world already "felt to be doomed to an arbitrary play of forces (natural or supposedly supernatural, individual and social) . . . there came the *a priori* of the rights of man understood as intellectual *a priori*, and becoming in fact the measure of all law."[46]

---

45. Ibid., 117.
46. Ibid., 116–7, 119.

The question that haunts Levinas's essay on the originary status of the rights of man is this: "But do not the rights of man (that is, individual freedom, the uniqueness of the person) also run the risk of being belied or infringed upon by the rights of the other man?" Echoing the sentiments of Paine's treatises on the possibilities of a republican justice, Levinas answers that the "rights of man" signify an authority prior to the existence of historically conceived government. To acknowledge the antecedent freedom of the Other is not, in an absolute sense, to restrict or obscure that same right of freedom for the I. Prior to the appeals of freedom is the fact of a given proximity where "immediately, one and the other is one *facing* the other," and where the encounter between these specific human beings reveals each to be the "only one of its kind." And this becomes the "myself *for* the other." Because of this nonnegotiable event and experience of proximity, these persons are already "non-indifferent" to one another; in their proximity, they are already in the mode of a facing that cannot be denied. It is this posture of "non-indifference" that lies at the origins of an original sociality, issuing from the "wish for peace" that frees the I "from its auto-affirmation, from its egotism . . . *to answer for the other*." These are the initial terms of the encounter of meeting. This "wish for peace"—which initiates Levinasian "goodness" and characterizes Paine's biblical "fraternity"—emerges as the "first language" human beings discover. Levinas asks, "Should not the fraternity that is in the motto of the republic be discerned in the prior non-indifference of one for the other, in that original goodness in which freedom is embedded, and in which the justice of the rights of man takes on an immutable significance and stability, better than those guaranteed by the state? A freedom in fraternity, in which the responsibility of one-for-the-other is affirmed, and through which the rights of man manifest themselves concretely to consciousness as the rights of the other, for which I am answerable."[47]

The rights of the Other, Levinas argues, do not infringe upon the freedom of the individual. On the contrary, it is in honoring one's duty (as Paine might say) to the Other, whose very presence makes an appeal to one's responsibility, in which the freedom of the I is invested. Since the fact of one's responsibility for the Other is "irrecusable and non-transferable," then it is through the awakening to that responsibility that "I am instituted as noninterchangeable: I am chosen as unique and incomparable." To answer my

47. Ibid., 125.

call to responsibility for the Other who faces me, whose presence in proximity is inescapably and undeniably real, is to propose that my "freedom and my rights, before manifesting themselves in my opposition to the freedom and rights of the other person, will manifest themselves precisely in the form of responsibility, in human fraternity."[48]

The fact that Levinas speaks here of a "fraternity that is the motto of the republic" is no more accidental than Paine's first signatures in the name of "Justice and Humanity." In the terms of this study, this is the exquisite site of the ethical imagination in its disruptive intervention upon the human sphere of community, where politics is instituted. In *Common Sense* and *Rights of Man*, Paine's agenda is implicitly disruptive: he dares to contest the oppressive and totalizing forces of politics through which the previous narratives of history had been constructed. But Paine's political perspective is most radically defined by his persistence in envisioning an American republic that is committed to the commands of its specific "humanity," as well as being devoted to the originary "rights of man." If Paine's insurgent critique is disruptive, it is also prophetic. He emerges as one of the unique and singular voices that "will recall, to the judgments of the judges and statesmen, the human face dissimulated beneath the identities of citizens" (*EN*, 196). In this particular call and answer, as it presents itself at the dawn of the republic, Paine stands alone. And he speaks in a language that insists that the realm of politics must originate in the encounter with the Other (whose originary rights of freedom are beyond dispute) if it is to fulfill its potential for a legitimate and humane justice.

Here is where Paine's ethical *anschauung* leans towards the utopian. But his is a notion of utopia that takes as its object the interhuman modalities of encounter. It is not the utopia of the Hegelian dialectic, which posits a mastery of the interhuman connection in the prescription of a future state already delineated. Nor is it the concrete utopia of Marxist theory, grounded in its deterministic realization of scientific materialism. At the center of Paine's envisioned republic are "the people," positioned in their concrete proximity to one another as existing and distinguishable presences, separate through the specificity of their individual places, stories, and historical experiences, yet also (and simultaneously) bound and turned towards one another, united through the efficacy of a language in which the command of responsibility

---

48. Ibid.

reverberates. If the rights of man are to be instituted as the basis of government, then the people must insist upon their primacy, and they must act and speak to assure their protection.

The utopian aspect of Paine's political vision resides in his projection of the republic as inherently social. I have argued that it is possible to read Paine's political theory in terms of its construction of the republic as a site founded through discourse and which emerges as a polity based upon the interhuman encounter. As such, Paine's republic becomes a political entity in which the individual is recognized and protected, and one in which the originary (or biblical) responsibility of the I to the Other is simultaneously revived. In this sense, there is a promissory excess in Paine's republican dream. In privileging the social as the sphere of real relationships of human beings to one another, both government and politics become answerable not only to "the people," but also answerable for a construction of justice that refuses indifference before the faces of its respective citizens. This is the possibility resonant in the ethical relation, one we might think of as the "search for a Revolution which, far from the model of accomplishment or completion, would be a 'permanent revolution,' 'a rupture of frameworks,' [a] 'disorder.'"[49] This disruptive potential is the "disorder" so present in Paine's legacy; it is the lingering face of the Other. This is the possibility of a republic that thinks of justice in the name of humankind—that envisions justice not only as a higher goal than freedom, but conceives of justice as a relationship marked by obligation.

Where is the discourse of freedom in Paine's utopian republic? The protection of freedom emerges as a vigilance through which the originary rights of man are reestablished as the first cause, the first command, and where the freedom of the I becomes an investment in the protection of the rights of the Other. This is the originary site for the "new era" of human being and government that Paine so passionately envisions. It is perhaps the most radical contribution of Thomas Paine's humanistically ethical legacy.

49. Miguel Abensour, "To Think Utopia Otherwise," trans. Bettina Bergo, *Graduate Faculty Philosophy Journal* 20.2–21.1 (1998): 266.

3 STANDING IN THE "FIELD OF FREEDOM"
Thomas Jefferson and the Reverberations of that Declaratory Promise

The Declaration of Independence has always been America's most problematic document. Articulating the nation's founding claims of freedom and independence, the Declaration guarantees the "inalienable rights" of "life, liberty, and the pursuit of happiness," affirms "in the course of human events" the necessity "for one people to dissolve the political bands which have connected them with another," and expresses the "right of the people to alter or abolish" any government that restricts liberty and the pursuit of happiness or that has lost the "consent of the governed."[1] Thomas Jefferson was well aware that once such a revolutionary document was offered up as the basis for a nation, instability would become a way of life. Such freedom, once released, would never cease spawning new rebellions. "God forbid we should ever be 20 years without such a rebellion," Jefferson wrote a decade after the Declaration, as he expressed concerns with the way the new nation was turning its rebellious energy into lawmaking. "What country can preserve its liberties if their rulers are not warned from time to time that their people preserve the spirit of resistance? Let them take arms. . . . The tree of liberty must be refreshed from time to time with the blood of patriots & tyrants. It is its natural manure."[2]

Perhaps by May 1825, a little more than a year before his death, Jefferson already had an inkling of how the Declaration might inspire those within the new nation to begin to conceive of their own young government as the new tyrant that needed to be "altered or abolished." Perhaps he realized that his own slaves, along with slaves across the country, would be moved by the

---

1. Jefferson, "Autobiography," *Life and Selected Writings*, 22.
2. Jefferson, "Letter to Colonel Smith," ibid., 436.

Declaration's call to life and liberty, and that the Declaration would be invoked by slaves and abolitionists as they called for slave revolts to demand liberty for those the Constitution excluded from the rights of citizenship.

Jefferson died unaware of how his Declaration would be used by his fellow southerners as a justification for their own rebellion, their claim that the United States government had ceased to have the "consent of the governed." Over the span of American history, the Declaration has continued to be performed by many groups for many reasons. It is one of the telling paradoxes of our nation's history that slaveholders and slaves turned with an equal sense of entitlement to the Declaration of Independence. They did so because it valued freedom above all else. It asserted the right of the governed to dissolve its ties with the governing body, whether slaveholders or the Union itself. When freedom is perceived as a primary right, people with vastly different conceptions of who should enjoy that freedom can use the same document to support their revolutionary actions: justice follows those who exert the power to free themselves to act as they see fit, even if their freedom allows them to enslave others.

"The Declaration," Jefferson wrote to Henry Lee in 1825, had not been authored "to find out new principles or arguments," but "to justify ourselves in the independent stand we are compelled to take. Neither aiming at originality of principle or sentiment," it "was intended to be an expression of the American mind."[3] In this chapter, I will contemplate the implications of the Declaration as an "expression of the American mind," engaging its declaratory promise in ways that go beyond its revolutionary intent. Jefferson's phrase signals the Declaration as a philosophic text: one in which a way of being-in-the-world is first articulated and argued. The reverberations of that argument call for our attention, as they have done again and again throughout our history. From the perspective of ethics, the Declaration, with its celebrated promises of freedom, provides a unique window on this way of being-in-the-world. For in the final analysis, the ideal of freedom must be answerable to the demand for justice.

In moving toward that realization, we need to rethink freedom as something other than autonomy, independence, and unfettered self-sufficiency. Indeed, we need eventually to go so far as to find the place where freedom discovers its investment in the responsibility for the Other. Until that point

---

3. Jefferson, "Letter to Henry Lee," ibid., 719.

is reached, however, the presence and face of the Other must come forward to assert the primacy of justice before freedom. The fact of this other presence—the Other, whose very being is the origin of an ethical challenge—disrupts the "American mind" in its commitment to a promise of freedom in the absence of obligation. As Levinas warns, freedom as "autonomy" is the "*reduction of the Other to the Same,*" or, more simply, the "conquest of being by man over the course of history."[4] As a philosophic text, the Declaration of Independence encourages us to question American assumptions about freedom and justice from an ethical perspective.

When Jefferson authored the Declaration of Independence in 1776, there was no doubt about its revolutionary intent. It came into being to signal to the "tribunal of the world" the emergence of an unprecedented possibility: the creation of a political structure founded upon the ideal of freedom.[5] In this respect, it is a text founded on a violence of revolt, for at its core it disrupts the prevailing structures of property and law to assert the fundamental right of an oppressed people to craft the material conditions of their historical existence.

Writing to Jefferson in April 1776, John Adams articulated the extraordinary challenge facing the American people in those turbulent times: "You and I, my friend, have been sent into life at a time when the greatest lawgivers of antiquity would have wished to live. . . . When, before the present epoch, had three millions of people full power and a fair opportunity to form and establish the wisest and happiest government that human wisdom can contrive?"[6]

Adams's celebration of the novelty of the revolutionary moment is echoed in much of the literature of 1776, coming to voice in a score of political and populist texts: Richard Price's *Observations on the Nature of Civil Liberty, the Principles of Government, and the Justice and Policy of the War with America*, Jeremy Bentham's *Fragment on Government*, and Paine's *Common Sense*. But it was Jefferson who issued the greatest challenge, one that, as historian Bernard Bailyn writes, was "destined to transform the course of Western history." The exceptionalism of the Declaration, Bailyn argues, was

---

4. Levinas, "Philosophy and the Idea of the Infinite," 91.
5. Jefferson, "Letter to Henry Lee," *Life and Selected Writings*, 719.
6. Quoted in Bailyn, *Faces of Revolution*, 160.

that it "not only declared its participating thirteen states to be a separate nation equal to all other nations but gave reasons for doing so that were so utterly idealistic and so rational—and yet so manifestly practical—that they stood as a threat and a challenge to every political system that existed."[7] Jefferson's Declaration transcends its practical justification for the violence of revolt to announce the founding moment in the constitution of a political structure in which the ideal of human freedom would achieve its rightful sovereignty.

The Declaration's claim that the sovereignty of freedom constitutes a rupture in human history, demands a legitimate resort to violence, and justifiably transforms the relations of law (as *droit*) signifies its essential performativity as a text of revolution. As Hannah Arendt convincingly argues, "The modern concept of revolution, inextricably bound up with the notion that the course of history suddenly begins anew, that an entirely new story, a story never known or told before, is about to unfold, was unknown prior to the two great revolutions at the end of the eighteenth century. . . . Crucial, then, to any understanding of revolutions in the modern age is that the idea of freedom and the experience of a new beginning should coincide."[8] Arendt makes clear that the content of revolution can be contained neither in a pure ideal nor in sheer physical violence. Revolution is activity, having as its aim an absolute and radical transformation. An old, known world is shattered—and with it, its imposed and implied structures of person and place—to usher into being a previously unknown reality marked by an "eagerness to liberate and to build a new house where freedom can dwell."[9]

The Declaration is not a revolutionary text merely because it declares a people's intent to rebel and justifies their recourse to violence. Arendt argues that violence of itself can bring about change, but it cannot explain the phenomenon of revolution. Only when change occurs in the sense of a new beginning, when violence is used to constitute an altogether different form of government, when liberation from oppression aims at least at the constitution of freedom—only then can one speak of revolution. The revolutionary content of the Declaration lies in the actuality of the transformation that it declares is existent: from here and now, it proclaims, the equal rights of

---

7. Ibid., 158.
8. Hannah Arendt, *On Revolution* (New York: Viking, 1965), 21–2.
9. Ibid., 28.

human beings will be authenticated through civil and political institutions, and government will function to preserve those rights. Should it fail to do so, it relinquishes its authority and legitimacy over the lives of free human beings.

"We hold these truths to be self-evident: that all men are created equal; that they are endowed by their Creator with CERTAIN [inherent and] inalienable rights; that among these are life, liberty, and the pursuit of happiness." This is the critical message of the Declaration as it is reproduced in Jefferson's *Autobiography*.[10] If the concept of equal rights was not a novel one, it was one never before realized—one which never found its way into actual application. If the notions of freedom and equality first surfaced in the philosophical and political legacy of the Greeks, these notions were understood as attributes granted by the polis, not accorded by birth. The Declaration, however, placed political power in the hands of those previously destined to be laborers, demanding both their appearance and their accountability as active makers of their own historical and political existence.

Revolution is ultimately about bread and land: it must accomplish not merely the alteration of an abstract and philosophical *weltanschauung* but must strike at the material conditions of a given people's existence.[11] Arendt has argued that this is precisely what makes the American Revolution an authentic one. In 1776, the public ratification of the Declaration announced the categorical rejection of the idea that poverty and want are natural components of human existence. As Arendt puts it, "America had become the symbol of a society without poverty, its own incontrovertible evidence of the fallacy in a conventional wisdom, which held that the distinction between the few, who through circumstances or strength or fraud had succeeded in liberating themselves from the shackles of poverty, and the laboring poverty-stricken multitude was inevitable and eternal."[12]

This is the metamorphosis that Crèvecoeur celebrates in *Letters from an American Farmer* when he invests property with sovereign authority to bestow upon the dispossessed not only "name" (and therefore a sudden visibility) but also "place" and its real possibility of economic prosperity. This is also the promise offered in Jefferson's 1801 inaugural address as the "palpable

---

10. Jefferson, "Autobiography," *Life and Selected Writings*, 22.
11. Frantz Fanon, *The Wretched of the Earth* (New York: Grove, 1963).
12. Arendt, *On Revolution*, 15.

truth, that the mass of mankind has not been born with saddles on their backs, nor a favored few booted and spurred, ready to ride them legitimately, by the grace of God." It is a promise entwined in the founding violence of a new law, creating an egalitarianism of material pursuit, where a "wise and frugal government, which shall restrain men from injuring one another . . . shall leave them otherwise free to regulate their own pursuits of industry and improvement, and shall not take from the mouth of labor the bread it has earned."[13] Significantly, Jefferson's promise appeared capable of fulfillment, which accounts in no small measure for its revolutionary content: the American landscape in 1801 presents itself as an uncharted and unclaimed frontier, imaginatively empty and fertile in invitation, a "chosen country, with room enough for our descendants to the hundredth and thousandth generation."[14]

As a political text, the Declaration presents the rationale for self-rule and self-determination to an observing world. As a philosophic text, it bears a prophetic vision of what ought to be: human existence constituted through the autocracy of freedom. But one of the more problematic elements of the Jeffersonian frame through which the American idea of freedom takes shape is its privileging of enjoyment—the "pursuit of happiness"—among the inalienable human rights. In a historical context, the "pursuit of happiness" denotes a fundamental relationship between the individual and the polis, as that sphere in which recognition becomes possible. Through its insistence upon the primacy of the state and political society as precedent to individual desire, Aristotle's *Politics* makes clear that happiness is synonymous with recognition and freedom, both of which are possible only in the public sphere, and hence the exclusive province of a privileged, propertied few. Thus there is a historical legacy through which the concept of happiness is entwined with public activity, with an individual's participation in the arena of the performative, in and through which the individual attains visibility and recognition before the gaze of the Other. This is the essential logic of identity proposed in the Hegelian edict that "self-consciousness exists in and for itself when and by the fact that, it so exists for another; that is, it exists only in being acknowledged."[15] More simply, freedom is first merely a possibility, dependent upon one's participation in the public arena, where the recognition of one's peers confirms one's autonomy as an individual.

13. Jefferson, "Inauguration Address, 1801," *Life and Selected Writings*, 323.
14. Ibid., 321.
15. Hegel, *Phenomenology of Spirit*, 111.

In this regard, one can read the Jeffersonian inclusion in the Declaration of the inalienable right to the "pursuit of happiness" as a call for the construction of a public sphere in which the American, by virtue of nationality and not conditional upon privilege, is accorded recognition through the agency of political participation. Indeed, this would appear to be Jefferson's intent in an earlier text, *A Summary View of the Rights of British America* (1774), written to remind the chief magistrate of the British Empire that "our ancestors, before their emigration to America, were the free inhabitants of the British dominions in Europe, and possessed a right, which nature has given to all men, of departing from the country in which chance, not choice, has placed them, of going in quest of new habitations, and of there establishing new societies, under such laws and regulations as, to them, shall seem most likely to promote public happiness."[16] The particular freedom denied Jefferson's ancestors, as "free inhabitants" of British soil, consists in the "citizen's right of access to the public realm, in his share in public power—to be 'a participator in the government of affairs.'"[17] Jefferson's free British subjects were not wholly or authentically "free" because they were neither participators in the processes of government nor actors accorded visibility in the public sphere.

Two years later, however, when Jefferson drafts the Declaration of Independence, his terminology has changed. His previous notion of "public happiness" has been revised to claim the priority of the individual's intrinsic right to the "pursuit of happiness," a significant modification that transfers the ambit of happiness from the public to the private realm. This change is both monumental and transformative. It signals an ontological bent in which the specific conditions of one's freedom are predicated upon an ideal of separation (what Levinas calls "ipseity") in and through which an isolate self affirms its independence, its egoism, as if it owes nothing to the Other whose presence precedes it and remains transcendent to it.

In his fascinating treatise on the Declaration, *Inventing America*, Garry Wills makes the argument that Jefferson's inclusion of the pursuit of happiness as an unalienable right "had nothing vague or private in mind. He meant a public happiness which is measurable, which is, indeed, the test and justification of any government." Wills traces the influence of moral-sense philos-

---

16. Jefferson, "A Summary View of the Rights of British America," *Life and Selected Writings*, 293–4.

17. Arendt, *On Revolution*, 124.

ophers—particularly Francis Hutcheson and (later) James Wilson—on Jefferson's intellectual development. He offers compelling evidence that, for Jefferson, "happiness" refers not to an individual yearning, but rather embraces the eighteenth-century notion of benevolence, in which the "surest way to promote private happiness is to do publicly useful actions." Wills continues, "Since man finds true happiness only in society, his pursuit of happiness will lead him, if nature is not obstructed, to desire the greatest happiness and perfection of the largest system, of those with whom he is associated. This provides the basis for all social organization, including that of the state: 'The general happiness is the supreme end of all political union.'" If we accept Wills's conclusions—and certainly the evidence of Jefferson's indebtedness to a score of moral-sense thinkers is impressive—then we must read this tenet of the Declaration as one that prioritizes and, at least in theory, ensures the responsibility of the individual to the whole. Jefferson's ideal citizen, in the pursuit of his particular happiness, discovers that happiness is dependent upon the well-being and happiness of those with whom he is associated through the "silken bands" of government and society. Wills concludes that Jefferson's inclusion of "'the pursuit of happiness' as the natural right to rank with life and liberty is not a vague or 'idealistic' or ill-defined action," but rather one which consistently echoes his moral-sense theory of public and political action, through which government achieves its validity and justification.[18]

And yet, as Wills himself acknowledges, the challenge inherent in this interpretation of the Jeffersonian construction of happiness reveals itself in its confrontation with the problem of difference. Even if we accept the claim that underlying Jefferson's understanding of the "pursuit of happiness" is a moral philosophy privileging benevolence before individual desire, benevolence is nonetheless unashamedly conditioned by affection. Ultimately, the "political bands are those of benevolence, formalized by compact to continue an existing affection." Herein resides the difficulty. This notion of "compact," which might otherwise be expressed as "amity," necessitates an affection mediated through the rule of sameness, and Wills freely admits Jefferson's "admiration for social cohesion" as well as his pivotal "desire to preserve homogeneity in America."[19]

18. Garry Wills, *Inventing America: Jefferson's Declaration of Independence* (Garden City, N.Y.: Doubleday, 1978), 164, 252.
19. Ibid., 292.

But the American landscape in 1776 is marked neither by amity nor affection in terms of its dark and problematic Others. And the happiness of the free American self seems deeply invested in a "principle of individuation," of an enjoyment specific to an ideal of separation from the presence of his African and Indian neighbors. As Levinas would add, "Happiness is not an accident of being"; rather, "Happiness is independence" (*TI*, 112). Indeed, as Jefferson delineates in *Notes on the State of Virginia*, the identity of the American displays itself through a logic of opposition made manifest in its essential juxtaposition to the existence of the Other, hidden within the recesses of this benevolent republic. In response to that memorable Crèvecoeurian question, "What is an American?" we can imagine Jefferson answering, "He is not an Indian, and he is certainly not of African blood." In drafting the Declaration of Independence, Jefferson was not declaring independence for these Others.

What marks Wills's elucidation of the historical and philosophical sources that inform Jefferson's writing of the Declaration is the apparent sincerity that motivates his inquiry. Wills insists that Jefferson's perspective on slavery and the condition of "people of color" consistently conformed to an Enlightenment belief in benevolence, which enables us to understand, if not agree with, Jefferson's ideas regarding difference. Wills is no apologist for a Jeffersonian defense of slavery—yet neither does he endorse the view of historian Paul Finkelman, who concludes that Jefferson was essentially a "failure." Writing on the occasion of the 250th anniversary of Jefferson's birth, Finkelman was moved to assert:

> Even historians who have concentrated on his faults argue that Jefferson, along with Lincoln, "is the central figure in the history of American democracy." Yet this "apostle of liberty" could never reconcile the ideals of freedom, expressed in the Declaration of Independence and his other writings, with the reality of his ownership of men and women and his leadership of a slaveholding society. . . . Scrutinizing the differences between Jefferson's professions and his actions does not impose twentieth-century values on an eighteenth-century man. Because he was the author of the Declaration and a leader of the American Enlightenment, the test . . . is not whether he was better than the worst of his generation, but whether he was the leader of the best . . . whether he was able to transcend his economic interests and his sectional background to implement the ideals he articulated. Jefferson fails the test.[20]

---

20. Paul Finkelman, "Jefferson and Slavery: Treason against the World," in *Jeffersonian Legacies*, ed. Peter S. Onuf (Charlottesville: University Press of Virginia, 1993), 181.

This criticism of Jefferson emphasizes the conflict between Jefferson's public and private selves. Finkelman insists on the relevance of the connection between public and private, arguing that public virtue does not absolve Jefferson but rather reinscribes his accountability. Yet if Jefferson was not wholly a "failure," he was nonetheless a man troubled by contradiction and denial—particularly regarding the presence of the Other.

In contrast, Wills argues that Jefferson's inability to embrace the presence of difference, as displayed upon the body of the African and the Native, is linked to and arises from his ideological and/or philosophical perspective on the issue of benevolence. Wills offers abundant evidence that Jefferson acted in concert with his own ideals for benevolence and self-rule. Most interesting is Wills's defense of Jefferson's plan for the deportation "into freedom" of African peoples. Jefferson's rationale for deportation, offered in his *Notes on the State of Virginia*, is grounded in the premise that slavery constitutes an essentially unconquerable experience, through which the European American and the African have become unalterable enemies. To extend freedom to the African would be to initiate racial war, or "genocide," as Wills names it, and Jefferson's reasons are succinctly "scientific": "deep rooted prejudices entertained by the whites," "ten thousand recollections, by the blacks, of the injuries they have sustained," and "fresh provocations" occasioned by the exclusion of African people from the compact of American "*fraternité*" all signify the existential impossibility of the African's sudden social integration, thus reinscribing the "real distinctions which nature has made."[21] Wills argues that Jefferson's rationale is informed not by an inherent belief in the inferiority of the African, but rather reflects his belief in the "need for a shared ethos—for '*fraternité*,'" which made him "doubt that blacks could ever be incorporated into Virginia society." To put it slightly differently, persons of African blood and lineage, if transported to some other place, might enact the same rules of self-determination that informed the American model. Indeed, Wills tells us, "His deportation scheme was meant to assure for blacks the same rights Americans were asserting. But the blacks had first to have a *separate* station, for that to become an *equal* one."[22]

Wills's argument is predicated upon his reading of *Notes on the State of*

---

21. Thomas Jefferson, *Notes on the State of Virginia*, ed. William Peden (New York: Norton, 1982), 138.

22. Wills, *Inventing America*, 306.

Virginia, in which Jefferson elucidates a theory of difference through which the identity of the African finds articulation. Thus, before we can judge the veracity of Wills's claims for Jefferson's benevolence, we must turn to *Notes*, as the seminal text in which Jefferson first encounters the presence of the Other and articulates a philosophical inquiry into the nature of human difference in its appearance in the New World.

From its opening lines, in which Jefferson attempts an "exact description of the limits and boundaries of the state of Virginia," *Notes* posits the existence of a natural world that is discoverable, measurable, and rationally knowable. In the very first "Queries" of the text, Jefferson offers an exhaustive description and analysis of the Virginia terrain and speaks in the voice of the natural scientist, confident of a Newtonian world regulated by a rational and discoverable order. But as the Virginia of the *Notes* is transformed into the sign of an emergent American landscape, Jefferson's intent undergoes a similar transformation. *Notes on the State of Virginia* is not simply the investigation of a newly explored natural habitat, but the vindication of a New World territory against the charge of "degeneracy" so prevalent in European intellectual circles. Intervening in the discussion on the relationship between "climate and civilization," *Notes* is determined to establish the demonstrable superiority of the New World terrain.

Jefferson's methodology in the initial "Queries" of *Notes on the State of Virginia* emphasizes reason and experience as the primary vehicles through which the laws of Nature can be uncovered. Underlying the Jeffersonian insistence upon exactitude and specificity is an acceptance of the Newtonian supposition that the natural world, grasped in its phenomenal appearance, can be rendered comprehensible through a logic of inductive analysis. As Henry Steele Commager has pointed out, Jefferson's *Notes* is a "typical Enlightenment inquiry . . . on the geography, the minerals, the cascades and caverns . . . for with these it mingled questions about 'all that can increase the progress of human knowledge,' 'the administration of justice,' 'the different religions,' and the 'customs and manners of the people.'"[23] Yet in those moments when Jefferson's gaze moves beyond the sphere of natural phenomena to encompass the presence of the Other—and therefore to anticipate the question of justice—his system falters, undermining the objectivity of his scientific inquiry.

23. Henry Steele Commager, *Jefferson, Nationalism, and the Enlightenment* (New York: Braziller, 1975), 37.

Investigating the ontological assumptions that inform Jefferson's *Notes*, we discover the ruling presence of an enlightened subjectivity engaging its world as an exteriority open to examination and reflection. Experience yields truth, Jefferson repeatedly asserts, revealing his faith in the abilities of an educated aristocracy of scientists and philosophers to uncover the essential content of a natural world governed by reason. As historian John H. Randall suggests, however, the conflation of the "rational" and the "natural" constitutes a particular problem in Enlightenment thinking: "What was rational was ipso facto natural, and what was natural was what appealed as reasonable to the enlightened commonsense of the progressive thinker—especially, for the middle-class business man, what led to prosperity and wealth."[24]

One of the problems revealed by Randall's insight is that the imposition of a rational law upon the realm of natural phenomena works to subjugate Nature to the mastery of human conceptualization and comprehension. This process of subjugation ultimately divests the world, and Being itself, of its essential mystery, of its absolute Otherness, to enable the translation into property—as that which can be known and subsequently owned. Levinas puts it this way: "As knowledge, thought relates to what is thinkable, that is, the thinkable called being. Relating to being, thought is outside itself, but remains marvelously in itself, or returns to itself" (*OG*, 138). When we peruse the pages of Jefferson's *Notes*, we find that Virginia is neither a mysterious nor a treacherous terrain. Both literally and figuratively, it is a propertied landscape firmly under the command of Jefferson's possessive knowledge. As Levinas argues, "That which thought knows, or what it learns in its 'experience,' is at once the *other* and the *property* of thought" (*OG*, 138). The greater difficulty in Jefferson's methodology resides in its privileging of ontology before ethics. As a result, his thinking privileges his experience and specularity, so that the alterity of the land, and ultimately the Other, becomes the "property" of his thought.

In Jefferson's text, the "natural" otherness of the Native and the African must also lend itself to rational explication: it must be penetrable and systematically comprehensible. Indeed, Jefferson's methodological inquiry into the nature of human difference manifests the same philosophical orientation that previously has been suggested: *Notes on the State of Virginia* is a text in which

---

24. John H. Randall, *The Career of Philosophy*, vol. 1 (New York: Columbia University Press, 1962), 567.

the primacy of knowledge promotes the priority of freedom. In other words, the spirit of inquiry that motivates Jefferson's *Notes* might be understood as the "unity of the *I think*," such that this unity of thought constitutes the "ultimate form of spirit as knowledge. And to this unity of the *I think* all things are referred, constituting a system." But, as Levinas warns, the "system of what is intelligible is, ultimately, a consciousness of self" (*OG*, 139).

Thus what Jefferson accomplishes in *Notes* can be understood as the articulated performance of the subject in search of its own identity—as an act of sojourning in and through which the American self derives its very certainty. As readers, we bear witness to the narrative presence in *Notes* that journeys out into the world, as Jefferson does on the parapet at the Natural Bridge, where "few men have resolution to walk," and where "looking down from this height about a minute" gives him a "violent head ache." The potential dissolution of self that this experience precipitates is resettled only moments later in an act of recovery, as the I resumes its consistency of identity: "If the view from the top be painful and intolerable, that from below is delightful in an equal extreme. It is impossible for the emotions arising from the sublime to be felt beyond what they are here; so beautiful an arch, so elevated, so light, and springing as it were up to heaven! The rapture of the spectator is really indescribable!"[25] This is the movement that Jefferson's authorial "I" accomplishes: he is the indigenous subject, engaging the Virginia terrain as an object of exteriority, but in such a way that the alterity of the natural landscape is suspended before his gaze and thus integrated into the totality of thought, where the I reclaims its integrity and freedom. As Levinas writes, "In thinking, the being situated within the totality is not absorbed by it. It exists in relation to a totality, but remains here, separated from the totality: me" (*EN*, 15).

The predominance of ontology in *Notes* is most clearly demonstrated through Jefferson's encounter with the alterity of the Other. In the eighteenth-century American landscape, the Native and the African constitute the presence of the Stranger—the Other whose difference in being threatens to disrupt the cohesion of the totality in which freedom and thought prevail. Ontology privileges freedom by enacting a relation with difference, manifested in the presence of the Other, in order to make possible its comprehension. Yet if, as Levinas argues, the system of knowledge and thus "of what is

---

25. Jefferson, *Notes on the State of Virginia*, 25.

intelligible is, ultimately, a consciousness of self," then the Other's very being disrupts that unity of intelligibility; it is only the Other who "does not affect us by means of a concept." More specifically, the relation to the Other "certainly consists in wanting to understand him, but this relation exceeds the confines of understanding, not only because, besides curiosity, knowledge of the other also demands sympathy or love, ways of being that are different from impassive contemplation," but also because the Other, unlike the exteriority of landscape, cannot be subsumed through the imposition of a concept. "The other is a being and counts as such" (EN, 5).

This ethical flaw permeates the inquiry into the alterity of the Other in Notes. Jefferson approaches the Other as if the Other's otherness is comprehensible, as if the presence of alterity can be represented in a language that reflects understanding. This, Levinas emphasizes, is why "ethics and comprehension are not on the same level" (OG, 99). The Other exceeds the "confines of understanding" because the Other—Native or African—does not belong to the horizon of perception, existing as a "thing" among things. Rather, the Other exists as a being who bears a face and thus is not reducible to the language of representation. As Levinas clarifies, in "every attitude toward the human being there is a greeting—even if it is the refusal of a greeting. Here my perception is not projected toward the horizon (the field of my freedom, my power, my property) in order to grasp the individual against this familiar background" (EN, 7). But Jefferson's Notes situates the Other within the horizon of perception (and within the "field of [his] freedom"); as a result, the activity of understanding "carries out an act of violence and of negation" (EN, 9).

As soon as the Other becomes an object of contemplation upon whom an I exerts the powers of his understanding, a particular kind of violence and negation is instituted. Insofar as the activity of understanding is predicated upon vision, it imposes a logic of equivalence that returns the Other to the field of the Same. As Levinas points out, while "vision certainly exercises power" over the Other, the "meeting with the other person consists in the fact that, despite the extent of my domination over him and his submission, I do not possess him. He does not enter entirely into the opening of being in which I already stand as in the field of my freedom" (EN, 9). This is one of the key difficulties that plagues Jefferson's inquiry into the alterity of the Other: his desire to subsume that alterity under the faculties of the understanding. Through that process, the face of the Other is obliterated. And, in the optics of ethics, the "face is the very identity of a being; it manifests itself in it in terms of itself, without a concept. The sensible presence of this chaste bit of skin with brow, nose, eyes, and mouth, is neither a sign allowing us to approach a signified, nor a mask hiding it" (*EN*, 33). With this in mind, let us turn to Jefferson's representation of the Native and the manner of difference he discovers there.

Query XI, "Aborigines," begins in the voice of a dispassionate and interested investigator: "When the first effectual settlement of our colony was made, which was 1607, the country . . . was occupied by upwards of forty different tribes of Indians." Jefferson compiles a table of enumeration—a "state of these several tribes, according to their confederacies and geographical situation, with their numbers when we first became acquainted with them"—and notes the "melancholy sequel of their history": judging by their numbers in the 1669 census, "we discover that the tribes therein enumerated were, in the space of 62 years, reduced to about one-third of their former numbers."[26] The Indian of America is already something of an endangered species, Jefferson implies, and so the inquiry into the nature of the Indian's *being* is both necessary and important. Jefferson's investigation is more than an effort of comprehension, more than an act of reduction through which the Indian disappears. As Native writer and critic Gerald Vizenor suggests, "Jefferson created a presence of natives, a representation that was not common in narratives; in earlier journals the *indian* was an absence in histories" (*FP*, 11). Jefferson's Indian is not absent in the history that *Notes* rewrites, but she is nevertheless a figure consumed by tragedy and a disappearing entity in the landscape.[27]

It is thus not surprising that Jefferson next turns his attention to the actual presence of an absence: "I know of no such thing existing as an Indian monument: for I would not honor with that name arrow points, stone hatchets, stone pipes, and half-shapen images."[28] Why is this absence so critical, so revealing, to Jefferson? The answer lies in the notion of "monument" as that which survives as testimony and record, and "that by surviving, repre-

---

26. Ibid., 92, 96.

27. While the term *Indian* is inherently problematic in the ethical context of naming the Native Other, I use it here to designate the language of classification that dominated nineteenth-century American discourse. The term *Native* refers to the original and essential presence of the Other, whose alterity supersedes its representation in language.

28. Jefferson, *Notes on the State of Virginia*, 97.

sents or testifies to the greatness or achievement . . . of an individual or age."[29] In the context of the *Notes*, the absence of an Indian monument becomes testimony to the lack of "greatness" that marks this particular race and culture.

The closest Jefferson can come in uncovering the existence of an Indian monument are the tribal "barrows, of which many are to be found all over this country." In order to discover the nature of these crude "repositories" and "on what occasion [they were] constructed," Jefferson investigates: "There being one of these in my neighborhood, I wished to satisfy myself. . . . For this purpose I determined to open and examine it thoroughly."[30] Jefferson's intent is to contribute to the scientific effort to penetrate the veil of Indian and of "savage" existence itself and, in so doing, to offer a more definitive explanation of the habits and customs of the North American Indian.

That Jefferson was well aware of the violative nature of his experiment has been most effectively established by historian Richard Drinnon, who argues, "As he had to know, he would have been guilty of grave robbing, *pro confesso*, had he entered a Charlottesville cemetery, dug up skeletons, counted the bones, and published his findings in *Notes on Virginia*. Yet he had no hesitation in excavating the mound near his home and putting the results before members of the American Philosophical Society. Had he respectfully studied the ways of his red neighbors, he would have known that they considered burial grounds sacred."[31]

Jefferson himself acknowledges that even as they are repositories for the dead, the barrows constitute a significant and actively sacred presence in the living memory and cultural life of Native peoples. On the basis of his personal knowledge, Jefferson testifies that "on whatever occasion [the barrows] may have been made, they are of considerable notoriety among the Indians; for a party passing, about thirty years ago, through the part of the country where this barrow is, went through the woods directly to it, without any instructions or inquiry, and having staid about it for some time, with expres-

---

29. Philip Babcock Grove, ed., *Webster's Third New International Dictionary* (Springfield, Mass.: G. C. Merriam, 1966).

30. Jefferson, *Notes on the State of Virginia*, 98.

31. Richard Drinnon, *Facing West: The Metaphysics of Indian-Hating and Empire-Building* (Norman: University of Oklahoma Press, 1997), 93.

sions which were construed to be those of sorrow, they returned to the high road, which they had left about half a dozen miles to pay this visit, and pursued their journey."[32] Jefferson's decision to explore the burial ground is not only a physical violation; it is also an ethical one. In exhuming the barrow, Jefferson commits an act of "negation which is violence" because it "denies the independence" of the Other's being, as if to assert, in the case of those remains, "they are mine" (*EN*, 9).

What permits the ethical violence of Jefferson's exploratory conquest lies in an earlier process of conversion, through which the Indian emerges as a being whose presence is marked by the inevitability of his (soon-to-be) absence. As with Crèvecoeur's *Letters,* the Indian of *Notes* exists primarily as a specimen and relic of a time already being overwritten by the newly initiated history of the free American subject. Whether regarded as specimen or relic, the Indian ceases to be. In the factual ground of human relations, the conversion into "relic" makes one an object, not a subject. The Indian is made into an object, just as the burial mound is converted into the site of an inquisitive interrogation. In Levinasian terms, this conversion of the sacred into artifact becomes the act of a "partial negation, which is violence. And this partialness can be described by the fact that, without disappearing, beings are in my power" (*EN*, 9). While "everything that comes from him" and all evidence of his otherness in difference "offers itself to my understanding and my possession," this is the posture of an I who can only understand the Other "in terms of his history, his environment, his habits," as Jefferson so valiantly attempts to do. But the face of the Native Other defies and exceeds both the language of representation and the conclusions of scientific expertise: "What escapes understanding in him is himself, the being. I cannot deny him partially, in violence, by grasping him in terms of being in general, and by possessing him. The other is the only being whose negation can be declared only as total: a murder" (*EN*, 9).

Here, more transparently than one would expect, the Jeffersonian inquiry into the alterity of the Native Other reveals its bias, its participation in a system of intelligibility that is, "ultimately, a consciousness of self." Cognition, or the activity of comprehension, "consists in grasping the individual . . . not in its singularity which does not count, but in its generality, of which alone there is science." But the idealized reign of science can be ethically

---

32. Jefferson, *Notes on the State of Virginia,* 100.

dangerous, for "here every power begins. The surrender of exterior things to human freedom through their generality does not only mean, in all innocence, their comprehension," but, far more insidiously, "their domestication, their possession." In Levinas's view, the law of science is the rule of reason, but "reason, which reduces the other, is appropriation and power."[33] If the Indian can be philosophically constructed as the aboriginal relic of an earlier, pre-American and New World landscape, then the Jeffersonian inquiry surely grounds her (and the mysterious content of her existence) in a past history whose reality has been superseded—as evolutionary law must dictate—by the enlightened humanity and culture of a superior race of beings. In other words, when Vizenor argues that "Jefferson created a presence of natives," it is a "presence" achieved through death. The very effort to "know" the Indian is an act of negation, one in which (as we shall see) his death is made imminent.

Johannes Fabian pinpoints this same problem with the concept of alterity, arguing that in a historical context, "Anthropology's efforts to construct relations with its Other by means of temporal devices implied affirmation of difference as *distance*."[34] To construct and to situate the Indian as an Other removed in time and distance is to disrupt the possibilities of cultural dialogue or collaboration. If the Indian, as represented by Jefferson, belongs to another time—one pre-American—then insofar as one encounters her, she is beyond recovery. The denial of contemporaneity establishes the Indian as an Other outside the reality of Jefferson's historical present. As Vizenor frames it, "Natives were represented in narratives and in the comparative notions of race, but not in the foundational sense of the nation" (*FP*, 12).

With respect to Jefferson's treatment of the Indian, arguably one of the more complex moments in *Notes* is the presentation of the speech attributed to Chief Logan. Logan's words, Jefferson argues, "may challenge the whole orations of Demosthenes and Cicero, and of any more eminent orator." As Jefferson subsequently asserts, Logan's speech constitutes a specific moment of refutation of the "contumelious theory of certain European writers" who argue for the "degenerated animal nature, in general, and particularly the moral faculties of man." Logan's oratory is offered as a "specimen of the talents of the aboriginals of this country, and particularly of their eloquence."

---

33. Levinas, "Philosophy and the Idea of the Infinite," 98.
34. Johannes Fabian, *Time and the Other* (New York: Columbia University Press, 1983), 16.

In this respect, it constitutes a rare moment in the text in which the Indian is given voice. It is important to note, however, that Logan's speech is offered in defeat—in the aftermath of the slaughter of his family, reportedly at the hands of Captain Cresap along the Ohio River. While the series of documents appended to *Notes* makes plain that Jefferson's sympathies lie with Logan and that he wishes at least in part to acknowledge the moral complexities that inhere in the murder of Logan's kin, there is nonetheless a far greater emphasis in *Notes* placed upon Logan's distinction as an orator. Furthermore, Jefferson's revision of the account of the murders underscores Logan's distinction not only as an aboriginal orator, but as also an Indian "long distinguished as the friend of the whites."[35]

If one is tempted to read Jefferson's inclusion of Logan's speech in *Notes* as a sympathetic gesture, it is necessary to place that gesture within the expository tradition to which it belongs. As many scholars (Roy Harvey Pearce in particular) have noted, there was a compelling need among post–Revolutionary War American thinkers to devise a theory of the Indian that would enable them to refute European misconceptions of the Native presence, as well as allowing them to construct a particularly American idea of savagism—one that would include the Indian's tragic but inevitable demise. Logan's appearance in *Notes* is qualified by the dual assertion of his nobility in speech (and therefore emotion) and his inherent ignobility as the "savage." He is the Other whose eloquence is revered in the approaching moment of his destruction. The fact that Logan is both a chief—whose words are reported to have been uttered in tears—and the "friend of the whites" marks his particularity, his uniqueness in opposition to the faceless Indian against whom the war for civilization would be waged. Significantly, however, Logan's nobility is founded in his position as one already-in-defeat. He speaks from the ground of the conquered; even as his voice is permitted inclusion in *Notes*, it signifies what Pearce has designated as the "inferior kind of nobility of the savage, a nobility which achieved its ends by emotion rather than reason, by action rather than thought, by custom rather than by law."[36] The fact that Chief Logan speaks suggests the tremendous complexity of the problem of difference in *Notes*. While Logan's speech can be read as evidence of a specifically American inquiry into the nature and essence of the Indian, it is

---

35. Jefferson, *Notes on the State of Virginia*, 62, 226, 230.
36. Pearce, *Savagism and Civilization*, 79.

simultaneously constructed as evidence of an inferior sensibility, one which paradoxically assures his defeat and ultimate erasure.

Jefferson's Indian is already destined for removal—he is the Other whose actual presence must disappear, whose stubborn resistance must be overcome, whose symbolic value is primarily what Derrida has named "the remains." Indians, as Vizenor argues, were a threat to the republic politically because, as Native peoples, they "had negotiated treaties and formed alliances with other governments" that were "considered to be dangerous to the new constitutional democracy" (*FP*, 12). Philosophically, however, the Indian was an obstacle in the way of freedom and the expansion of the frontier. This is the Other-to-be-defeated, to be retired through death. "But the dead have no rights," Jefferson would later remark, in a statement that could serve as a fitting conclusion for his investigation of the "Indian of North America" in *Notes*. He carried this attitude with him into his writing of the Declaration of Independence. Indians appear in the Declaration, albeit in one of its less frequently quoted passages, as simply and purely the dangerous and disposable Other who stands as the impediment to the free movement of "We, the people": the "present King of Great Britain" has, among other tyrannous atrocities, "endeavored to bring on the inhabitants of our frontiers the merciless Indian savages, whose known rule of warfare is an undistinguished destruction of all ages, sexes, and conditions."[37]

While the Indian in *Notes on the State of Virginia* and the Declaration of Independence is cast as the Other-to-be-defeated, the African comes to presence as the Other-already-in-defeat. Africans do not even appear in the Declaration, though Jefferson had tried to include them; during the Congressional debate on the document, Jefferson's draft came under attack because he included a section excoriating slavery, calling it a "cruel war against human nature itself, violating its most sacred rights of life and liberty" (though he blamed this racist war on George III). The entire passage was deleted. Jefferson later remarked, "The clause reprobating the enslaving of the inhabitants of Africa, was struck out in complaisance to South Carolina and Georgia, who had never attempted to restrain the importation of slaves, and who on the contrary still wished to continue it. Our northern brethren also I believe

---

37. Thomas Jefferson, *Writings*, comp. Merrill D. Peterson (New York: Literary Classics of United States, 1984), 18.

felt a little tender under those censures; for tho' their people have very few slaves themselves yet they had been pretty considerable carriers of them to others." Jefferson, the owner of as many as 175 slaves, spoke out against slavery, though he believed the practice would only gradually fade away; in one of his last letters, he wrote that the end of slavery is "not to be expected in a day, or perhaps in an age; but time, which outlives all things, will outlive this evil also."[38]

In *Notes*, Jefferson encounters the African not as the vestige of an evolutionary past that deserves inquiry, but as pure alterity. As Merrill Peterson has suggested, Jefferson's partial "'vindication of the Indian'" might be understood "as a 'vindication of the American environment.'" But since the African had no "place" in the natural landscape, Jefferson's "solution for them was not amalgamation but expulsion" (quoted in *FP*, 12). The African in *Notes* is the Other whose conversion into object has been previously effected. He is the Other whose objectification through the imposition of enslavement prevents his appearance in the human realm of presence and identity, thus ensuring his intentional erasure from the Declaration.

As with the "North American Indian," Jefferson attempts a catalogue of the observable traits of the African. In this instance, however, he does not feel compelled to offer an account of the source of his knowledge. The authority which informs the Jeffersonian treatise derives, it would seem, from a "self-evident" proposition: Jefferson is the thinking subject whose existence is rooted in freedom, while the African is the absolute Stranger whose presence is contained in and through his brute objectivity. The African is animality indistinct from his material physicality. Configured beneath the gaze of Jefferson's inquiry, the African is abstract individuality—what Marx would distinguish as a "freedom *from* being, not freedom *in* being," as what "cannot shine in the light of being" because its "individuality loses its character and becomes material." The African can only exist "in the void," in the "realm of absence and concealment."[39] For Jefferson, the African takes shape as an "animal" whose "existence appears to participate more of sensation than reflection," who "when abstracted from [his] diversions, and unemployed in labor," is revealed as an "animal whose body is at rest, and who does not

---

38. Ibid., 18, 1516.

39. Quoted in Cornel West, *The Ethical Dimensions of Marxist Thought* (New York: Monthly Review, 1991), 22.

reflect, must be disposed to sleep of course."[40] In sum, Jefferson's African is unreflective, nonthinking "being." The extent and content of his humanity is undiscoverable, for it remains hidden beneath "that immovable veil of black." If the African possesses subjectivity, at least in Jefferson's terms, it is a subjectivity in absentia.

Numerous contemporary scholars have provided extensive analyses of the obvious contradictions in a logic of racial identity that begins with the assertion of a human equality grounded in the "brotherhood of man as imbedded in the story of Genesis" in order to demonstrate that "mankind consisted of a single species and that human varieties had come to differ in appearance through the operation of natural causes."[41] This argument enables Jefferson to assert that the "blacks, whether originally a distinct race, or made distinct by time and circumstances, are inferior to the whites in the endowments of both body and mind," permitting the conclusion that "it is not against experience to suppose, that different species of the same genus, or varieties of the same species, may possess different qualifications."[42]

Modern scholarship notwithstanding, perhaps one of the most revealing accounts of this logic of identity comes from the nineteenth century. In *Democracy in America*, Alexis de Tocqueville offers a stunningly simple and profound observation in his chapter "The Three Races that Inhabit the United States." On the differences in racial presence and identity, Tocqueville comments:

> The men scattered over [America] are not, as in Europe, shoots of the same stock. It is obvious that there are three naturally distinct, one might almost say hostile, races. . . . Among these widely different people, the first that attracts attention, and the first in enlightenment, power, and happiness, is the white man, the European, man par excellence. Below him come the Negro and the Indian. . . . Seeing what happens in the world, might one not say that the European is to men of other races what man is to the animals? He makes them serve his convenience, and when he cannot bend them to his will he destroys them.[43]

40. Jefferson, *Notes on the State of Virginia*, 139.

41. Winthrop Jordan, *White over Black* (Chapel Hill: University of North Carolina Press, 1968), 195.

42. Jefferson, *Notes on the State of Virginia*, 143.

43. Alexis de Tocqueville, *Democracy in America*, trans. George Lawrence (New York: Harper, 1966), 292.

What Tocqueville reveals here is the essential element of relationality: the triumph of democracy is the triumph of the European self constituting its own happiness and freedom. But freedom is a relative experience; one discovers the certainty of one's freedom only through an opposition to the Other who is not free. In other words, Tocqueville unmasks the necessity for a hierarchical differentiation of race in the American consciousness. Through the paradigm of opposition, the European demonstrates his privileged and providential place in the creation of a new world order.

At this point, it is appropriate to return to Hannah Arendt's argument and to revisit the question of the Declaration's revolutionary content. It is clear that the Declaration calls into being a new body politic, one whose aim is the creation of a different form of government that is specifically founded in freedom. Arendt's celebration of the unique accomplishments of the American revolution is unconditionally linked to the sense of a new beginning. As Bonnie Honig has suggested, this sense of a new beginning is characterized by the "modern disappearance of traditional political authority," initiating an opening for "new possibilities of innovative political action, revolution and foundation."[44] These new possibilities, especially as Arendt formulates them in *On Revolution*, return one to the Declaration of Independence as a text that achieves greatness not for its natural-law philosophy but for its revolutionary performativity as both language and monument.

The profound revolutionary significance of the Declaration resides in its "performative utterance" as a "speech act that in itself brings 'something into being which did not exist before.'"[45] This is what Arendt terms the "grandeur" of the Declaration, which is neither philosophic nor "even so much in its being 'an argument in support of an action' as in its being the perfect way for an action to appear in words." The Declaration is revolutionary, Arendt contends, because of what it performs: the creation of a political possibility through which the conceptual reality of the republic is born. The notion of the republic is founded in the language of action, a language invested in the performance of promise through which the citizen makes a "mutual pledge"

---

44. Bonnie Honig, "Declarations of Independence: Arendt and Derrida on the Problem of Founding a Republic," in *Rhetorical Republic: Governing Representations in American Politics*, ed. Frederick M. Dolan and Thomas L. Dumm (Amherst: University of Massachusetts Press, 1993), 201–2.

45. Ibid., 204.

with a community of other citizens, with whom one promises the "right to become a 'participator in the government of affairs,' the right to be seen in action." In other words, the Declaration is performatively revolutionary because it articulates—and thus births—an alternative source and foundation of power. For the "men of the American revolution," Arendt writes, "power came into being when and where people would get together and bind themselves through promises, covenants, and mutual pledges; only such power, which rested on reciprocity and mutuality, was real power and legitimate." As opposed to previous conceptions of power, understood as the consent to rule by "kings or princes or aristocrats," the American revolution emerged from, and translated into the realm of fact, the novel ideal of mutuality, in which power was understood to originate "from below, [from] the 'grass roots' of the people, and the source of law, whose seat is 'above,' in some higher and transcendent region."[46]

As Bonnie Honig explains, Arendt locates the performative power of the Declaration as act and text in the opening words of its second paragraph: "We hold these truths to be self-evident." The *"We hold"* works to "empower . . . an existing community inasmuch as it constitutes a free coming together and publicly expresses a shared agreement to abide by certain rules in the community's subsequent being together. The *We hold* is a promise and a declaration; it signals the existence of a singularly human capacity: that of world building." The revolutionary content of the Declaration is specifically this act of speech as performative founding: it is both that which brings into being what was not before and that which subsequently acts as (and becomes) its own foundation of authority. In its performative power, the Declaration is inherently revolutionary because it founds an authority grounded in the promise of its citizens, who pledge themselves to the community and are bound by the reciprocity that community entails. Most importantly, however, this pledge replaces the rule of the absolute with the mutuality of fraternity, in which the "plurality of participants who subscribe to a shared authoritative practice of promising" works to reinscribe the authority of their own words and actions.[47] The people themselves must ultimately become the authoritative guarantors of the promise that they performatively "speak" in the public arena.

46. Arendt, *On Revolution*, 127, 181–3.
47. Honig, "Declarations," 206, 210.

Yet as Honig's analysis suggests, the difficulty in this reading of the revolutionary content of the Declaration is its circularity. If, as Arendt has argued, the Declaration founds an authority—a beginning—that does not exist prior to its linguistic utterance, Honig asks, how does this "'We' stand as the guarantor of its own performance? How can it function as the sole source of stability for the Republic?"[48] To resolve this question, Honig turns to Derrida's "Declarations of Independence," where the issue of authority is returned to the authoritative signature(s) that necessarily demand interrogation.

Derrida asks the critical question: "Who signs, and with what so-called proper name, the declarative act which founds an institution?" He answers that the "signer is thus the people, the 'good people'" who "declare themselves free and independent by the relay of their representatives." The problem, Derrida argues, is one of a circuitous performative: "Is it that the good people have already freed themselves in fact and are only stating the fact of this emancipation in [par] the Declaration? Or is it rather that they free themselves at the instant of and by [par] the signature of this Declaration?" According to Derrida, given the Declaration's performative power of initiation, there could not have been any "signer, by right, before the text of the Declaration which itself remains the producer and guarantor of its own signature." Yet there is and must be "another 'subjectivity'" who will sign—who will, through its authoritative intervention, make possible the guarantee of signature. That Other is the "name of God."[49] In essence, Honig writes, "God is the name Derrida gives to whatever is used to hold the place of the last instance, the place that is the inevitable aporia of founding (or signing or promising)."[50]

In Derrida's words, the revolutionary act and simultaneous utterance/signature of freedom that would declare that "these united Colonies are and of right ought to be free and independent states" engage and call upon the constative word and presence of God. The signers of the Declaration recognized the necessity of a higher authority, one that could anchor the promise of revolution in an authority beyond the activity of revolution itself and that could secure the "what ought to be." We can comprehend the meaning of

---

48. Ibid., 212.

49. Jacques Derrida, "Declarations of Independence," trans. Thomas Keenan and Thomas Pepper, *New Political Science* 15 (1986): 8, 9, 10.

50. Honig, "Declarations," 213.

the Declaration, in all its revolutionary intent, as a "vibrant act of faith," Derrida suggests, because "for this Declaration to have a meaning *and* an effect, there must be a last instance. God is the name, the best one, for this last instance and this ultimate signature."[51] As Honig elaborates, the authority of the Declaration cannot be wholly performative, because "in every system (every practice), whether linguistic, cultural, or political, there is a moment or place that the system cannot account for. Every system is secured by placeholders that are irrevocably, structurally, arbitrary and prelegitimate. They enable the system but are illegitimate from its vantage point."[52]

Yet Derrida's turn to God as the "proper name" in and through which "the 'good people' of America call *themselves* and declare *themselves* independent" is itself problematic. If the "good people" of America "invent (for) themselves a signing identity," they do so in the name of that God who "comes, in effect, to guarantee the rectitude of popular intentions, the unity and goodness of the people."[53] But is this God to whom Derrida refers, whose authority "founds natural laws" and thus secures the revolutionary promise of an independent and free republic, One who privileges linguistic performativity—that is, privileged utterance and signature—over the call of humanity? It would seem that this God signs on behalf of those "good people" who are capable of declaration, those whose singularity of person is translatable into the rhetoric of community, informed by a unity of intention, righteousness, and representation. What of the Other, of the face excluded through the fact of its essential alterity and marked by its unequivocal silence, its lack and absence of representation? What of the Other who is denied representation or signature, whose presence, according to natural law, does not count in the realm of signs and referents?

A partial answer is provided by Jay Fliegelman in *Declaring Independence*. Fliegelman situates the Declaration as a specifically performative event that derives its meaning not from the sanctimony of the text itself but rather from its public iterability. While we think of the Declaration as a text to be read in private, Fliegelman asserts, it was actually a performative document in the most genuine sense. Its reality and resonance emanated from the act of its performativity: "The public readings made the Declaration an event rather

---

51. Derrida, "Declarations of Independence," 12.
52. Honig, "Declarations," 215.
53. Derrida, "Declarations of Independence," 11.

than a document. They gave it a voice, which like 'the voice of the people [that] drove us to it,' the delegates' 'voices for it,' and 'the voice of justice & consanguinity,' to which 'our British brethren' have been 'deaf,' was experienced emotionally and responded to vocally. Read out loud, the document that denounced a false community would galvanize the bond of a true one."[54]

For Arendt, the Declaration was revolutionary because it called into being a form of political association previously unimaginable and therefore historically unique; for Fliegelman, that revolution was also oratorical and elocutionary. To be an American had much to do with a "particular cultural code whose audibility signified the possession of a sensibility others lacked; in turn, possession of that sensibility was the very test definition of being an American, the principle of national differentiation."[55] Thus, the Declaration was performatively revolutionary. Its reiteration across counties, districts, and states was both foundational and authoritative because, in each utterance, its meaning gained significance and fortitude, initiating the creation of a national community that was otherwise impossible.

But—as Fliegelman acknowledges in the first pages of his text—this is a revolution in kind and in sameness. In its emphasis on oratory and the "culture of performance," it must concede the presence of that which remains unsayable, as well as that which exists as the unsaid. In this sense, the particular elocutionary sensibility that defines the American character in the late eighteenth century simultaneously denies, silences, and obliterates the face of the Other. If the "oratorical revolution," as Fliegelman names it, has something to do with the "larger history of the social and psychological meanings and consequences of self-expression," then it is also a revolution that leaves out its problematic Other, who does not and is not permitted speak. Indeed, Fliegelman acknowledges that the "oratorical revolution had its own deeply racist dimension, especially because of its roots in physiognomy."[56]

And it is not simply the fact that the Other cannot speak, but that speech itself is grounded in an aesthetics of *face*. This is Vizenor's point as well. As he writes, Native peoples "were named in connection with the vast distances of an unexploited nation, and as a potential threat to the government. . . . Natives, in other words, were removed as a vindication of the environment.

---

54. Jay Fliegelman, *Declaring Independence* (Stanford: Stanford University Press, 1993), 25–6.
55. Ibid., 191.
56. Ibid., 192.

The *absence* of the *indian* in the histories of this nation is an aesthetic victimry" (*FP*, 12). The face of the African, as Jefferson's *Notes* makes clear, also becomes its own argument for an "aesthetic victimry" and hence an epistemological inferiority. As Fliegelman suggests in the closing pages of his provocative study, the "oratorical revolution," given its nonnegotiable link between public performance and public virtue, had "no meaning" for the disenfranchised and unrepresented Other. "Full membership in the republic of letters," the "republic of taste, or the republic of virtue—either as producer or consumer—required prior political enfranchisement."[57] If authentic membership in the republic is predicated upon utterance and/or signature, then it is the privilege of freedom that signifies both authenticity and inclusion. In other words, freedom comes only for those who sign and perform the Declaration and not for those who are declared as Other, whose very alterity renders them unfit or ineligible to sign.

One can argue that the revolutionary content of the Declaration resides in its historical precedent. As text and event, the Declaration initiates a new era in the political experience of a historically repressed people, and its declarations of independence render possible the founding of a republic crafted through the promise of mutuality and freedom. Insofar as Jefferson lays some claim upon its authorship, we must read his role as representative rather than originary. As author, Jefferson "is representative of the signers, who are representative of the people, who are being created by the document they have not technically authored, but which, in public forums, will re-authorize it with every performance."[58] But despite this revolutionary achievement, a rupture reverberates at the heart of this declaratory promise.

The schism that resounds in the Declaration lies in what it fails to account for: the relationship between the "right to be" of a free subject and his inalienable responsibility "for the death of the other." From the stand of Levinasian ethics, this responsibility distinguishes and signifies the identity of the I, in its uniqueness and humanity. It is not a question of whether the I chooses to be responsible; one is already, through the experiential reality of proximity, situated in an event of facing the Other. This reality of proximity does not permit one's indifference to the Other's suffering. The question of one's "right to be and the legitimacy of this right," Levinas contends, is

---

57. Ibid., 195.
58. Sarah Pelmas, "Freedom's Performative Legacy," *Qui Parle* 7.1 (1993): 33.

"inseparable from the for-the-other in me," and "it is as old as this for-the-other." Given that the Other already exists as a being in the world, then "whether he looks at me or not, he 'concerns me.'" While Levinas concedes that this question of one's "right to be" is a "question against-nature, against the naturality of nature," it is nevertheless a "question of meaning *par excellence,* prior to or beyond all the meaning games that we happen upon in the reference of words, the ones to the others, in our writing pastimes. It is a question of the meaning of being: not the ontological meaning of the comprehension of this extraordinary verb, but the ethical meaning of the justice of being" (*OG*, 171).

To the extent that the Declaration finds its authority in the public performance and utterance of its words, those words establish an existential context in which the "right to be" of free subjects is separated from the individual's prior responsibility of a nonindifference towards the Other's presence and persecution. Given that the Declaration prioritizes freedom for the "good people" of America, it also performatively confers that freedom "in the reference of words," where the "ontological meaning" of being has been permitted to displace the "ethical meaning of the justice of being." Ultimately, even the language of freedom—notwithstanding its resonance, power, or urgency—does not "exonerate" the individual from a responsibility that precedes his arrival in the cherished "field of freedom." Nor can it. For the face of the Other remains in the world—if only as an absence—and in the reality of being that transcends language, it is her presence to whom and before whom the free subject is already answerable.

If we return to Derrida's claim that the name of God is the "ultimate signature" through which the Declaration's "meaning *and* effect" are secured, we must inquire how that signature—and therefore the "word of God"—enters the realm of human activity and meaning. In the context of the ethical meaning of being, Levinas argues that God "comes to mind" through the face of the Other. It is solely the face of the Other that is "exposed to my gaze in its weakness and its mortality" and is simultaneously "also the one that orders, 'Thou shalt not kill.'" This is the command in the face of the Other that must, in the "justice of being," interrupt the "spontaneity, without circumspection, of my naïve perseverance," to supersede the linguistic legitimacy and conference of my "right to be." In Levinasian ethics, "There is, in the face, the supreme authority that commands," and "this is the word of God. The face is the site of the word of God"; importantly, it is a "word not thematized." If the word of God comes to presence, or "comes to mind" in the experience of human beings, it must be signified through the face of the Other. The Other is the only entity both "wholly weakness and wholly authority. This order which it exposes to the other also concerns the demand for responsibility on my part." For in the final analysis—even in the presence of language—Levinas answers, "I am never exonerated before the other."[59]

If the covenant of the republic is sealed in the name of freedom and not in the prior responsibility and obligation that the possibility of justice entails, it runs the risk of becoming a linguistic promise that permits and, at its worst, sanctions the persecution and death of the Other. It matters not whether the Other—as tragic Indian or enslaved African—is permitted to "look back": she is already there, living in the hidden recesses of the republic, and it is her presence and her death that disrupt the discourse on freedom to sound the call for justice. As long as the I is the subject standing in the "field of my freedom, my power, my property," a new situation is required to raise the possibility of justice: "Someone must ask me for an accounting." That "someone" is the face of the Other whose death cannot be purchased through my right to freedom, my right to be. For "justice does not result from the normal play of injustice. It comes from outside, 'through the door,' above the fray; it appears as a principle exterior to history" (*EN*, 30).

Here is the real challenge of the ethical perspective in the American discourse on freedom: it is the disruptive call for the articulation and institution of a binding, national law that privileges justice before freedom. It is the insistence upon the irreducible inviolability of the face of the Other, which always and absolutely reveals itself as that essential freedom before whom one is not free to commit murder. As we will discover in the performative legacies of Frederick Douglass, Sarah Winnemucca, and John Brown, law and justice—at least in a specifically American context—have not necessarily shared the same points of origin. But each of these particular human beings will ask for an "accounting," and their entry upon the American scene will appear as the disruptive manifestation of a "principle exterior to history."

59. Emmanuel Levinas, "The Proximity of the Other," in *Is It Righteous to Be? Interviews with Emmanuel Levinas*, ed. Jill Robbins (Stanford: Stanford University Press, 2001), 215.

4   Fugitive Poseurs
The Native Eloquence of Frederick Douglass and Sarah Winnemucca

In the opening paragraphs of Frederick Douglass's sole novella, "The Heroic Slave," Douglass focuses our gaze upon the impressive figure of Madison Washington, standing concealed in the midst of a "dark pine forest." In the presence of God and under the protective grace of Nature, Washington utters a series of "scathing denunciations of the cruelty and injustice of slavery," which is soon followed by painful testimony, first of his own suffering and then that of his people—each story culminating in an impassioned and "emphatic declaration of his purpose to be free." Not far away, but sequestered from Washington's view, Mr. Listwell, the northern traveler, is the reluctant and cautious witness to Washington's moving soliloquy. In the presence of Washington's voice, riveted by the emotional intensity of his words of despair and declaration, Listwell is called towards an experience of recognition in which Washington's true humanity is revealed to him: "'Here indeed is a man,' thought he, 'of rare endowments,—a child of God,—guilty of no crime but the color of his skin.'"[1]

In that scene in the forest, Washington's speaking, his vocal and dramatic presence, is not merely rhetorical. Even as the words of the fictionalized fugitive slave fulfill the sentimental expectations of Douglass's abolitionist audience, through the dramatic activity of speech he becomes more than mere "slave." Indeed, Washington's speaking disrupts the categories of his nonpersonhood to become both transformative and inherently performative. When one reads this artistic moment as a self-reflexive gesture in Douglass's literary oeuvre, "The Heroic Slave" begins to suggest something

---

1. Frederick Douglass, "The Heroic Slave," in *Violence in the Black Imagination*, ed. Ronald Takaki (New York: Putnam, 1972), 40–1.

important about Douglass's faith in the poetics of the performative to alter the political relations between human beings and, more specifically, in the power of language to change the world.

In the context of Douglass's fictional world, the presence of the voice and the performativity of language distinguish themselves in a profound manner. In "The Heroic Slave," Washington's speech overwhelms the spheres of rhetoric and mere confession to create a performative context through which transformation ensues. Listwell eventually emerges to acknowledge Washington's authentic humanity—for Washington's speaking lifts him beyond the racial and categorical designation as slave. Listwell sees him as a man and, more importantly, as a "child of God." Washington's speech thus initiates a conversion, both existentially and dramatically radical. In the performative presence of this African stranger, Listwell is propelled towards the realm of action and its possibility for the crafting of justice. In the aftermath of Washington's departure, the previously indifferent Listwell offers his own version of a liberatory declaration: "'From this hour I am an abolitionist. I have seen enough and heard enough, and I shall go to my home in Ohio resolved to atone for my past indifference to this ill-starred race, by making such exertions as I shall be able to do, for the speedy emancipation of every slave in the land.'"[2]

By investing Washington's words with this power of transformation, Douglass suggests the profound respect that he accords the human voice, particularly in its service to the call of justice. In that moment in the woods, Washington "exists in and achieves essential being" in language.[3] His speaking is the performance of a freedom wholly prior to and perfectly independent of Listwell's knowledge or experience. Washington's words possess the power to affirm the reality and authenticity of his own existence, as well as to call into being a catalytic change in the legitimate American observer, who suddenly becomes a participant in Washington's mission of freedom. From the moment Washington is heard and his face is seen, he is revealed as the Other whose alterity is absolute, whose authenticity of being both defies and exceeds whatever ideas the northerner Listwell may have harbored regarding

---

2. Ibid., 41–2.

3. This is an idea that characterizes the relationship between language and being in the work of N. Scott Momaday. See, for example, *The Man Made of Words* (New York: St. Martin's Press, 1997).

the identity of the slave. The fact that Washington's speech disrupts Listwell's sojourn in the world to convert him to the cause of emancipation—and therefore to the command of justice—reveals Douglass's faith in the efficacy of language and the power of the performative dimension in which ethical transformation may occur.

Five years after that pivotal encounter in the woods, in the dark of a winter's night, Listwell and Washington actually meet face to face. There, Listwell admits, "'Oh sir, I know not your name, but I have seen your face, and heard your voice before. I am glad to see you. *I know all.*'" If we doubted the impact of Washington's earlier words, Listwell's hospitality in the presence of this African stranger stands as testimony to the authenticity of his conversion. Even before he recognizes Washington per se, he extends the graciousness of welcome: he opens his home and offers it as a gift of refuge to the fugitive slave, whose homelessness and hunger command his response. Only later, in response to Washington's inquiry, does Listwell reveal the reasons for his generosity of welcome. "Describing the place where he first saw him; rehearsing the language which [Washington] had used; referring to the effect which his manner and speech had made upon him," Listwell confesses the "secret" of their earlier encounter and his subsequent conversion to an abolitionist stance. Listwell's conversion, initiated by the transformative power of language, is simultaneously predicated upon the priority of the face and the ethical efficacy of the face-to-face meeting. As he subsequently testifies to the fugitive slave, "'From that hour, your face seemed to be daguerreotyped on my memory.'"[4]

I start with this moment in "The Heroic Slave" because it suggests the extent to which Douglass prioritizes the human voice and thus privileges the orator as a critical agent in the cause of social and political change. But it is also possible to regard the fictionalized figure of Madison Washington as a model for Douglass's notion of his own potential efficacy as an orator. If so, then "The Heroic Slave" can be read as a significant mise-en-scène, indicative of why Douglass chooses the stage as such a pivotal arena for his crusade against the brutal injustices of slavery.

Admittedly, Washington's power of transformative speech occurs within the dimension of fiction and not in the sphere of everyday life. In that sense, "The Heroic Slave" is primarily an "aesthetic drama," one in which the audi-

---

4. Douglass, "Heroic Slave," 45.

ence, as reader, is "separated both actually and conceptually from the performer," which in this case is Douglass as writer. But "The Heroic Slave" is an antislavery novella, one whose fictive reality is intrinsically grounded in the overriding politics of everyday life, and Douglass clearly intends that his novella will precipitate a transformation (both individually and collectively) in his audience of readers. As Richard Schechner points out, aesthetic drama does not necessarily take place in a realm independent of sociality, politics, or even ethics. Rather, the "function of aesthetic drama is to do for the consciousness of the audience what social drama does for its participants: providing a place for, and means of, transformation."[5]

Douglass writes "The Heroic Slave" in order to effect a change in the consciousness of his readers—so that they, like Listwell, are moved towards the possibility of awareness and action. His goals in the creation of that fictional drama can thus be read to overwhelm literary aesthetics in order to engage the domain of everyday life and existence. His expectation is that fiction and the realm of the theatrical imagination are actually and conceptually transformative acts that refigure the relationships between aesthetics, social existence, and the performative dimension in which ethics is enacted.

I am thus interested in revisiting Douglass's performative legacy: not simply the content of the many distinguished speeches he authored, but the theatrical and performative dimension in which those words achieved sound and shape. Above all, I am interested in conceptualizing performativity in terms of its disruptive impetus and potential. I want to rethink performativity in the larger dimensions of a theatrical space: the stage at Corinthian Hall, where Douglass steps forward as a teacher in the ethics of democracy and difference, and the stage at San Francisco's Platte Hall, where Sarah Winnemucca first captures a western American imagination. In reassessing the performative legacies of Douglass and Winnemucca, this chapter explores the potentially fertile connections between art and artifice, the theatrical and the performative, and the possibility of the theatrical domain as an ethically disruptive site: one where the space of an individual and communal transformation—and with it, the invitation to justice—opens forth.[6]

Numerous literary critics have richly mined Douglass's literary and auto-

---

5. Richard Schechner, *Performance Theory* (New York: Routledge, 1988), 171.

6. In the following discussion I am indebted to Gerald Vizenor's seminal work *Fugitive Poses*, whose influence on my thinking in this chapter is acknowledged in the chapter's title.

biographical texts, but few scholars have ventured truly to explore his performative legacy. Yet Douglass's speeches and their performative context comprise a significant aspect of his final legacy. One of the difficulties, however, in revisiting Douglass's oratorical achievements is that we cannot fully recover the material context of his performances—the specificity of place and audience or the temporality of a given historical moment—either in his private or the nation's public life. In the very nature of performance, there is an element of the ephemeral and the evanescent. What is more accessible to us are the texts themselves, the small, anecdotal histories of their occurrence, and the critical temptation to read them as "texts," as though their textual existence is fully separate from the theatrical context of their performative utterance.

This theatrical dimension may have made Douglass's performative legacy less critically compelling than his literary oeuvre. A peculiar suspicion surrounds the idea of the theater, perhaps founded in its evocation of "make-believe," the unreal, and the substitution of a virtual reality for the more realistic business of material, everyday life. Yet Douglass's theatricality can be approached as evidence of those moments of rupture when he finally does break through the expectations imposed upon him by the competing interpretive narratives of abolitionism and "representative blackness."[7] If so, Douglass's employment of the theatrical is worthy of investigation.

On the other side of the continent, Paiute activist Sarah Winnemucca also took to the stage as a contestatory platform from which to mount her own version of a political critique. But then and now, the theatricality of Winnemucca's performative poses cost her greatly, particularly in the eyes of her critics, who have condemned her as being either fraudulently Indian or conciliatorily guilty in reproducing negative representations of Native people's dispossession. Such readings of performativity, however, overlook its ability to disrupt the logics of identity that return the Other to the province of the Same. Through reconsidering the performative and theatrical legacies of Frederick Douglass and Sarah Winnemucca, I hope to demonstrate that there is a poetics of theater specifically linked to ethical activism. I also hope to show that it is possible to regard Douglass and Winnemucca as collaborators and comrades whose command of the nineteenth-century stage made the theater a space of confrontation and identity disruption.

7. I am borrowing here the language of Henry Louis Gates Jr., *Figures in Black: Words, Signs, and the Racial Self* (New York: Oxford University Press, 1987), 103.

Indeed, Douglass and Winnemucca were disruptive presences even before the onset of their performative careers. Simply by virtue of being African and Indian, Priscilla Wald argues, neither Douglass nor Winnemucca was an authentic "citizen nor [a real] alien," but a representative emissary from the ranks of those "who had not consented to the laws by which they were bound."[8] Because Douglass was the more accomplished agent in the narrative of nineteenth-century cultural activism, his choice of the stage as a primary vehicle for insurgent action is important for our historical reflection. Like Winnemucca, Douglass opted to engage the potential of theater to disrupt the narratives of identity through which the alterity of the Other had been figured. The fact that Douglass and Winnemucca, both fugitives, utilized the stage as an arena for contestatory politics serves to call into question the political and cultural assumptions of the nonpersonhood of the racialized American Other.

Perhaps Douglass and Winnemucca each embraced the power of the theatrical arena in its ethical force—in its specific ability to transport its audience and actors beyond the prescribed frames of everyday life, where one was either master or slave, legitimately American or mysterious Indian and African Other. This is the space of theater that critic Alan Read proposes. Drawing on de Certeau's notion that ethics "defines a distance between what is and what ought to be," and that "this distance designates a space where we have something to do," Read asserts that the space "where we have something to do" is the "space where theatre occurs." Read argues that "both ethics and theatre are concerned with possibility," noting a critical distinction between theater and representation: "Representation is the reflection of an 'existing' proposition as though it were fact, and this is never what the theatre achieves. The theatre image unlike any other is always a possibility without closure, like the ethical relation that awaits creation."[9]

What distinguishes the theater in its connection to ethics is the face-to-face encounter that it imposes. If theater engages representation and the realm of play, it also insists upon that leap of the imagination in which one becomes willing to put oneself in the other's skin, to momentarily inhabit the Other's place. As Read suggests, this is the "classic 'as if' of theatre," and it opens the space of possibility for the theater to become one of the pivotal

---

8. Priscilla Wald, *Constituting Americans* (Durham, N.C.: Duke University Press, 1995), 17.

9. Alan Read, *Theatre and Everyday Life* (London: Routledge, 1993), 90.

sites of engagement in the interrogation of cultural theory and practice. When we take seriously Read's argument for an ethics of theatrical performance, the poetics and politics of Douglass's and Winnemucca's performativity are rich indeed. In that regard, they invite us to reconsider the disruptive and ethical power of the American fugitive's performative pose. Let us return, then, to "The Heroic Slave," where Douglass envisions a powerful connection between language, performance, and their transformative possibility.

In a literary context, the initial scene between Washington and Listwell recalls Douglass's experience with the text of the *Columbian Orator*. As he recounts in his 1845 autobiography, it was there that Douglass first discovered the power of oration to provoke change. In that text, the effect of the slave's words "resulted in the voluntary emancipation of the slave on the part of the master."[10] And while Listwell is not a slaveowner, he is nevertheless implicated in the politics of slavery by virtue of the privilege that his whiteness accords. Like his literary predecessor, Washington's words achieve a similarly emancipatory effect. Listwell goes forth from the forest to "be" an abolitionist: that is, to act in the pursuit of freedom for the African, whose native freedom he now recognizes to be unjustly enslaved.

Later in the novella, as Washington is being taken aboard ship, Listwell passes him the "three strong files" that become the tools by which he will break the shackles from himself and eighteen enslaved Africans. Even if the sympathetic reader concludes that Listwell's actions enable the success of Washington's liberatory revolt, it is nonetheless Washington's performativity in speech that is the first event that makes his revolt viable. The fact that Douglass makes Listwell an indispensable character in the crafting of the mutiny aboard ship seems to support Richard Yarborough's reading. Yarborough contends that not only does "Listwell give . . . the white audience a figure with whom to identify," but that "Douglass doubtless intends the white audience to see that they should not only sympathize with the slaves' plight but work actively to help them gain their freedom." For Yarborough, however, Douglass's investment in Listwell's actions signals a certain failure of imagination. His choice of Listwell as the one who supplies Washington with the

---

10. Frederick Douglass, *The Narrative of the Life of Frederick Douglass, an American Slave* (New York: Anchor, 1989), 42.

tools of his eventual freedom "implies that even the most self-reliant and gifted black male slave needs white assistance."[11]

It is also possible to read this scene as an indication of Douglass's faith in the performative tradition and the power of the spoken word to alter the external realm of human reality. If Douglass's portrayal of Washington bears the echo of the imaginatively heroic slave he encountered in the *Columbian Orator,* then Washington's speaking exceeds the eloquence of oratory, for here Douglass represents speech as a living presence, as a force exerted upon the world through which the transformation is initiated. Listwell is not merely a witness to Washington's words; he is psychologically and physically changed by them. As Douglass writes, "The speech of Madison rung through the chambers of his soul, and vibrated through his entire frame."[12] Within the frame of Douglass's fictional theater, Washington's speech lingers and reverberates in the secretly shared neutrality of the forest, not simply overcoming the boundaries of difference, but creating an acoustic space where sound and the performative elements of word and presence signify an essential dimension of human "being."

Washington's words immediately reveal the authenticity of his presence as a human being who has been wrongfully condemned—and one who "has not consented" to the authority of law that would make him either slave or fugitive. In that sense, his oratory constitutes the performative evidence through which his uniqueness of person is rendered visible. In the activity of speech, Washington transcends the imposed boundaries of his racial categorization. In the performative dimensions of language, he exists in his own right: of African blood, distinctly American by virtue of his enslavement, and wholly critical of a deeply flawed human reality that legally sanctions the blatant injustice of slavery.

But Washington's speaking does more than satisfy the literary expectations of a sympathetic abolitionist readership. His words act upon Listwell and effect change in the interiority of Listwell's being: they exert the force of transformation. In this sense, Douglass situates Washington's speaking

---

11. Richard Yarborough, "Race, Violence, and Manhood: The Masculine Ideal in Frederick Douglass's 'The Heroic Slave,'" in *Frederick Douglass: New Literary and Historical Essays,* ed. Eric J. Sundquist (New York: Cambridge University Press, 1990), 179.

12. Douglass, "Heroic Slave," 41.

within the performative dimensions of an oral tradition in which "words are intrinsically powerful. They are magical. By means of words can one bring about physical change in the universe."[13] And Washington's words bring about a powerful change, for his speech calls Listwell to responsibility. Washington's words are the catalyst for Listwell's conversion from an outside observer to an engaged ethical activist. Indeed, the performative force of Washington's speaking becomes the originary event that leads to Listwell's participation as a collaborative agent in the Creole revolt against the tyranny of a republic steeped in the wars of injustice and genocide.

Henry Louis Gates Jr. suggests that the initial encounter between Washington and Listwell can be read as a "model of the function that all of the slave narratives were to have upon their American and European audiences." Implicit in the literary desire of the slave narrator, Gates argues, is the "creation of a face, 'daguerreotyped on memory,' that the strong black speaking voice was intended to create."[14] Given the ideological intentions of the novella, Douglass succeeds in creating, through Washington, a literary character "of face"—both in Gates's and Levinas's sense of that term. Extending this argument, I believe that Douglass's "The Heroic Slave" can provide a model for reading Douglass's own performance as an orator. As the exemplary black orator, Douglass becomes the face of African Otherness. His privileging of the spoken word places him within an oral tradition in which language performs a specifically ethical function. In speech, Douglass becomes the contestatory face before whom an American republic is called to consciousness.

In his preface to the *Narrative of the Life of Frederick Douglass,* William Lloyd Garrison writes of his first encounter with Douglass at the Nantucket antislavery convention in August 1841. It is Douglass's first appearance as a speaker. While he will later confess, "My speech on this occasion is about the only one I ever made, of which I do not remember a single connected sentence," the magnitude of his performance is documented through Garrison's written testimony.[15] It is significant that Garrison first identifies Douglass as a "stranger to nearly every member of that body," representing Douglass as a foreigner whose specific identity in person is unknown.[16] But

---

13. Momaday, *Man Made of Words,* 16.
14. Gates, *Figures in Black,* 108.
15. Frederick Douglass, *My Bondage and My Freedom* (New York: Dover, 1969), 358.
16. Douglass, *Narrative,* ix.

Douglass steps forward under the veil of another condition as "stranger": he is an escaped slave, whose status renders him one of the "excluded subjects" dwelling in the hidden recesses of the republic. Priscilla Wald makes this point in noting the contradictions that permeate the constitution of personhood in nineteenth-century law. As a fugitive, Douglass exists outside the law: he is both nonperson and subject simultaneously. As Wald argues, to inhabit the body of the Other, whether of Native or African blood, is to exist in that "metaphysical void wherein excluded subjects dwelled: persons *de jure* and *de facto* without natural rights, human beings whom the law would not fully and equally represent."[17]

In fact, had the law intervened upon that closed meeting room in Nantucket, Douglass would have been captured and returned to the irons of enslavement. His foreignness is reinforced through his status as this excluded subject; as a fugitive under the law, his humanity in being is de facto and legally denied. In this sense, Douglass begins to embody the Levinasian Stranger: from the moment in which he speaks, he can be seen as the "Stranger who disturbs the being at home with oneself [*le chez soi*]. But Stranger also means the free one. Over him I have no *power*" (*TI*, 39). Douglass's words are inherently disturbing. Despite his position as a fugitive, Douglass is nevertheless that presence who escapes full thematization under the laws that seek his possession.

It is therefore not surprising that the disruptive moment initiated by Douglass's speaking must be categorized and interpreted through Garrison. Garrison's mediation is ultimately dualistic. In print, he intervenes upon the literary text of the *Narrative* to grant its legitimacy of authorship; in person, Garrison converts Douglass into his "text," an act of appropriation that not only consigns Douglass's actual speaking to the sphere of pure rhetoric but tries to render his alterity translatable. As Eric Cheyfitz has pointed out, Garrison's interpretive description of Douglass in the activity of speech attempts to cast Douglass in the "figure of the eloquent orator," while "Garrison's use of the classical opposition between a natural and a cultivated, or ornamental, eloquence implicitly places Douglass in the position of the savage, no matter what Garrison intends."[18]

But despite Garrison's intentions or the rhetoric of his paternalistic in-

---

17. Wald, *Constituting Americans*, 23.
18. Cheyfitz, *Poetics of Imperialism*, 128.

tervention, the performative efficacy of Douglass's appearance defies reduction in simplistic terms. Even Garrison is moved to remark upon the extraordinary phenomenon of Douglass in speech: "There stood one, in physical proportion and stature commanding and exact—in intellect richly endowed—in natural eloquence a prodigy—in soul manifestly 'created but a little lower than the angels'—yet a slave, ay, a fugitive slave."[19] Garrison objectifies Douglass through the discourse of sameness; he is determined, as Sidonie Smith suggests, to reassert the values of a liberal humanism so that the "exceptional can be incorporated and neutralized."[20] But in assuming the stance of the fugitive slave who speaks, Douglass remains performatively transcendent. This is what Levinas suggests when he asserts that to be the "Stranger also means the free one. Over him I have no power." Douglass cannot be both slave and the Other who speaks, and it is this disparity that ruptures the correspondence between idea and existent, the rhetorical and the ethical, and which works to reinforce the ethical contention that "to show the *relation* between the same and the other—upon which we seem to impose such extraordinary conditions—is language" (*TI*, 39).

From the moment that Douglass mounts the stage in Nantucket, he initiates a performative legacy through which his freedom, even as it is denied by law, is shown through language and face. In the midst of the violence implicit in Garrison's assertion that "by the law of the land . . . by the terms of the slave code, he was only a piece of property, a beast of burden, a chattel personal," and dramatically refuting all logic and law through which property can be constituted, Douglass *speaks*. It is without question a moment of inception, one that reverberates with the symbolic significance of what Gates terms a "metaphorical birth."[21] In this respect, Douglass's subsequent amnesia regarding his first speech makes sense. What is at stake here is not so much what Douglass might have said, but the fact that he *says*. In his act of saying, in the revelation that speech makes possible, Douglass presents himself as an interiority that is absolute. As an alterity that signifies its own meaning, he fulfills the Levinasian edict that "the absolutely other is the Other. He and I do not form a number." The "collectivity" in which Douglass

---

19. Douglass, *Narrative*, x.

20. Sidonie Smith, "Performativity, Autobiographical Practice, Resistance," *a/b: Auto/Biography Studies* 10.1 (1995): 27.

21. Gates, *Figures in Black*, 102.

and his audience exist "is not a plural of the 'I,'" because "these are not individuals of a common concept" (*TI*, 39). Douglass's speaking arrestingly disrupts his false designation under the nomenclature of "slave"—for in the riveting theatrical dimension that surrounds his first appearance, new possibilities, "whole worlds otherwise not lived," are created.[22]

Alan Read makes the argument that theater occurs when there are more than two: when the expectations of an audience necessarily and in the "simultaneity of equality" alter the one who speaks and the one who witnesses. Specifically, Read conceives of theater in terms of three. As long as there are three, he argues, the "ethical relationship with the other becomes political." This entry into the domain where politics, ethics, and orality unite is the "privilege of theatre." In true Levinasian spirit, Read conceives of theater as the "shadow and the echo of the everyday," turning it into a site where "the saying" prevails over "the said," and where the relational structures of cultural and social practice are unmasked and challenged. Theater, Read contends, "inaugurates" an ethical situation precisely because it is so fully invested in "the saying" and thus "replaces the inert object of literature and language with the process of enunciation."[23] This "process of enunciation" is fully engaged in the dialectic of audience, place, time, and performer.

This argument for the ethical urgency of "saying" in opposition to the rule of "the said" is a distinctly Levinasian concept. Even though Douglass appears onstage as a fugitive slave, once he begins speaking, he challenges his audience to see him differently. "Speech," Levinas explains, "refuses vision, because the speaker does not deliver images of himself only, but is personally present in his speech, absolutely exterior to every image he would leave" (*TI*, 296). When Read juxtaposes the activity of theater as a "process of enunciation" that "replaces the inert object of literature and language," he thus marks the distinction between the realm of "the said" and "the saying." As Adriaan Peperzak clarifies, "the Said encompasses all discourses or narratives in which beings are identified and essence verbalized," so that "written texts are the clearest examples of the Said." Douglass's identification as fugitive slave places him within the context of "the said," since the "very structure of thematization makes every being into a said, i.e., into a being that is identified as a phenomenon within the context of a story or discourse." As Peper-

22. Schechner, *Performance Theory*, 184.
23. Read, *Theatre and Everyday Life*, 94, 95.

zak suggests, however, the act of "saying resists becoming a theme"; speaking, as saying, "can never become a theme or noema because its structure is radically different: it establishes a *contact* and *proximity* which are neither forms of knowledge nor possible themes of a theory."[24]

When Douglass speaks, his language creates a relationship between him and his audience that, as Levinas writes, "breaks up the unity of a genus." In speech, Douglass overwhelms his thematization as slave. It is here that language can disrupt the narrative of history—the province of "the said"—to emerge as the "very power to break the continuity of being or of history." As speech addressed to another being, language establishes "contact and proximity" and thus "cuts across vision." As Levinas argues, "The formal structure of language thereby announces the ethical inviolability of the Other" (*TI*, 195). As "slave," Douglass is not a presence but an idea, an object. As speaker, he becomes a face whose reality cannot be comprehended. Levinas contends that only in speech does the "Other remain infinitely transcendent, infinitely foreign; his face in which his epiphany is produced and which appeals to me breaks with the world that can be common to us" (*TI*, 194). This is the activity of saying that, for Read, makes the theater one of few cultural sites that "relates ethics back to a poetics and out to a politics of performance."[25] In his performances, Frederick Douglass demonstrably achieves full presence: he is writer, actor, witness, instigator, and the representative presence of the contestatory African face, come forth to demand not only accountability but justice from a promisingly young republic.

Yet to name Douglass as the "representative presence of the contestatory African face" is problematic. In such a naming, I become guilty of subjecting the very essence of the face, its very authority beyond the terms of representation, to a language that already betrays the significance of Douglass's face. Such language reconsigns the ethical significance of Douglass in speech into a logic where even the "otherness of the Other" enters the spheres of intelligibility and intellectual access, which Levinas has identified as "the said." What I want to highlight here is that to speak of Douglass's performativity is to think and imagine beyond what is "thinkable." It is to attempt to raise the issue of the "surplus"—"that does not represent itself . . . but signifies in the imperative with authority" (*EN*, 151)—that simultaneously inheres in and exceeds the face of Frederick Douglass that his audience first sees.

24. Peperzak, *Beyond*, 60, 61, 67.
25. Read, *Theatre and Everyday Life*, 96.

Douglass was not the first African Other whose face appeared on the stage of white American spectatorship. The African face had been contemplated in the European and American gaze since the inception of the auction block, and so it is not simply the particular presence of the African face that bears the potential for ethical disruption. Rather, it is Douglass's performativity as the Other in speech that signifies the fissure between object and alterity. Douglass's performative presence, which exceeds the expectations of his witnesses, can transport him and them beyond not only their respective social roles, but beyond the clear dimensions of time in which those roles are lived. This conception of performativity implicates the ways that the face, speech, presence, and performance, considered holistically, challenge the existent logics of representation and the modes of perception that impose the illusion of intelligibility.

The "process of enunciation" that Read designates as vital to the theatrical context reaffirms the primacy of orality in the ethical equation. Douglass's emergence as the Other who speaks is implicitly defiant. Not only does he—much like Madison Washington in the forest scene—disrupt the possibility of his containment and thematization as slave, but his whole being exerts the command for response and responsibility. As Walter Ong has demonstrated, the voice, by asserting the primacy of sound before surface, signifies the presence of a "beyond" before which phenomenology falters: "Sound is more real or existential than other sense objects, despite the fact that it is also more evanescent."[26] Ong's insight suggests the extent to which sound and (more specifically) the human voice exceed their apparent genesis through a visually perceptible form.

The "beyond" to which Ong refers implicates both the sphere of vision and the sphere of intelligibility that "seeing" founds. As Levinas asserts, there is an intricate web of connection between the modalities of vision and the priorities of "intellectual accession" and knowledge through which "everyday life as well as the tradition of our philosophic and scientific thought maintains itself." Levinas further points out that modes of vision rely upon the "structure of a *seeing* having the *seen* for its object or theme" (*EN*, 159). In other words, vision easily facilitates the conversion of "the seen"—in this case, Douglass as the presence of the face of the slave—into the structures of knowledge and experience that inform the gaze of a subject, indifferent to

---

26. Walter Ong, *The Presence of the Word* (New Haven: Yale University Press, 1967), 111.

the experience of the Other whose face he sees. This is also Ong's point: voice disrupts the surfaces of phenomenology and the categorical certainties of ontology. Sound, voice, and the performative pose open into an interhuman dimension where the living presence of the Other commands the nonindifference of her observing witness. And in Read's concept of theater, Douglass's performativity, which is first manifest in the activity of enunciation, invites an opening into that interhuman dimension in which the primacy of sight is displaced by the efficacy of performance. It becomes the site where the individual subject as spectator-witness becomes a participant, a self or an I distinct from the citizen of the republic, an awakened respondent to the authority of the Other's face and its insistent plea for justice.

Let us consider Douglass's words of self-introduction before the expectant audience gathered at Faneuil Hall in January 1842: "I rejoice to be permitted, as well as to be able to speak upon this subject in Faneuil Hall. I will not detain you long, for I stand here a slave. (No! no! from the meeting). A slave at least in the eye of the Constitution. (No! no! *with emphasis from the meeting*). It is a slave by the laws of the South, who now addresses you."[27] Douglass's repeated insistence that "it is a slave . . . who now addresses you" unmasks the blatant fallacy in logic that constitutes the law of the republic. In the terms of the republic's legal distinctions, a slave is chattel, not a being, and thus even the possibility of an address from a slave to a master—used here to signify the ultimate privilege that whiteness bestows, whether actualized or not—is foreclosed.

Yet as Douglass speaks, the performative effect also initiates a dimension of human relation otherwise than that which the republic's ideology of representation deems possible. The adamant and repeated "No!" that his audience speaks back to him suggests their transition from disinterested spectators to awakened participants, now capable of responding beyond the limited phenomenology of sight. This is that "theatrical space" Read envisions, where aesthetics instigates an interhuman community, receptive to the performative dynamic that invites personal and social transformation.

Three years later, although now legally free, Douglass again chooses to inhabit the fugitive pose of the Other. Before a "densely crowded" assemblage at the Cork courthouse in Ireland, he says: "I stand before you in the

---

27. Frederick Douglass, *The Frederick Douglass Papers*, ed. John W. Blassingame (New Haven: Yale University Press, 1979), 1:16.

most extraordinary position that one human being ever stood before his race—a slave. A slave not in the ordinary sense of the term, not in the political sense, but in its real and intrinsic meaning."[28] Like his speech in Faneuil Hall, and despite differences in place and legal politics, Douglass speaks to incite change; his words are clearly intended to be disruptive. "I stand before you . . . a slave," he says, knowing full well that slaves are not legitimate persons, recognized speakers, or reputable cultural commentators. In those few words, he disturbs the sanctity of personhood grafted upon whiteness, so as to contest its logic of equivalence and perception. And this is Ong's point: "Sight reveals only surfaces. It can never get to an interior as an interior, but must always treat it as somehow an exterior."[29] To be in the presence of the voice is to be in the presence of the Other whose difference exceeds thematization; it is to experience the beyond of appearance, and it is also to be summoned by the immediacy and urgency of an address that demands an answering.

Thus we can begin to understand Douglass's point when he argues, "Humanity, justice and liberty demand the service of the living human voice."[30] Just as voice makes visible the presence of alterity, Douglass's insistence and faith in the potency of oral language signifies its potential as an explicitly ethical discourse. Language reveals interiority because it presupposes plurality: in speech, the performative effect of Douglass's voice creates a relationship that defies reduction between himself, as the African who speaks, and his audience of European and American listeners.

This is the experience of revelation that Douglass himself notes in the closing moments of the *Narrative*. Reflecting upon his first oratorical performance in Nantucket, Douglass perceives the invitation to speak as being charged with contradiction. Even as he feels "strongly moved to speak" and is actively urged to do so by his white supporters, the performative responsibility of speaking confronts him as a "severe cross" that he bears "reluctantly." The reason for his reluctance is critically important: "The truth was, I felt myself a slave, and the idea of speaking to white people weighed me down."[31]

28. Ibid., 1:39.
29. Ong, *Presence of the Word*, 74.
30. Quoted in Gates, *Figures in Black*, 106.
31. Douglass, *Narrative*, 114.

That Douglass first thinks of himself as a slave is itself an extraordinary testament to the relationship between language, voice, and personhood. Only through speaking can Douglass discover and enact a claim to freedom that is essential, primordial, and inviolable. Thus he can say, in spite of the burden his performance imposes upon him, that in speech he comes to know and experience a "degree of freedom" sufficiently compelling to elicit the declaratory promise that will call him towards the particular "cause of his brethren" and the larger pursuit of American justice. His experience recalls Levinas's contention that language is "perhaps to be defined as the very power to break the continuity of being or history," since its efficacy is reciprocally transformative. This kind of transformative possibility leads Levinas to cite language as the opening through which the transcendent presence of the Other emerges: "In discourse the divergence that inevitably opens between the Other as my theme and the Other as my interlocutor, emancipated from the theme that seemed a moment to hold him, forthwith contests the meaning I ascribe to my interlocutor" (*TI*, 195). Indeed, as Douglass himself confesses, it is solely through speech that he makes the move from the "Other as theme" to become the "Other as interlocutor" who calls the world of shared experience into question.

As many scholars have noted, Douglass's appearance in Nantucket constitutes an originary moment. Peter Walker has remarked that it serves as the "great reference point in Douglass's post-Baltimore life, not only because it was at Nantucket that he first entered the public life, but because it was there that he was first able to become the person he believed himself to be." In that initial appearance, Walker argues, Douglass recognizes that his real identity and freedom are no longer "defined by the others' whiteness." The call to abolitionist activity thus presents itself as a "way to break clear of the stigma of color."[32]

The Nantucket appearance is clearly of pivotal significance. It is the nascent moment of what Douglass later describes as the "open[ing] upon me of a new life"—a life constructed in and through language, as well as one invested in the theater of performative possibility.[33] It is a defining moment in Douglass's transformation into the iconic voice and face of the African's alter-

---

32. Peter Walker, *Moral Choices: Memory, Desire, and Imagination in Nineteenth-Century American Abolition* (Baton Rouge: Louisiana State University Press, 1978), 236–7, 242–3.

33. Douglass, *My Bondage*, 359.

ity. At Nantucket, Douglass's face enters the American imagination. He will later become the face of the African-blood interlocutor who steps forth to disrupt the discourse on freedom and to reassert the primacy of justice.

I agree with Henry Louis Gates Jr. that it is of particular importance that Douglass chooses to append the texts of his speeches in his last two autobiographies. Indeed, one can argue that Douglass's performative posture calls those written texts into being. In the 1855 *My Bondage and My Freedom*, Douglass writes, "People doubted if I had ever been a slave. They said I did not talk like a slave, look like a slave, nor act like a slave." As a result, he was "induced to write out the leading facts connected with my experience in slavery . . . thus putting it in the power of any who doubted, to ascertain the truth or falsehood of my story of being a fugitive slave."[34] One might concur with Peter Walker that Douglass's experience in Nantucket initiates those written texts, necessitating their origin and the logic of their rhetorical technique. Whereas Gates reads the successive autobiographies in terms of Douglass's concern with his public representation and thus his autobiographical desire to revise his past in ways that create a series of "fictive selves," Walker argues for their origination as "oratorical efforts." For Walker, Douglass's written expression is birthed through his actual experience in the performative arena. The autobiographies aim "to move, justify, and persuade. They do not propose to tell."[35]

As Walker acknowledges, Douglass's written texts do "tell." They simply constitute a different dimension through which Douglass enters the cultural memory. In the autobiographies, Douglass reconstructs his life through a succession of fictive portraits. Yet, as Gates maintains, this representation does not "suggest any sense of falsity or ill intent," but rather the "act of crafting or making by design . . . a process that unfolds in language," and over which Douglass undoubtedly exerts considerable control.[36] In the performative context, however, Douglass must relinquish that sole authorial control; the theater is predicated on its engagement in the dialectic of call and response as a shared experience. Assuming, as Walker proposes, that we should read the story of Douglass's life "as an extended historical metaphor," then his theatrical performances assume an increased critical importance. Specifically in the

---

34. Ibid., 362–3.
35. Walker, *Moral Choices*, 226.
36. Gates, *Figures in Black*, 103.

dimension of performance, Douglass comes to embody the American face of African alterity.

Levinas has argued that the face is already its own discourse; its signification is primordial because the "face of the Other at each moment destroys and overflows the plastic image it leaves me, the idea existing to my own measure and to the measure of its *ideatum*—the adequate idea" (*TI*, 51). In the presentation of his face, Douglass's presence is its own indisputable proof of the violation that persists in his being seen as slave. Walker, however, reads Douglass's appearance in speech somewhat differently. For Walker, Douglass's willingness to enter the arena of abolitionist activity, particularly given the personal risk it imposes upon him, is directly tied to the experience of freedom that speech permits. This freedom, Walker argues, extricates Douglass from the burden of his body: "He was 'made to forget' that he was Harriet Bailey's son. He was divested of his dark skin and crisped hair. He had ceased to be a Negro. The agency, the 'good cause,' was the literal escape from his physical features and from everything that tied him to his black mother."[37]

The difficulty here is that Douglass, for Walker, quickly becomes a "passive participant in his own drama." If in speech Douglass first achieves the experience of his own freedom, that same freedom is eclipsed by his role of speaker, through the Garrisonians' insistence upon his performance as specimen. As Douglass himself testifies, Garrison would remind him at each performative occasion, "'Tell your story, Frederick.'" Douglass answers, "I could not always obey, for I was now reading and thinking. New views of the subject were presented to my mind. It did not entirely satisfy me to *narrate* wrongs; I felt like *denouncing* them."[38] Initially, Douglass's freedom in speech is constricted by the expectations of an audience that is desirous to see the slave perform.

The key insight of Walker's analysis is the extent to which the relations between Douglass and Garrison become marked by a dual sense of betrayal. Douglass refuses to perform as a specimen, and the abolitionists refuse him the assertion of an interiority that exceeds the category of slave. Walker argues that Garrison and his entourage refuse Douglass the implicit promise that "he could now live without the attributes of blackness," and that the real

---

37. Walker, *Moral Choices*, 244.
38. Douglass, *My Bondage*, 361–2.

betrayal of the Garrisonians was their failure to "let him be what he desperately wanted to be," which was Douglass's internal desire "to be white."[39]

What is interesting about Walker's reading is both its inquiry into the motives and experiences that led Douglass to choose to become an abolitionist orator, and its conclusions that equate Douglass's search for an authentic—i.e., nonideational—identity with his desire for "whiteness." Walker maintains that previous critics and interpreters of Douglass's entrance into the arena of abolitionist discourse have failed to answer the question of why he undertakes such a particularly dangerous public persona. As Walker rightly points out, to become an antislavery "agitator and spokesman" is hardly "synonymous with fleeing slavery, nor are the motives informing them the same."[40] In that sense, Walker's study of the external circumstances that surround Douglass's emergence as an abolitionist spokesman is provocative.

Yet Walker's conclusion that Douglass's desire to be seen as a human being is equivalent to a hidden desire for whiteness is problematic. What does it mean to reread Douglass's admission that his enthusiasm for entering the "ranks of freedom's friends"—a space that enabled his transcendence of the name of slave, and one in which he could write, "For a time I was made to forget that my skin was dark and my hair crisped"—is equivalent to an expressed desire to be white?[41] According to Walker, the primary appeal of the abolitionist stage was its extension of a performative space where Douglass not only felt himself to be no longer a slave, but where "he had ceased to be a Negro." Such an analysis of Douglass's motives draws upon Eric Cheyfitz's argument that Douglass "conceives of the mechanics of slavery . . . as a differential in the power of language possessed by master and slave." In Cheyfitz's view, it is again through speaking that Douglass comes into being. If authentic existence resides in language, then once Douglass masters the language of the "master," his identity is translated from the shadow of invisibility (as enslavement) into the visible space of the polis—where to be free is signified by "whiteness." Cheyfitz explains, "To become white, that is to become a real human being, is not a physical problem, it is a political problem: the problem of mastering the master's language, of speaking the language of the capital. It is the problem of the difference in power between the center and the periphery."[42]

39. Walker, *Moral Choices*, 246.
40. Ibid., 237.
41. Ibid., 360.
42. Cheyfitz, *Poetics of Imperialism*, 33, 125.

Cheyfitz's statement that "in the colonial situation, the desire of the colonized to master the master's language is a desire to be white" gives Walker's reading some legitimacy.[43] Within the American landscape of the mid-nineteenth century, blackness is equated with the absence of speech and the absence of an interiority that signifies legitimate humanity. Whiteness becomes representative of the linguistic mastery equated with freedom, and thus the sign of a presence that is authentic and visible. In this context, Walker and Cheyfitz both read Douglass through the figure of the "eloquent orator," seeing the betrayal of the Garrisonians as a refusal to permit Douglass this equity in being. For the Garrisonians, Douglass is never eloquent enough to be granted full recognition: he is destined to remain always the outsider, who even in speech—indeed, whose very performativity in speech—must conform to the ideas that constitute the authority of being and therefore the right of address, here signified through whiteness. Hence the necessity of the paternal translator whose authoritative eloquence mediates the "natural" (but flawed) eloquence of the slave.

But Douglass's performativity in speech is precisely what disrupts this equation. On those innumerable occasions when Douglass mounts the stage to speak, his interiority is made evident. The primacy of his voice—as the revelation of the specific and profound experience of a self—makes possible the event of his address. Walter Ong would equate Douglass's capacity for address as engaging the interiority of the Other who listens, but not necessarily as an event of Levinasian "facing." Ong nevertheless acknowledges the power of the spoken word as "curiously reciprocating not only intentionally, in what it is meant to do (establish relationships with another), but also in the very medium in which it exists. Sounds bind interiors to one another as interiors. . . . Because the spoken word moves from interior to interior, encounter between man and man is achieved largely through voice."[44]

Perhaps the more pertinent intention behind Douglass's speaking lies in his desire to create this kind of "encounter between man and man" that opens into the nonindifference of a response: one in which the sound and "expression" of the face "speaks to me" beyond the politics of the polis "and thereby invites me to a relation incommensurate" (*TI*, 198) with power, knowledge, or racial designation. To read Douglass's desire in performance

---

43. Ibid., 126.
44. Ong, *Presence of the Word*, 125.

through the metaphor of whiteness is to restrict the significance of his appearance to the order of politics, as if it were the only reality. But the "order of politics . . . that inaugurates the 'social contract' is neither the sufficient condition nor the necessary outcome of ethics" (*EN*, 101). In other words, the interhuman dimension of address and response in which ethics is enacted is distinct from the political and from the prescriptions of identity one adopts in the social drama. Whiteness has meaning only within the social and political realm—and even there, only as an existential attribute through which subjectivity might be signified. In itself, whiteness is merely an ideational representation—and thus ultimately a false category of human being. Were Douglass merely to desire whiteness, his would be a desire for equity, equivalence, and incorporation within the "exercise of the same." More importantly, it would reflect a desire satisfied with the existing modes of power as privilege, one entirely indifferent to the "useless suffering" and persecution of those who, in skin and face, differ from his. In a world where whiteness is coeval with privilege and difference is equated with the absence of human right, both concepts resonate as metaphors of illusion. To be Other is not, finally, a designation that race can fulfill. Rather, it is to be that independent Stranger over whom the I has no real power: it is to be a face who "speaks to me." Even if, in the worst of social realities, the I desires her death—even then, her difference, her alterity is irrefutably evident. As Levinas repeatedly argues, the desire to "kill is not to dominate but to annihilate," because "murder exercises a power over what escapes power." But it is "still a power," because the "face rends the sensible. The alterity that is expressed in the face provides the unique 'matter' possible for total negation" (*TI*, 198). Douglass desires neither whiteness nor its privilege of power to condone the Other's murder. In speaking, Douglass reveals himself as an I situated in the theoretical context that his blackness entails, but, more importantly, existing as an I hungry for the political transformation that justice would render possible.

I am arguing that Douglass's speaking, his emergence as orator, originates a language desirous to "address and invoke the other," to intervene upon the very play of representations (as in "blackness" and "whiteness") in order to create the possibility of a community founded in responsiveness and responsibility. As Levinas writes, "It does not, to be sure, consist in invoking [the other] as represented and thought, but that is precisely why the *écart* between the same and the other, the gap in which language stands, cannot be reduced to a relation between concepts, one limiting the other, but describes the transcendence in which the *other* does not weigh on the *same*, but only obligates him, makes him responsible, that is, articulate" (*EN*, 32).

If Douglass actually intends his audience to become articulate, obligated, and responsible agents in the war against slavery, then his performative ambitions must be reconceived in terms of an explicitly ethical imperative. Compared to the fictional example of Madison Washington, Douglass seems far more invested in the disruptive potential of language as speech to shatter the discourses and delineations of identity. He is perhaps even more invested in the power of language to initiate an interhuman perspective that transcends the representational (and racial) language of the republic. When Douglass unequivocally states that "justice and liberty demand the service of the living human voice," he asks us to consider the unique relationship between the power of speech to open the way towards an ethical calling (as command) and the accountability that leads to the invitation to justice.

Returning to Douglass's dramatic refrain, "I stand here a slave," and his repeated insistence that it is a "slave who now addresses you," we begin to appreciate the performative efficacy of those simple words that situate Douglass beyond the frame of his individual experience. From his first Nantucket appearance, it is clear that Douglass is already seen as the exceptional Other. To some extent, this grants his story, his fugitive presence, the possibility of inclusion in the narrative of history. When Garrison prefaces Douglass's remarks to the Massachusetts Anti-Slavery Society by dramatically declaring, "It is recorded in holy writ that a beast once spoke. A greater miracle is here tonight. A chattel becomes a man," he incorporates Douglass's story into the narrative of abolition and so mediates the effect of his Otherness.[45] By constructing Douglass as the "miraculous" Other, Garrison extricates Douglass from the mass of unknown African others who remain faceless behind the veil of enslavement.

But Douglass's choice to speak in the name of the slave is intended to subvert his exceptionalism. Instead, he steps forward to become the interlocutor, the "face [that] breaks the system" (*EN*, 34), in order to demand an accountability that exceeds the compelling immediacy of his story. In other words, we might think of Douglass as the "primary" Other whose performative pose reveals the "apparition of a 'third'" who is not Frederick Douglass

---

45. Douglass, *Douglass Papers*, 1:15–6.

per se, "nor directly an *alter ego*, but another Other who is *beside* or *behind* this one here and now." The real ethical significance in Douglass's performative legacy involves the fate of all those equally persecuted African American Others whose faces are not seen, who do not speak, but who, in their necessary anonymity, should not be degraded "into a secondary species of human beings."[46]

It would be relatively easy for European and American audiences to see Douglass as the exceptional African Other towards whom a "just" response is reasonable. His face commands their respect and the urgency of response. Yet the relationship between Douglass and his audience is not justice, but one aspiring more towards intimacy: an accountability only before the face of the Other that one knows is to exist within a privacy of relation, where the injustice of one's actions can be pardoned. Only in relation to "the third"—the Other hidden beneath the invisibility of her enslavement—does justice enter the equation: "The word 'justice' applies much more to the relationship with the third party than to the relationship with the other. But in reality, the relationship with an other is never uniquely the relationship with the other: from this moment on, the third is represented in the other; that is, in the very appearance of the other the third already regards me" (*OG*, 82).

Here is the real efficacy of Douglass's performative legacy. Each time that Douglass takes the stage to assume the face of the American slave, he disentangles himself from the potential embrace of intimacy to place his audience in the presence of "the third": those three million Others of African blood who stand beside and behind him. The possibility of justice requires that one become accountable before the faces of the Other that one never sees or confronts. This is what Levinas means when he says that the "social wrong is something committed without my knowledge, against a multitude of third parties whom I will never face, whom I will never find in the face of God, and for whom God cannot answer."[47] God cannot answer for the Other as slave because the institution of slavery is not the work of God: it is the irreparable violence that human beings legislate and enact against one another. To work in the name of liberty and justice is to work in the name of accountability and in the cause of the Other whose face is never known.

46. Peperzak, *Beyond*, 127.
47. Emmanuel Levinas, *Collected Philosophical Papers*, trans. Alphonso Lingis (Dordrecht: M. Nijhoff, 1987), 33.

In the presence of the third, one must answer to the Other who stands outside the circle of dialogue and familiarity that Douglass's performativity invites. This may well be the greatest achievement of Douglass's oratorical legacy. He succeeds where others before him did not or could not. Despite his personal fortune in attaining freedom, Douglass never permits his audiences to forget that what is really at stake is the continuous persecution of those unknown African-blood "third parties," who remain hidden under the genus of slave, and who—just like Douglass himself—demand their right to freedom. In Douglass's oratorical presence, language creates the community of care; language breaks up the continuity of history, challenging his audiences to become engaged partners in the ethical command that permits justice to disrupt the privilege of freedom.

Yet while Douglass's abolitionist audiences were at least imaginatively capable of recognizing the hidden face of "the third," this was not necessarily the case in the West, where Sarah Winnemucca sounded her voice in the crusade for liberty and justice. For Douglass's audience, the image of the Other as "the third" was the face and body of the slave of African blood, and even though that body of slaves constituted a difficult and frightening specter in the American mind, their presence in the republic was indisputably tangible. On the western frontier, however, when Sarah Winnemucca mounts the stage in the name of the American Indian, the faces of "the third" (who stand beside and behind her) have all but vanished from the republic's imagination.

For Winnemucca's audiences, the Native Other is either presumed dead or is thought to be quickly disappearing from the territorial contours of the landscape. By the late 1800s, the Indian was more fantasy than real, a romantic presence encapsulated in cultural spectacle, an Other whose face has been effectively displaced under the sign of "the Indian." Unlike Douglass, Winnemucca speaks before an audience for whom the Indian is primarily a curiosity, not a cause.[48] Her task is thus especially formidable. And her decision to turn to the theatrical arena as her primary platform complicates her project even further. The theater, as Alan Read has convincingly argued, can be-

---

48. Despite the committed efforts of Winnemucca's northern patrons, Elizabeth Peabody, Helen Hunt Jackson, and Mary Mann, I want to suggest here that there was not the cultural equivalent of an abolitionist movement on behalf of Native peoples, and thus Winnemucca appeared before a public lacking in the ideological solidarity that more clearly informed Douglass's public.

come a critical site for catalytic instigation, creating an opening into the ethical possibilities of relationship. In more than three hundred performances during the 1880s, Sarah Winnemucca Hopkins claimed the stage in order to reassert the face of the Indian in the American mind and to argue her native right to inclusion in the national discourse on freedom and justice.

In late November 1879, when Sarah Winnemucca arrived in San Francisco aboard the steamer *California*, she had already achieved a peculiar notoriety. Known primarily for her efforts as a scout and interpreter in the Bannock War (1878), her arrival captured the attention of the local press, and she was immediately ushered into the space of public spectacle. First heralded for her bravery and "native eloquence" and subsequently demeaned for her "extensive and diversified matrimonial experience" (a reference to the "numerous" white men she was reputed to have married), Sarah Winnemucca emerged full-blown in the mind and imagination of a national public obsessed with the conflicting images of Indian dispossession and disappearance.[49]

In retrospect, it seems clear that Sarah Winnemucca was a woman of genuinely dramatic proportion, a natural and practiced actor, whose theatrical inclinations propelled her into the public eye. As early as twenty years old, Sarah, in concert with her father and sister, gave public performances designed to dramatize the Paiutes' peaceful ambitions and their desperate need for federal assistance. In 1864, the Winnemuccas took the stage at Virginia City's Sutcliff Music Hall, where they enacted a series of tableaux depicting Indian-white relations from the advent of "supposed scalpings" to "Pocahontas saving the life of Captain John Smith." Eventually they took their show to San Francisco, where, prior to the evening performance, they rode through the streets in full Indian regalia: "The warriors were painted with ochre and vermilion, and all of the party wore buckskins and bright-colored feather headdresses." One might say that Sarah Winnemucca inherited the notion of a political theatricality from her father. According to contemporary newspaper reports, Chief Winnemucca's first objective was political: "to make a show" of his tribe's plight in order to raise money to "buy food and blankets for his people."[50] The daughter learned from her

---

49. Gae Whitney Canfield, *Sarah Winnemucca of the Northern Paiutes* (Norman: University of Oklahoma Press, 1983), 163.

50. Ibid., 40, 39, 42.

father that the business of playing "Indian" was far more politically effective (and lucrative) than merely being the real thing.

It is not surprising that Winnemucca's return visit to San Francisco in 1879 once again captured the attention of a western public, or that within days of her arrival, the local papers dubbed her the "Princess Sarah." Numerous reviewers remarked upon her dress and appearance, noting her "beautifully-rounded brown arms, and scarlet leggings . . . her flowing black locks," and marveling at the "spontaneous flow of eloquence . . . accompanied by gestures that were scarcely ever surpassed by any actress on the stage."[51] By the end of November 1879, Sarah Winnemucca had triumphantly conquered the stage at San Francisco's Platte Hall.

If her first motivation had been to lecture about the recent Bannock War and to renew her service as an interpreter between oppositional racial and cultural communities, she soon realized the larger effects of her performative presence. "I would be the first Indian woman who ever spoke before white people," she is reported to have said, "and they don't know what the Indians have got to stand sometimes."[52] And there begins Sarah Winnemucca's compelling and complicated performative career. Between 1879 and 1884, Winnemucca would travel across the country to lecture, to be seen, and ultimately to enact one of the genuinely unique performative renditions of Indian and female otherness since the romantic narrative of Pocahontas first provoked the American imagination.

Renowned as the Princess Sarah, spectacularly attired in fringed buckskin and a "headdress of eagle feathers set in a scarlet crown," Winnemucca captivated an American imagination hungry for "savage nobility" and "natural eloquence." The press celebrated the Princess Sarah for her theatricality, applauding her performative pose as "Nature's child," whose words were "unlike anything ever before heard in the civilized world." Yet then and now, her critics scorned her decision to drape herself in the mythology of the Indian princess. Despite the complex and controversial legacy through which Sarah Winnemucca comes to presence, her accomplishment was of enduring significance. In the guise of the Indian princess, she placed her face in the mind and memory of an American republic that was resolved to deny Native peoples both the legitimacy of their historical past and the contemporaneity of the present, in which recognized subjects live and speak.

51. Ibid., 164.
52. Ibid., 162.

In the midst of her appearances as the Indian princess, Sarah Winnemucca accomplished two further achievements of national significance. In 1883, she published the first autobiographical narrative grounded in the experience and perspective of a Native woman. Later, primarily as a result of her phenomenal theatrical success, she chose to situate herself before the eye of the camera, and thus to participate in the photographic record of Indian survivance in the latter moments of the nineteenth century. Between 1879 and 1884, Winnemucca posed for a series of nine photographic studio portraits, most of which present her in the "elaborately decorated nontraditional clothing," indicative of her performative pose as the Princess Sarah.[53] That series of photographic images projects Winnemucca's performative legacy beyond the frames of the stage. The photographs remain and linger in the national archive, returning us to the face of Sarah Winnemucca, where we once again become accountable respondents and readers.

Sarah Winnemucca is best known in a literary context for her memoir, *Life among the Piutes: Their Wrongs and Claims*. On its initial printing, editor Mary Mann articulated the significance of its appearance in American print culture by declaring *Life among the Piutes* to be the "first outbreak of the American Indian in human literature," whose "single aim" was "to tell the truth as it lies in the heart and mind of a true patriot, and one whose knowledge of the two races gives her an opportunity of comparing them justly."[54] Winnemucca's memoir bears significantly upon the history of nineteenth-century American autobiography; yet, not unlike Douglass's venture into the textuality of autobiographical narrative, *Life among the Piutes* is a literary work called into being through the performative success of Winnemucca's oratorical efforts.

Indeed, much like Douglass's experience, Winnemucca's emergence into print was essentially the result of her theatrical performances. She discovered onstage the enthusiastic presence of a national audience interested in hearing her story. Recognizing the fertile possibilities of that public reception, she soon "became determined to write about her people at length."[55] In that re-

---

53. Joanna Scherer, "The Public Faces of Sarah Winnemucca," *Cultural Anthropology* 3 (1988): 170.

54. Sarah Winnemucca Hopkins, *Life among the Piutes* (Reno: University of Nevada Press, 1994), "Preface," n.p.

55. Canfield, *Sarah Winnemucca*, 201.

spect, *Life among the Piutes* originates in Winnemucca's experience as a speaker; it is a text birthed in the dimension of the performative context. But *Life among the Piutes* is also a testimonial text. Winnemucca's story is implicitly the story of her people, and, as such, it disrupts the ideal of autobiographical individualism to assert the validity of "the first-person plural" through which the presence of a tribal "We" comes to voice.[56] In that sense, both Winnemucca's print and theatrical presences constitute an autobiographical stance (and storytelling) that is inherently performative. Winnemucca performs not only her own interiority of person: the fact that she speaks in the voice of the first-person plural signals the performance of an interiority inclusive of those standing beside her who are Paiute. But this is a competing notion of interiority already grounded in the foreignness of alterity that signifies the Indian.

If Douglass, in his initial appearances as the fugitive slave, is the Stranger—the Other whose alterity is unknown—Winnemucca comes closer to embodying the figure of the foreigner. She is the Other whose presumed demise signifies her very being as both exceptional and foreign. I am playing a bit here with the Levinasian notion of the Other, for it is precisely the Other's otherness that makes her "strange" and "foreign." That is what alterity means. But I want to emphasize the dramatic and conceptual differences that distinguish Winnemucca's public persona from that of Douglass's. While Douglass speaks in the name of the slave, Winnemucca's emergence as the "Indian Princess" signifies the absence of the Native self in the cultural consciousness of the new republic.

At the beginning of *Life among the Piutes,* Winnemucca announces, "I was born somewhere near 1844, but am not sure of the precise time." Resounding through those words is the evidence of an uncertainty, an inconclusiveness, through which her story comes to presence. In its very first words, Winnemucca's text signals that it is marked by the presence of an absence—an absence not unlike that of Douglass's *Narrative,* where he is both the subject and the Other. But the greater absence that informs Winnemucca's story reveals itself through the problem of the name and the critical significance

---

56. Hertha D. Sweet Wong, "First-Person Plural: Subjectivity and Community in Native American Women's Autobiography," in *Women, Autobiography, Theory,* ed. Sidonie Smith and Julia Watson (Madison: University of Wisconsin Press, 1998), 171.

borne by acts of naming. Indeed, one of the distinguishing components that informs Douglass's and Winnemucca's alterity is that each must come to presence under the burden of lost names. In Winnemucca's case, the deletion of the name is inextricably bound up with the intended erasure of Native peoples and the substitution of the Indian to designate that space of absence.

In *Life among the Piutes*, Winnemucca bears several names; through them, she bears the reminder of contradictory realities and competing identities. Her authorial name is "Sarah Winnemucca Hopkins," but its legitimacy is contested by a prior name, her tribal name, which we can only know in translation. That first name, in which the trace of an originary identity resides, is "Thocmetony," and this is her name before her conversion into the province of Indian Otherness. This is the name closest to her authentic and native self, and it bears little relation to the names that follow, through which Winnemucca becomes visible. In "Thocmetony," whose sounds and meanings and nuances ultimately elude us, reside the real stories of identity, presence, and lineage that indicate a self whole and intact, in her rightful being and historical continuity. But even as we acknowledge its precedence, "Thocmetony" is a name that reflects an existence, a reality, that is no longer recoverable.

This is one of the points that Gerald Vizenor elucidates in his reflection on the story of Ishi, the "last wild Indian" of the northern California coast. In "Ishi Obscura," Vizenor recovers the story of Ishi, the last Yana (Yahi) Indian, whose small tribe of people had lived undetected in the forests near Mill Creek, California. Prior to his discovery and capture—which was inevitable, due to the clearing and logging of the California forests—Ishi and his people persisted in the seclusion of their invisibility.[57] It was in the terrain of his forested homeland that Ishi's authentic self and real name would remain. Vizenor accordingly begins his essay by asserting, "Ishi was never his real

---

57. I am drawing upon Gerald Vizenor's concept of the "manifest manners" that mark and characterize the historical processes through which Native peoples are subject to the rules and politics of colonial dominance. Ishi's "discovery" is inextricably bound up with the "manifest manners" of the new republic, and specifically, that imperative through which the landscape itself must be translated into the sphere of domesticity, or the site of dwelling. The fact that Ishi and the remaining members of his tribe lived undiscovered for fifty years after the "American" settlement of California is testimony to their determination to remain rooted in their homeland. His discovery is evidence of the violence that manifest destiny, as an ideological imperative, enacted upon the lives of Native peoples.

name. Ishi is a simulation, the absence of tribal names." From the moment of his "discovery," Vizenor argues, Ishi existed through the names of his conquerors, and those names were neither real nor authentic. As Vizenor writes, Ishi "never told the anthropologists, reporters, and curious practitioners his sacred tribal name, not even his nicknames." "Ishi" is the name imposed on him, the sign of his conversion from freedom into Indian survivor. Between his discovery in 1911 and his death on March 25, 1916, he would be named the "last of his tribe," the "last 'uncontaminated' aboriginal American Indian in the United States," and the "last wild Indian" uncovered in the dark recesses of the republic.[58]

Ishi was captured long after the Paiutes had been defeated, but his story mirrors that of Sarah Winnemucca's in terms of its politics of the name. Like Ishi, Sarah Winnemucca's tribal people were "discovered" by settlers moving from California through Nevada in pursuit of new land. Early in her narrative, Winnemucca tells of being buried alive by her mother, with "sage brushes over our faces to keep the sun from burning them, and there . . . left all day," for fear that if they were discovered, they would "all be killed or eaten up."[59] Who and what her people had been before the event of their discovery ended in that act of symbolic burial. Who they had been we cannot know, for that "truth" and its reality of everyday life would have resided in the oral stories and the nuances of a native language resistantly untranslatable.

And it is not only Sarah Winnemucca's personal name that bears the weight of absence and inauthenticity. Early in the pages of *Life among the Piutes*, Winnemucca contests the naming of her people and her tribal community, unmasking the layers of misrepresentation that distort the Native face and presence: "I do not know how we came by the name of Piutes. It is not an Indian word. I think it is misinterpreted. Sometimes we are called Pine-nut eaters, for we are the only tribe that lives in the country where Pine-nuts grow."[60] Here is one of the amazing moments in this difficult and labored text. Winnemucca exceeds the politics of "civilization and savagism" that necessarily are at play in her narrative to reveal the hidden connections between "Indianness" and linguistic invention.

58. Gerald Vizenor, *Shadow Distance* (Hanover, N.H.: University Press of New England, 1994), 184.
59. Hopkins, *Life among the Piutes*, 11.
60. Ibid., 75.

That "Piute" is itself already an aberration, a missed translation, and a false naming, goes directly to Vizenor's point that the "*indian* is a simulation, the absence of natives; the *indian* transposes the real, and the simulation of the real has no referent, memories, or native stories" (*FP*, 15). In Winnemucca's revelation that "Piute" is the "Indian" name superimposed upon the faces of her people, she compels her readers to acknowledge that "Piute" is a word without resonance, meaning, or history in the experience of those that it purports to render visible. It is, quite literally, a name for whom there is no existent referent, cultural memory, or native story. In other terms, the discourse that culminates in the invention of the northern Nevada Paiutes works to transpose the real and living presence of those tribal peoples among whom Winnemucca belongs. Here Vizenor's choice of language is especially astute. The true violence residing in acts of transposition is less an issue of linguistic inaccuracy than an issue of the intention of a removal in time and place, such that the very alterity of the Other is eclipsed by the imposition of a foundational corruption exercised through language.

Yet this violence is difficult to see, precisely because it has always informed the words through which the Native presence and face have been represented. In that seemingly innocent moment when Sarah Winnemucca Hopkins contests the naming of her people, she exposes the violence of injustice that saturates the language through which the American Indian has been seen. Each act of naming and renaming the Native presence reveals a linguistic process that takes place independently of the Other who is identified as Indian. From an ethical perspective, this is the imposition of a rhetoric that "approaches the other not to face him, but obliquely"; the "specific nature of rhetoric" thus masks an injustice. For the specific nature of a language that "consists in corrupting [the Other's] freedom" is violence. "It is preeminently violence, that is, injustice," Levinas argues, because it is not a "violence exercised on an inertia (which would not be a violence), but on a freedom, which, precisely as freedom, should be incorruptible" (*TI*, 70).

The trace that remains of Sarah Winnemucca's "incorruptible freedom" lingers in her first name, Thocmetony, even as the nuances of its signification remain buried in the desert terrain of Nevada, where her people lived authentically in their natural freedom. There is an inviolable connection, N. Scott Momaday asserts, between the originary name and the human being who proceeds from it. Momaday's second autobiographical narrative is appropriately entitled *The Names,* and in its prefatory pages he marks the distinction between his name in translation and his real name, given to him by the elder, Pohd-lohk: "My name is Tsoai-talee. I am, therefore, Tsoai-talee; therefore I am." The significance of the name "Tsoai-talee" is not simply its evocative power to return Momaday to the circle of his Kiowa past; its real meaning has to do with the efficacy of language and imagination, which, for Momaday, animates the very core of human identity. In his words, "The storyteller Pohd-lohk gave me the name Tsoai-talee. He believed that a man's life proceeds from his name, in the way that a river proceeds from its source."[61]

For Momaday, there is something indivisible in the relationship between the name given and the essential identity of the one chosen to honor and live it. But equally important is the absence manifest in the name imposed from the outside, the name issued in order to impose upon an indigenous freedom the nomenclature of category, as if to supply an answer to the question already "contradictory in its terms" but nevertheless posed, as in, "What is the nature of this freedom?" (TI, 70). In the case of Winnemucca's people, discovered living "in the country where Pine-nuts grow," they emerged into the national lexicon as "Piutes."

And so we return to the "preeminent violence" that language can initiate against the Other whose face it approaches "obliquely," as if that Other bore no sign of a freedom. Vizenor argues that "Indian is a simulation and loan word of dominance," illuminating Derrida's insight into the relationship between ontologies of power and the language that inscribes them. According to Derrida, "There's no racism without a language. The point is not that acts of racial violence are only words but rather that they have to have a word. Even though it offers the excuse of blood, color, birth—or, rather, because it uses this naturalist and sometimes creationist discourse—racism always betrays the perversion of a man, the 'talking animal.' It institutes, declares, writes, inscribes, prescribes. A system of marks, it outlines space in order to assign forced residence or to close off borders. It does not discern, it discriminates."[62] It is precisely this invention of a "system of marks" that permeates the nomenclature of the American Indian. To be named "Indian" means explicitly to be removed, spatially and temporally, from the interior map of the

---

61. N. Scott Momaday, *The Names* (Tucson: University of Arizona Press, 1976), n.p.
62. Jacques Derrida, "Racism's Last Word," trans. Peggy Kamuf, *Critical Inquiry* 12 (1985): 292.

republic, and to "be assigned forced residence" in the constructed spaces of the reservation (itself a term implicated in the poetics of concealment and limitation). Returning to Vizenor's point, we can say that neither Paiute nor Sarah Winnemucca were ever the "real names" of this Other, whose freedom is first corrupted (and violated) in the imposition of a false language.

But the problem of the name is not restricted to Sarah Winnemucca and the experience of Native peoples: we know that the African self was also denied privilege to its originary name. Like Winnemucca, Douglass must live and speak under the weight of lost names. In the *Narrative,* Douglass reveals that the "name given me by my mother was, 'Frederick Augustus Washington Bailey,'" and that he was first known as "Frederick Bailey." In the course of his fugitive travels and poses, he became "Stanley Bailey," and upon his arrival in New York, he reinvented himself in the name of "Frederick Johnson." Having taken up residence in New Bedford—where there were numerous Johnsons of African descent—Frederick Johnson became the Frederick Douglass we now know. And yet Douglass's emergence through this name was a matter more of chance than destiny. "Frederick Douglass" was a name birthed in the mind of Nathan Johnson, the New Bedford abolitionist who took him in and attended to his safety. As Douglass writes, "I gave Mr. Johnson the privilege of choosing me a name, but told him he must not take from me the name of 'Frederick.' I must hold on to that, to preserve a sense of my identity. Mr. Johnson had just been reading the 'Lady of the Lake,' and at once suggested that my name be Douglass. From that time until now I have been called 'Frederick Douglass'; and as I am more widely known by that name than by either of the others, I shall continue to use it as my own."[63] Douglass's story should make us acutely aware of the linguistic violences that inform and constitute conquest, for the relocation and reconstruction of the Other in the narrative of dominance hinges upon this pivotal erasure that arbitrarily denies that individual even the sanctity of his name.

Let us return to Ishi, whose story introduced this caesura between name and presence. "Ishi was never his real name," Vizenor reminds us, "and he is not the photographs of that tribal man" who "posed at the borders of the camera" in the "best backlighted pictures of the time." In similar respects, neither is Sarah Winnemucca the real name of the Native woman whose face comes to us through her performative poses as the Princess Sarah, onstage

---

63. Douglass, *Narrative,* 110.

and in photographs. She is no more the "Indian Princess" of the camera than Ishi is the "stout pretense of a wild man lost and found in a museum."[64] Winnemucca's real self, her tribal self, stares "over the camera, into the distance"; only in her eyes, "in the stare of the shadows," Vizenor argues, can we discover an "elusive native presence" (*FP*, 156). I now want to turn to the Winnemucca photographs. If Vizenor is right, then there is an "elusive native presence" lingering behind the simulation of Indianness through which Sarah Winnemucca has been seen and judged. If so, perhaps we can recover the trace and the remains of an ethical resistance through which the face of Thocmetony still speaks.

On at least nine occasions between 1874 and 1884, Sarah Winnemucca posed before the camera to place her face in the national archive and its documentation of Indian survival. There are nine known studio portraits of Sarah Winnemucca, and with the exception of three, she appears through her performative pose as the Princess Sarah. In two of the remaining three, she is dressed in clothing typical of the period, which represents her as a woman of class and education. The last of these photographs is a formal portrait of the 1880 Paiute delegation, taken on their trip to Washington in pursuit of federal recognition and relief. Here Sarah poses with her father, Chief Winnemucca, "her brother Natchez, Captain Jim, a Paiute headman from western Nevada," and one Other, an unnamed tribal plaintiff. As Joanna Scherer comments, "The Paiute men wear new suits, gifts of the government," and Sarah "appears as a middle-class matron in a simple but typical Euro-American suit with her hair in fashionable 1880's coiffure." That Sarah is a member of the Paiute delegation again signifies her unique presence in the cultural record: "Few Indian women appear in formal delegation photographs, and her inclusion underscores her important status in her family and her position as a spokesperson for her tribe."[65] Yet Sarah Winnemucca lingers in the cultural imagination not because she was one of the few Native women whose face disrupts the gender bias of delegation photography, but because her performative pose as the Princess Sarah captivates the American mind and assuages its nostalgic longing for its exotic (and tragic) Indian Other.

In turning to the Princess portraits, the first thing one must see is their

64. Vizenor, *Shadow Distance*, 184.
65. Scherer, "Public Faces," 184.

seminal inauthenticity. In nearly all of the photographs, Winnemucca's dresses are comprised of the kinds of materials that were often used to decorate lampshades or curtains (such as beaded tassels and manufactured fringe). She wears necklaces that combine sequins, assorted beads and yarns, and bracelets fashioned from coins, beads, and shells. Sometimes she wears a feathered headdress; in other photographs, she is adorned with a small bow or netted cap. In the most famous of the Princess images, she wears a gold crown studded with stars and tassels. There she stands as if facing center stage, with a beaded purse draped at her hip, "decorated with a cupid figure holding a bow and arrow and edged with what appear to be heavy wooden beads."[66] This is the "Princess Sarah of the Northern Piutes." And in the face, in the eyes that stare out at us from the photographic frame, is the trace of the Native presence now become the performative poseur. For her critics, this image resonates with her acquiescence and complicity. This is the pose that has been read to signal Sarah Winnemucca's willing participation in the degradation of the Indian and the betrayal of tribal peoples. And if one sees and reads the portraits through this lens, then Winnemucca's decision to represent herself under the sign of the "Indian Princess" might suggest the politics of racial and cultural betrayal.

In one of the very few commentaries that consider the Winnemucca portraits, Joanna Scherer asserts that "formal portraits make purposeful statements of how the subject wanted to be known, and can be as revealing as a personal diary." Scherer argues that Winnemucca's studio portraits comprise a body of visual evidence that clearly demonstrates that she "pretended to be an American Indian Princess and promoted herself in this image. . . . In creating this image, however, she joined herself to a stereotype that on the one hand would make her acceptable to Euro-American mentality, but on the other hand tied her to the nineteenth-century notion of 'Indian Princess,' an expression of what Rayna Green has called the 'Pocahontas perplex.'" Because all but three of the studio portraits play upon the Princess image, Scherer concludes that "her image [as] seen through the formal portraits was of her own creation." In making such a choice, Scherer writes, Winnemucca worked against her own integrity of person: "That this early advocate of American Indian activism presented herself as an Indian Princess was perhaps the most detrimental public relations strategy she could have adopted.

66. Ibid., 180.

Rather than strengthening her credibility it may well have undermined it by presenting an image that was incompatible with her political message."[67]

It is important to note, however, that although Scherer's critique of the Winnemucca photographs initiates a number of provocative questions and issues—particularly in terms of how we read photographs of the Native face, and what they can be said to tell us—her approach to these photographic texts is explicitly anthropological. And, as Elizabeth Edwards clarifies, what makes a photograph "anthropological" is not its "subject-matter as such, but the consumer's classification of that knowledge or 'reality' which the photograph appears to convey." Edwards further argues that "material can move in and out of the anthropological sphere and photographs which were not created with anthropological intent or specifically informed by ethnographic understanding may nevertheless be appropriated to anthropological ends."[68] Scherer's reading of the Winnemucca Princess portraits thus seems to be grounded in an anthropological desire to represent the photographic images of Sarah Winnemucca as the visual evidence of a given and specific reality, one that corresponds both to Sarah Winnemucca as presence and the Paiutes as a discernable, definitively Indian alterity.

In other words, Scherer's reading grants a certain truthfulness to these images, one where the "signifier is treated as if it were identical with a pre-existent signified and in which the reader's role is purely that of consumer."[69] Of course, Scherer is more than a mere "consumer," but her approach to the photographs nevertheless depends upon a "phenomenology of images" that "insists on their transparency," in which the "intention of one who contemplates an image is said to go directly through the images, as through a window, into the world it represents, and aims at an *object*."[70] Scherer's reading, however, is genuinely problematic in multiple ways. While the photograph itself may be an object in the world—whether defined as art or as ethnographic evidence—the trace of the Other seen here, the Other we know as Sarah Winnemucca, is not. In these trickster images, Winnemucca is neither

67. Ibid., 178, 196.

68. Elizabeth Edwards, "Introduction," *Anthropology and Photography, 1860–1920*, ed. Elizabeth Edwards (New Haven: Yale University Press, 1992), 13.

69. John Tagg, *The Burden of Representation* (Amherst: University of Massachusetts Press, 1988), 99.

70. Emmanuel Levinas, "Reality and Its Shadow," trans. Alphonso Lingis, in *The Levinas Reader* (New York: Blackwell, 1989), 134.

the object of our contemplation nor the image through which she seems to appear. The image refers to her through a resemblance taken for the real, but the image is the "very event of obscuring" her reality, and the nature of the photograph is that it "consists in substituting the image" for the being who is real.[71] But Scherer's interpretation of these photographs invites the question of whether and what kinds of truth might resonate here—in the image, in the photograph itself—that nevertheless returns the face of Sarah Winnemucca to our gaze and to our national memory. If the photographs were only "image," if they could be said to possess no truth at all, no resonance except their reflection of the "event of obscuring" the face and presence of Sarah Winnemucca, then they would be unworthy of inquiry and critical reflection. Thus Scherer is certainly right to claim that there is some persistence of a truth that lingers in the images of Sarah Winnemucca and her performative poses. What is at stake, then, is how we conceive and imagine that truth and what it proposes to tell us of this Other whose face now returns to command our response.

When Scherer asserts that the Princess portraits reveal some truth of how Winnemucca, as subject, "wanted to be known," she constitutes the photographs in terms of a "phenomenology of images" that invests a positive correspondence between image and reality, representation and being. Scherer thus reads the photographs as portraits that indicate the free will of a subject deciding how she "wanted to be known." But John Tagg argues that despite the realism we ascribe to portraiture, the portrait is actually only a sign of the Other—a "sign whose purpose is both the description of an individual and the inscription of a social identity." And therein is one of the problems: Sarah Winnemucca is not an "individual" in Tagg's sense, nor is she a subject with the kind of free will in choices of representation that Scherer implies. Sarah Winnemucca is an Indian, which means that she appears first and foremost under the sign of "Indianness"—itself both the "inscription of a social identity" and an erasure of the freedom of the original being whose image has since replaced her. Despite the realism that portraiture appears to evoke, Tagg argues for its unreliability, its participation in the illusion of representation: "What lies 'behind' . . . the image is not reality—the referent—but reference: a subtle web of discourse through which realism is enmeshed in a complex fabric of notions, representations, images, atti-

71. Ibid.

tudes, gestures and modes of action which function as everyday know-how, 'practical ideology,' norms within and through which people live their relation to the world."[72] In the case of the Winnemucca photographs, it is these interrelationships between reference and the referent, the prevailing practical and cultural modes of ideology, and the politics of representation that are so acutely at stake.

It is possible to refute any trace of reality that could be said to inhere in these photographic portraits. When we focus on the most famous of the Princess images, it is absolutely clear that Winnemucca's dress is a costume and that her stance is artificially contrived; there is little, if any, anthropological authenticity. Scherer registers and acknowledges this image as an aberration, noting in detail Winnemucca's departure from "traditional Paiute women's" dress and modes of appearance. Scherer concludes that Winnemucca's "clothing is made up of cultural symbols that allow the observer to quickly recognize the American Indian princess image."[73] But the "traditional Paiute" women to whom Scherer refers are already entrapped in a photographic nightmare: for eternity, they are destined to exist as the objects of an acquisitive gaze that assigns to their nakedness and vulnerability the unmitigated evidence of their Indian alterity.

Rather than evincing some truth or knowledge of the Paiute Other, this image marks their death and seals their fate as prisoners in a representation both false and wickedly violative. Despite the traditional elements supposedly visible in this image (their bared breasts and their skirts of "woven sagebrush bark, rushes, or bird or mammal skins"), one must agree with Levinas that these "elements do not serve as symbols" of the Paiute's alterity. Rather, in the absence of the Other, "they do not force its presence, but by their presence insist on its absence. They occupy its place fully to mark its removal, as though the represented object died, were degraded, were disincarnated in its own reflection." The three women captured in this image have been "degraded" and "disincarnated" through the violent imposition of the camera, which under the pretense of documenting their alterity only succeeds in mutilating it. What we see is not an image of Paiute authenticity, but an image that is "already a caricature." Even worse, "This caricature turns into something tragic."[74]

72. Tagg, *Burden*, 37, 100.
73. Scherer, "Public Faces," 179, 187.
74. Levinas, "Reality and Its Shadow," 136, 138.

This photographic turn towards caricature and the tragic is an essential aspect of Levinas's arguments against the truthfulness of art. It is not simply that the photograph as a medium "is a mode of bereavement," where its subject, "seized by the camera," is "mortified—that is, objectified, 'thingified,' imaged."[75] Levinas argues that in the substitution of the image for the existent, which characterizes not just photography but all art, the "world to be built is replaced by the essential contemplation of the shadow. This is not the disinterestedness of contemplation but of irresponsibility."[76] In the photograph of the three Paiute women, "myth takes the place of mystery." As viewers, we are free to gaze upon the image, to catalogue or debate its ethnographic or anthropological value, even to marvel at the "cold splendor" of its depiction of the Other's difference. But this is an image of difference bordering on the inhuman, and the image itself frees us from the weight and the reality of our responsibility in the presence of the Other whose face should command us.

If the "poet exiles himself from the city," as Levinas argues, then one can argue that the photographer extricates himself from the command of the Other's face to betray it, to convert its transcendence as face into the darkness of the shadow, where the presence of alterity is obscured. "An image does not engender a *conception*," Levinas insists, writing that "art does not belong to the order of revelation." Rather, because "art brings into the world the obscurity of fate," the image of the Other is trapped and immobilized in the "eternal duration of the interval—the meanwhile." This is one of the violences that photography perpetrates. The unnamed Paiute women "thingified" in the image of their authenticity are forever imprisoned in that moment of their nakedness. They cannot get up to cover themselves; they cannot speak to mediate the meaning assigned and attributed to the image that now substitutes and stands in for them. They are trapped in a "stoppage of time," fated to be naked before every single eye that turns to see them. This is the violence of the "meanwhile" because it is "never finished," and in its "still enduring," it is, quite simply, "something inhuman and monstrous."[77]

But there is another level of violence at play here, involving the manner in which the violation against the Other is further complicated: we can gaze

---

75. Eduardo Cadava, *Words of Light* (Princeton, N.J.: Princeton University Press, 1997), 8, 11.
76. Levinas, "Reality and Its Shadow," 142.
77. Ibid., 132, 141.

upon this image of their nakedness without responsibility, accountability, or even the necessary pretense of a respectable and civilized modesty. Levinas argues that this is the way that art "frees." The image solicits our "disinterestedness," and we may even be charmed by its curiosity or its tragic beauty. But in the encounter with this image, we are "essentially disengaged." In a "world of initiative and responsibility," where we are answerable in the face of the Other's death, art in general, and this photograph in particular, grants its viewer the freedom of a gaze that in its disinterested "objectivity" constitutes an existential and ethical "dimension of evasion."[78]

I can think of few other photographic images that so explicitly illustrate Levinas's critique of the ways in which our contemplative appreciation of the photograph (and its artistry of substitution) is more than disengagement and irresponsibility. This image suggests that representation can signify for presence, which it absolutely cannot. This particular picture, especially in its efficacy as a peculiar kind of anthropological proof, reminds us that there is "something wicked and egoist and cowardly" in our enjoyment of the photographic images through which the face of the Other who is Indian is seen. For to gaze upon this image of the Other, constructed under the sign of the Indian as Paiute—as if, through it, we might know something of the truth of her difference—is shameful. It is to be as guilty, in Levinasian terms, "as of feasting during a plague."[79]

These multiple violences of substitution, evasion, and the eternally enduring duration of "the meanwhile" lead Robert Eaglestone to conclude that for Levinas, "art is not transcendent, nor does it bear any sign of the ethical." As Eaglestone argues, "A work of art is literally 'timeless,' trapped outside of time. As such, as 'timeless,' it can play no part in our world, which involves the constant taking up of a position in time. For Levinas, there is nothing art, in its hither, time-less world of resemblances, can teach us about the real world."[80] Here Herman Rapaport intervenes in the discussion of whether art can bear either "truth" or the "sign of the ethical," arguing that even in a reading of "Reality and Its Shadow" (Levinas's primary text on the failure of art), "One has to be careful not to assume that Levinas has taken a position

---

78. Ibid., 141.

79. Ibid., 142.

80. Robert Eaglestone, *Ethical Criticism: Reading after Levinas* (Edinburgh: Edinburgh University Press, 1997), 115, 108.

against the arts that simply reprises Socrates' condemnation of art as mimetically false, affectively infectious, and morally deleterious." Rapaport delineates the "spell of the image"—its ability to impose itself upon the viewer—and reveals the potentialities of a dimension beyond passivity and timelessness: "Nevertheless, because the image is passive and neither my subjection nor my freedom is being engaged, the image succeeds in imposing itself on me without my consent. Hence, it is aggressive."[81] Rapaport is specifically interested in the photograph. His inquiry, along with that of Vizenor's, opens up the space of possibility through which I hope to recover the ethical trace that persists in the Princess portrait of Sarah Winnemucca.

Thinking about the cultural legacy of the photograph and the Native face, Vizenor asks, "What can we see in the photographic representations of the racial other that is not dominance? Portraiture as evidence, or even postindian pasticcio, must be more than the eternal silence of a fugitive pose; there, in the stare of the shadows, is an elusive native presence" (FP, 156). As if in dialogue, Rapaport answers, "What Levinas can help us appreciate is the way in which an auxiliary appearance such as a photograph surreptitiously irrupts into the world and in so doing interrupts an event from a transcendental and ethical standpoint. Our consideration of the photograph, then, would mark a position from beyond or outside the event that nevertheless irrupts into the phenomenality of its historical unfolding."[82]

Were Vizenor to consider the Princess photographs of Sarah Winnemucca, he would surely note that "from beyond or outside the event" of her appearing through the myth of the Indian princess, the "crucial stories of natives in photographs are in the eyes and hands, not in the costumes or simulations of culture." The crucial story that Winnemucca tells, even in the midst of her "racial enactment" of Indian alterity, resides in the eyes turned on us, in the face that speaks still. "The eyes that meet in the aperture are the assurance of narratives and a sense of native presence" (FP, 156). Answering the condemnation of her critics, who see Winnemucca's costume and simulation as the evidence of a betrayal, Vizenor redirects our gaze, insisting that we must also see the politics of "surveillance" at work to recognize that "those natives captured as *indians*," as Winnemucca is here, in the "stoical poses of the

---

81. Herman Rapaport, *Is There Truth in Art?* (Ithaca, N.Y.: Cornell University Press, 1997), 50.

82. Ibid., 201.

other, are the cultural fugitives of desire and dominance." We cannot know how Sarah Winnemucca might have "wanted to be known," but we can be certain that hers is indeed a "fugitive pose" before the camera, and "one more weapon in the course of discoveries and cultural dominance"(FP, 157).

Sarah Winnemucca may be trapped in a pose that seems to betray her, in an eternal and timeless silence from which she cannot exit "to complete her task," as Levinas would say. But there is also here the activity of a defiance, of an "irruption" and, in Vizenor's terms, an "act of survivance": "The fugitives of manifest manners learned to pose in silence as an act of survivance" (FP, 156). According to Rapaport, this is precisely how the photograph comes to encompass a truth linked to the ethical: "In the coming to appearance of this face to consciousness, a power makes itself known that escapes the exercise of brutality: the power not of the individual to survive catastrophe or to meet his or her fate with honor, but of the ethical to persist in its exceeding the life of the individual wherein it appears as only a momentary epiphany, as nothing more than the appearance of a face before an other, of what Levinas calls the 'me voici.'"[83]

What survives beyond the moment of the photograph is not the significance of the costume (for its significance has already been deconstructed), but the coming to appearance of this face, in which we discover the persistence of an ethical law that signifies not only beyond the illusions of the pose, but beyond even the being and death of Sarah Winnemucca herself. What we encounter in the photograph is the persistence of the trace of the Other's face that still speaks to us "from beyond the finitude of its appearance and from the beyond of its being." If, as Herman Rapaport suggests, we can read the photograph as an "auxiliary appearance," then we can also understand it in Levinasian terms, where the "phenomenon which is the apparition of the other is also a *face*."[84]

What this means is that the photograph might exceed its stasis of representation to become the opening, the occasion, of a facing. Insofar as the photograph can be said to bear the "phenomenon which is the apparition of the other," then it harbors the potential, albeit differently from the encounter that is face to face, to recall us to a consciousness of the persistence of an ethical law that signifies even from the beyond of image, being, and death.

83. Ibid., 206.
84. Ibid., 216.

"The type of consciousness the photograph involves is indeed truly unprecedented," Roland Barthes has argued, "since it establishes not a consciousness of the *being-there* of the thing (which any copy could provoke) but an awareness of its *having-been-there*. What we have is a new space-time category: spatial immediacy and temporal anteriority, the photograph being an illogical conjunction between the *here-now* and the *there-then*."[85]

In this "new space-time category" that the photograph ushers into being, the ethical law remains intact; it is discoverable there in the eyes that meet us, in the trace of the face that lingers through its apparition. In Levinasian terms, the law that signifies beyond Sarah Winnemucca's place in the *"there-then,"* that speaks beyond her being and death, is the command of the face, which says that "you shall not kill" in the pursuit of your own freedom. This, Levinas would argue, is the trace of the face that is, first, the "other before death, looking through and exposing death. Secondly, the face is the other who asks me not to let him die alone, as if to do so were to become an accomplice in his death. Thus the face says to me: you shall not kill."[86] Were we to see only the performative pose, the substitution of an image for the reality of Sarah Winnemucca's *having-been-there*, and were we to fail or refuse to see also the trace of this face that looks back at us to expose the brutal politics of her death—in simulation, in extermination, in removal—then we become accomplices in a violence against alterity that persists beyond the facts of time.

Herman Rapaport's meditation on the ethical law that can persist through the photographed face is grounded in his reading of and reflection on one of the best-known photographs taken by "National Socialist forces during the destruction of the Warsaw Ghetto." It is the photograph of a child, perhaps eight or nine, who stands "alone and vulnerable in the foreground," a distinct presence and face standing separate, both from the Nazi soldiers who level their guns at him and from the adults and children whose fate he shares in being discovered as a Jew. Rapaport's interest in this photograph lies in the fact that this particular image still speaks; it transcends the temporality of its given moment of occurrence, as well as its translation into the timelessness of photographic representation. This photograph, whose meaning is brought home through the "arrested" face of this unknown child, con-

---

85. Roland Barthes, *Image, Music, Text* (New York: Hill and Wang, 1977), 44.
86. Quoted in Rapaport, *Is There Truth in Art?* 216.

tinues to resonate and serve as a "terrible indictment of those who committed crimes against humanity." As Rapaport has eloquently demonstrated, the face of this child signifies beyond his being and death: it eternally testifies against the unspeakable violence and brutality of a national and racialized injustice that the photograph will not permit us to forget or dispute.[87]

In much the same way, the portrait of Sarah Winnemucca signifies the fate of the Native Other who was "arrested" and violently silenced—and ultimately denied presence in the republic of freedom. In this context, even the performativity of the Princess pose becomes the sign of resistance rather than of betrayal or complicity. Once we understand that the "Indian Princess" is itself an invention of the politics of simulation, then Sarah Winnemucca's adoption of that pose testifies explicitly to the multiple deaths imposed and enacted against peoples indigenous to the American landscape. Rather than performing "Indianness," Winnemucca's Princess pose reveals the opposite: the intended "liquidation" of the Native Other through the cultural insistence that she become "the Indian," if indeed she is to survive at all. This is the concealed violence of simulation that Baudrillard describes as the "crossing into a space whose curvature is no longer that of the real, nor that of truth, the era of simulation is inaugurated by a liquidation of all referentials—worse: with their artificial resurrection in the system of signs" that ultimately "lends itself to all systems of equivalences, to all binary oppositions, to all combinatory algebra." The preeminence of that particular violence must be understood in this way: "It is no longer a question of imitation, nor duplication, nor even parody. It is a question of substituting the signs of the real for the real."[88]

Perhaps now we can read the photograph of Sarah Winnemucca in her performative pose as one that exceeds any notion of truthfulness that would impose an equivalence between image and being. In fact, to do so would make us accomplices who have tacitly sanctioned her death and who have "let her die alone." Can the photograph bear some trace of the ethical? In this case, yes, because the photograph of Sarah Winnemucca signs in the name of the first-person plural, in the name of an alterity that is Native, and it does so beyond her being and her death. Were Rapaport to consider this

---

87. Ibid., 196–7.

88. Jean Baudrillard, *Simulacra and Simulation*, trans. Sheila Faria Glaser (Ann Arbor: University of Michigan Press, 1994), 2.

photograph, I think he would still assert that "a photograph, such as the one we are considering, can be understood as a coming to perception of a trace that signs for alterity, not unlike a sacred name that is not 'proper.'"[89] In other words, here is the performativity of a resistance, of a presence that cannot fully "be said," nor represented and seen. But in the attempt to recover the trace of the face that we know as Sarah Winnemucca, there is nonetheless the presence of an ethical law that continues to assert itself. At the very least, revealed in the resistance that inheres in the performative pose is an "act of survivance" that serves to announce the "otherwise than being"— the existent whose being signifies for an alterity *otherwise* than the oppositional logic of identity that makes of the Native Other an "Indian" and the African a "slave." In Douglass and Winnemucca, we encounter a performative resistance that transcends the self to sign for all the Others who stand beside and behind them. We are returned to the consciousness of the injustices that are historical and existent. Insofar as even the trace of the face can sign for alterity, then the efficacy of its summons remains intact: "You shall not kill" in the pursuit of your own happiness or freedom.

The performativity, the indisputable "Native eloquence" of Douglass and Winnemucca, is genuinely disruptive, for they are each "fugitive poseurs," whose use of the theatrical dimension initiates a dialogue that commands their audiences towards responsibility and response. Douglass's innumerable orations in America and Europe serve to bring the mysterious and unknown face of American-born persons of African descent—those unwillingly condemned to enslavement—into the public consciousness. His performative eloquence, his magnitude in person, dramatizes the unjust persecution—the "useless suffering," as Levinas has named it—of the Other, whose integrity in being has been violated through his categorization as slave. At the heart of Douglass's oratorical legacy is the undeniable presence of the Other human, and the effect of his speaking constitutes an act of resistance and transcendence. For to be slave is to be an object, a "brute" capable of labor or "sleep" (as Jefferson determined), an Other living entity incapable of critique and argument. Yet when Frederick Douglass seizes the stage, his oratorical performances capture the minds and hearts of his listeners: indeed, his appearances fuel the transnational momentum towards abolition, and his face comes to signify the blatant injustices of a newly democratic state that

---

89. Rapaport, *Is There Truth in Art?* 209.

sanctions slavery. In the name of the slave, Douglass forever transformed the identity of the Other of African blood. Through the dialectic of theater, he challenges the prevailing assumptions of an uninformed, generally unknowing populace to assert the humanity of the Other person. In so doing, he becomes the Levinasian "absolute Other qua other," whose difference must not merit his willful persecution and murder.

In the case of Sarah Winnemucca, the dynamics of theater again become critically important. If, as Vizenor has suggested, the "*indian* is an imprinted picture, the pose of a continental fugitive" (*FP*, 145), then Winnemucca's performative presence both reinforces and disrupts her place in the historical narrative of "*indian* simulation." In the context of the photographic image, Sarah Winnemucca as the Princess of the Northern Piutes is indeed an image "poselocked in portraiture" and "poselocked in silence," but her pose, her decision to adopt such an image, is "not 'totally passive'" (*FP*, 147). As Vizenor later argues, photographs are "specious representations of the other, the treacheries of racialism. Pictures are possessory, neither cultural evidence nor the shadows of lost traditions" (*FP*, 154). The photograph of the Native face, albeit a simulation, is nevertheless potentially disruptive precisely because of the "special status" that the photographic image wields in our culture. When we look at the Winnemucca Princess portraits, we forget that the photograph is a "message without a code," that its real efficacy resides in its resistance to the very nature of photographic representation, one in which the real presence of the Native Other has already been eclipsed. "The fugitives of manifest manners learned how to pose in silence," Vizenor writes, but their doing so was implicitly an "act of survivance":

> The pictures of *indians* as the other, the wounded fugitives of the camera, are not the same as those nostalgic photographs of homesteaders and their families in a new constitutional democracy. The manifest camera created interimage fragments of fugitive poses that separated natives from their communities and ancestral land: the simulations of the other as *indian* turned the real into the unreal with no obvious presence in time or nature. . . . The *indian* in photographs should be seen in the shadows of the eyes and hands, an honorable invitation to underived narratives rather than public representations and closure. (*FP*, 157–8)

Vizenor's insights into the photographic representation of the Native face enable us to encounter the Winnemucca portraits as otherwise than images of Indian concession or racial betrayal. They are instead documented "acts of survivance." While the poses and costumes enact a specifically nostalgic dramatization of the transition between savagism and civilization that turned the Other human into "mere objects that bear material culture in photographs," it is in the eyes and hands that the Native presence perseveres. Had Sarah Winnemucca not posed for those portraits, her face would have disappeared in the cultural narrative of tragic victimry. Instead, it is through the photographic trace that the face of Sarah Winnemucca speaks beyond her death, beyond the politics of simulation. Indeed, it is the photograph that reveals the American drama of dominance that would distort the Native presence into the simulated representation of the "*indian*" as a cultural artifact. But the Winnemucca portraits testify to her presence. If, as Vizenor suggests, we "watch the eyes and hands in fugitive poses" like this one, we can still "hear the apophatic narratives of a continuous presence" (FP, 165).

5 IN THE PRESENCE OF THE GREAT AMERICAN CRIMINAL
John Brown's Triumphant Failure at Harpers Ferry

"I never thought that I should ever join in doing honor to or mourning any *American* white man," Charles H. Langston declared to a Cleveland audience in December 1859 when the state of Virginia brought to the gallows its most notorious criminal. There is little doubt that Langston spoke for many others of African descent—those like himself, whose "black face and curly hair doom me in this land of equality to a political damnation . . . beyond the possibility of redemption."[1] Earlier that year, Langston had served twenty days' imprisonment for his part in the conspiratorial effort to free fugitive slave John Price. A mere six months or so later, Langston would be among the first in the African American community to proclaim the revolutionary significance of Harpers Ferry and to assess the cultural significance of John Brown's actions.

My decision to cast John Brown in the "figure of the 'great criminal'" echoes the language of Jacques Derrida, who theorizes in "Force of Law: The 'Mystical Foundation of Authority'" about how a certain kind of violence can challenge and threaten the order of justice itself. John Brown seized the right radically to contest the order of law, attacking what Derrida calls the "legitimate authority of the state that summons" its citizens to obedience. With Derrida's help, we can begin to understand the critical significance of Brown's act by examining the implications of the figure of the "great criminal." Derrida explains that the "admiring fascination exerted on the people by the figure of the 'great criminal' . . . can be explained as follows: it is not someone who has committed this or that crime for which one feels a secret

---

1. Quoted in Benjamin Quarles, ed., *Blacks on John Brown* (Urbana: University of Illinois Press, 1972), 14.

admiration; it is someone who, in defying the law, lays bare the violence of the legal system [and] the juridical order itself."[2] This is precisely what John Brown did by defying the law at Harpers Ferry and then by verbally laying bare his country's violence at his trial. Derrida's insight into how this particular kind of criminality exposes systemwide violence and injustice moves us towards an understanding of the complex ethics involved in Brown's acts. Derrida's ideas will eventually lead us back to Levinas's striking insights about the relationship between violence and ethics. Together, these philosophers teach us how in 1859 John Brown forced the nation—and continues to force it—to confront one of the key questions of ethical philosophy: when is violence ethical?

From the moment the news of the attack on the Federal arsenal at Harpers Ferry reached the public, as Langston's comments indicate, John Brown's act became a highly contested interpretive site. The great criminal's revolutionary actions made him either a madman or a hero. Some, like Ralph Waldo Emerson and Julia Ward Howe, saw him as both. Regardless of the conflicting perceptions and assessments of Brown's Harpers Ferry strike, there is little question that he instigated one of the genuinely disruptive moments in nineteenth-century American history. Activists like Langston argued that Brown had acted in concert with the very principles of American democracy: "The renowned fathers of our celebrated revolution taught the world that 'resistance to tyrants is obedience to God,'" and Brown, in the spirit of those fathers, had acted on the founding principle that "when any government becomes destructive of . . . life, liberty, justice and happiness, it is the right of the people to abolish it," or, at the very least, to challenge its legal authority.[3]

Throughout the South, however, Brown's strike at Harpers Ferry was deemed "'an act of war' perpetrated by 'murderers, *traitors*, robbers, insurrectionists,' and 'wanton, malicious, unprovoked felons'" (*PLB*, 320). Brown's attack created widespread fears that further insurrections would occur. "Southern towns from Jackson to Richmond alerted militia units and local defense companies, [and] declared martial law"; *DeBow's Review* proclaimed

---

2. Jacques Derrida, "Force of Law: The 'Mystical Foundation of Authority,'" trans. Mary Quaintance, in *Deconstruction and the Possibility of Justice*, ed. Drucilla Cornell, Michael Rosenfeld, and David Gray Carlson (New York: Routledge, 1992), 33.

3. Quoted in Quarles, ed., *Blacks on John Brown*, 13.

Harpers Ferry to be "'the first act in the grand tragedy of emancipation, and the subjugation of the South in bloody treason'" (*PLB*, 321, 323). Whatever else Brown achieved at Harpers Ferry, it catapulted him to the forefront of American politics and debate. Throughout the republic, Americans were riveted by his name. Whether he was a madman or "'the bravest and humanest man in all the country'" (quoted in *PLB*, 318) had yet to be determined, but one thing was absolutely clear: John Brown had indisputably become the greatest American criminal of his era. His acts would cause the American people to shudder "not only with horror, but with awe" (*PLB*, 310).

The actual facts of the attack are relatively simple, belying the extraordinary event that would be initiated during the two days when John Brown and his comrades held the arsenal at Harpers Ferry. In the name of an insurgent violence that might (so they believed) work to free the enslaved African Other, Brown and his comrades attempted an impossible mission of radical intervention, one that was doomed to fail from the beginning. Paul Finkelman reports the facts succinctly: "On October 16, 1859, John Brown and eighteen followers seized the federal arsenal at Harper's Ferry, Virginia. Brown's plans were audacious, grandiose, even fantastic: he hoped to start an insurrection that would attract slaves to his guerilla force. His raid lasted about a day and a half. On October 18, United States troops under the command of Brevet Colonel Robert E. Lee captured Brown in the engine house on the armory grounds. By this time most of the raiders were either dead or wounded."[4]

The attack at Harpers Ferry lasted a total of thirty-six hours. In retrospect, what is most arresting about the incident was its utter failure to accomplish its ends. No slaves were freed, no coup d'état was accomplished, no slave revolt was initiated. By its end, Brown's cohorts had killed four people and wounded nine. Among his own forces, ten were dead, including two of his sons, and seven were eventually captured to stand trial. In fact, as historian David M. Potter argues, "Brown himself would have been killed if his assailant, Lieutenant Israel Green, in command of the detachment, had not been armed only with a decorative dress sword which inflicted some painful but not very serious wounds." Brown's strike at Harpers Ferry was a strategic

---

4. Paul Finkelman, "John Brown and His Raid," in *His Soul Goes Marching On: Responses to John Brown and the Harpers Ferry Raid*, ed. Paul Finkelman (Charlottesville: University Press of Virginia, 1995), 3.

failure, yet his symbolic triumph was rooted in the fact that he was not killed. As Potter writes, "John Brown never did develop the basic human capacity of making his means serve his ends, and his ultimate triumphant failure was built upon the accident of his survival to face trial after Harpers Ferry."[5]

Had Brown been killed at Harpers Ferry, the legacy of his presence (and the trace of his face) would likely not still haunt the American imagination and cultural memory. As numerous historians have repeatedly demonstrated, Brown's plan of attack at Harpers Ferry was poorly planned and ill-conceived. Potter concludes that the "most bizarre feature of all is that Brown tried to lead a slave insurrection without letting the slaves know about it. It is as clear as it is incredible that his idea of a slave insurrection was to kidnap a few slaves, thrust pikes into their hands while holding them under duress, and inform them that they were free."[6]

Yet despite the failure at Harpers Ferry, despite the "madness" of Brown's imagination and intentions, it is the event (or accident) of his survival that enables his triumphant survival in our national history, literature, and memory. As his biographer Stephen Oates reminds us, "He is still one of the most controversial figures in American history." Writing thirty years ago, Oates's words remain provocative: "One hundred and twenty-five years after Harpers Ferry, his name can still provoke rancorous debate about his motives and methods, even about his sanity. 'When the subject of John Brown comes up,' a historian said recently, 'we tend to get a little hysterical'" (*PLB*, vii).

That lingering and symbolic capacity to provoke a cultural and historically persistent "hysteria" is what interests me in the figure of John Brown. It is not merely Brown's actions per se that catalyze the American imagination, since his actions fail. Rather, it is his performative presence, his symbolic signification beyond death, that continues to haunt us. Perhaps the real significance of John Brown's irruption into the American mind lies less in the specifics of his failed expedition at Harpers Ferry and more in the problems of intelligibility and interpretation that his presence—and the enigmatic effects of his performance during his trial and up to his execution—continues to raise. In the final analysis, Potter is right: "The fact is that there was never

---

5. David M. Potter, *The Impending Crisis: 1848–1861* (New York: Harper and Row, 1976), 371, 357–8.

6. Ibid., 372.

as much uncertainty about *what* Brown proposed to do as about *how to interpret it*."⁷

One might argue that John Brown's greatest accomplishment is situated in the performative dimensions of language and theater, for it is there that Brown emerges to disrupt the national consciousness and to assert the absolute priority of the "monstrous moral contradiction" at the very heart of the republic (*PLB*, x). That contradiction is at the core of the drama that surrounds John Brown. His acts at Harpers Ferry raise the controversial issues of violence, justice, and the rights of a few individuals to wage war against the perceived tyranny of the state. As such, one can argue that he ultimately performs what Derrida calls a "strategy of rupture," one designed to contest the "given order of the law" (as well as its judicial authority) in order to open the way for the creation of a new and more just law.⁸

It is in his performance at Harpers Ferry at which John Brown, the man of many failed endeavors, finally excels. That performance spawns the enduring significance of his name, and it is there where we can find the trace of his face. During his trial, when Brown speaks to the nation, the power of speech exemplifies its disruptive efficacy: "to speak is to interrupt" the world and the temporal experience of its subjects. As Levinas argues, the "subject who speaks does not situate the world in relation to himself," nor does he "situate himself purely and simply at the heart of his own spectacle. . . . Instead he is situated in relation to the Other (*Autre*)."⁹ This is of special relevance in the case of John Brown.

I hope to recover an ethical efficacy in the legacy of John Brown, one residing in the performative stance and the transcendent quality of his words. In those words, a trace of the face of this Other named John Brown—no matter whether we call him "madman," "revolutionary," "criminal," or "prophet"—still confronts and accuses us. John Brown's words take us deep into the thicket of American injustice, and his revolutionary demand that we must better align America's laws to the ideal of justice persists beyond the events of 1859. It is ironic that his ethical legacy does not derive from his intended revolutionary revolt but rather from his legendary criminal stature.

7. Ibid., 365.

8. Derrida, "Force of Law," 33.

9. Emmanuel Levinas, "Transcendence of Words," in *The Levinas Reader* (New York: Blackwell, 1989), 149.

Only through his status as a "criminal" can he initiate the Derridian "strategy of rupture" that makes law answerable before the Other's unjust persecution.

In the immediate aftermath of Brown's capture and in response to the general panic and hysteria that characterized public perceptions of the Harpers Ferry incident, the *Baltimore American and Commercial Advertiser* announced that the "intelligence from Harper's Ferry has created an excitement in our community and throughout the whole length and breadth of the country that has scarcely been equaled by any preceding occurrence of the present century" (quoted in *PLB*, 307). In Virginia and Maryland, the virtually inconceivable audacity of his actions incited the rage and terror of the local townspeople, who were eager to undertake a vigilante retribution in the name of their notion of justice. As a result—and to prevent his death at the hands of an angry mob—Brown and his fellow captives were judiciously moved from Harpers Ferry to Charleston, where Governor Henry A. Wise chose to prosecute on the grounds that a federal trial would take far too long.

Within days of his transfer, Brown was formally charged by a grand jury "for murdering four whites and one Negro, for conspiring with slaves to rebel, and for committing treason against Virginia, even though he was not a citizen of that state and owed it no allegiance" (*PLB*, 308). John Brown's trial began on October 27, only ten days after the attack on the armory ended. When Brown was presented to the court, he was "composed and heroic, lying on a cot in full view of the crowded courtroom—and the nation beyond" (*PLB*, 309). Thus began John Brown's transformation from his designation as a "misguided, wild and apparently insane" madman into the figure of a great criminal. Brown was guilty of murder; more importantly, he was guilty of treason. He was now an identifiable enemy of the state. If at Harpers Ferry he had acted specifically against the state law of Virginia, he had by extrapolation waged war against the Union itself. Moreover, from the moment of his apprehension, he had resolutely defended his right to do so.

In Stephen Oates's account, the initial words that Brown utters in his preliminary interrogation by the government's primary representative—in this case, Virginia senator James M. Mason—seem intended to construct his crime as one authored in response to the first and greater violence of a state that would utilize its laws in the defense of slavery. Asked by Mason, "How do you justify your acts?" Brown's answer is specifically accusative: "I think, my friend, you are guilty of a great wrong against God and humanity—I say it without wishing to be offensive—and it would be perfectly right for any one to interfere with you so far as to free those you willfully and wickedly hold in bondage" (quoted in *PLB*, 304). Here, Brown alleges the criminal intentionality of the state, thus beginning to unmask the foundational violence inherent in a judicial order that sanctions and preserves the enslavement of the Other. He also asserts the right of the individual to rise against a state that is discovered to be unjust—to contest its authority of law and to question its accountability. Most interesting of all, however, is the fact that John Brown's contestatory authority is founded in his indisputable guilt and in his newfound criminal stature.

In the figure of the great American criminal, John Brown is catapulted onto the national stage, where he achieves a legitimacy of voice (and presence) categorically denied him in his prior endeavors. Suddenly, Brown's presence in captivity obliges the whole of the nation "to reconsider" and ultimately "to reinterpret the very foundations of law such as they had previously been calculated."[10] According to Bertram Wyatt-Brown, this is one of the reasons that "every generation of historians must wrestle with the meaning of this event and John Brown's relationship to the coming of the Civil War." For it was in the aftermath of Harpers Ferry—in fact, in blood, and in human sacrifice—that the "very foundations" of an American law that granted the right to enslave the African Other would be reinterpreted and revised.[11]

Virtually every historian, regardless of his final pronouncement on Brown's success or failure at Harpers Ferry, concurs in some measure with Wyatt-Brown's conclusion that the "assault at Harpers Ferry on October 16 was a dramatically symbolic act that proved to have far-reaching political and moral results."[12] At the center of that symbolic action, however, is the complicated dimension of violence. John Brown's embrace of a violent means of attack greatly problematizes and disrupts the reductionist arguments of his revisionist sympathizers, who award him an unqualified heroism—indeed, a heroism so constructed that the ends justify the means, even as they are stained by the blood of the innocent. This is the critical fracture at the heart of the Brown controversy that Frederick Douglass has to acknowledge, de-

---

10. Derrida, "Force of Law," 28.

11. Bertram Wyatt-Brown, "'A Volcano beneath a Mountain of Snow': John Brown and the Problem of Interpretation," in *His Soul Goes Marching On*, ed. Finkelman, 10.

12. Ibid.

spite his overarching desire "to pay a just debt long due" to a "brave and good old man" in his speech of vindication delivered at Harpers Ferry in May 1881, twenty-two years after Brown's attack. Douglass concedes that it "is not easy to reconcile human feeling to the shedding of blood for any purpose," because the "knife is to feeling always an offence."[13]

Douglass must go even further in his representation and critique of the raid, because the facts of Brown's violence are not negotiable. Douglass thus confesses that "viewed apart and alone, as a transaction separate and distinct from its antecedents and bearings, [the raid on Harpers Ferry] takes rank with the most cold-blooded and atrocious wrongs ever perpetrated."[14] His own implication in the raid further complicated his remarks. Brown had informed Douglass of his plans to attack the arsenal as early as February 1859. Douglass had chosen not to participate in the raid and had warned Brown of its almost certain failure. But in 1881, despite his earlier embrace of a nonviolent abolitionism, Douglass defends Brown's resort to violence in the aftermath of the raid, ultimately contextualizing that violence within the framework of an already existent state of war.

Douglass asserts that the violent eruption at Harpers Ferry did not take place in a vacuum; it was not a "transaction separate and distinct from its antecedents." In order to begin to interpret the symbolic and ethical meaning of John Brown's violent actions, Douglass argues, we must concede that "this raid on Harper's Ferry, no more than Sherman's march to the sea can consent to be thus viewed alone." Once again Douglass's critical acumen is evident, for Brown's violence demands an accounting and an evaluative interpretation. Yet any attempt to do so necessarily engages the complicated—and often conflicting—arenas of violence, law, and the ethical ideal of justice. It is significant that Douglass frames Brown's violence in the context of warfare. In his comparison of Brown's act to Sherman's devastating march towards Atlanta, Douglass situates the eruption at Harpers Ferry in the domain where violence can be legitimized through the declaration of war, so that, as Derrida argues, its "future anterior already justifies" its assault against the order of law and the rule of government. In Douglass's reading, Harpers Ferry must be understood in terms of the totality of a historical assault against the freedom of the Other who is of African blood. "To the

13. Douglass, *Douglass Papers*, 5:10.
14. Ibid.

outward eye of men, John Brown was a criminal," Douglass grants. But he also insists that the "bloody harvest of Harper's Ferry was ripened by the heat and moisture of merciless bondage of more than two hundred years. That startling cry of alarm on the banks of the Potomac was but the answering back of the avenging angel to the midnight invasions of Christian slavetraders on the sleeping hamlets of Africa."[15]

In other words, Douglass does not annul John Brown's guilt. Rather, he repudiates the seeming singularity and peculiarity of Brown's violence, as if it were an act of violence outside history or an act that was irrational and aberrant in the context of a society otherwise characterized by peace. Even as he admits that Brown made "war upon the peaceful people of Harper's Ferry," Douglass nevertheless insists that his audience remember that a "slave-holding community could not be peaceable, but was, in the nature of the case, in one incessant state of war." For John Brown, Douglass asserts, the legal existence of slavery was a "state of war," one in which the "slaves were unwilling parties and consequently they had a right to anything necessary to their peace and freedom."[16] Douglass positions Brown's act as one that did not initiate violence but rather responded to violence. In the optics that Douglass employs here, it is a violence necessarily conditioned by an already existent state of war physically waged against the African body, a war philosophically determined to ambush the native freedom of the African as Other.

One of the problems with Douglass's schema, however, is that John Brown was not himself a slave, and therefore he was not one of those "unwilling parties" tyrannized by the violence of enslavement, whose right to freedom could justify his resort to violence. This is one of the bizarre ironies that surrounds his insurrectionary intentions. As David Potter has suggested, Brown "tried to lead a slave insurrection without letting the slaves know about it," as if he actually expected them "to place their necks in a noose without asking for further particulars." Potter concurs with the initial judgment of Abraham Lincoln that Harpers Ferry was "'an attempt by white men to get up a revolt among slaves, in which the slaves refused to participate.'"[17]

But Douglass's, Lincoln's, and Potter's readings each return us to the

15. Ibid, 5:10, 11.
16. Ibid., 5:29.
17. Potter, *Impending Crisis*, 372.

problem and politics of interpretation at the center of the John Brown debate. It is no surprise—or accident—that Douglass and Lincoln radically differed in their evaluations of Harpers Ferry and John Brown. The interests of interpretation always involve the hidden logics of identity in which person and perspective are invested. Utilizing the language of Derrida, one might argue that the "order of intelligibility depends in its turn on the established order that it serves to interpret." As Derrida subsequently insists, this "readability will then be as little neutral as it is non-violent."[18] Thus is it possible that this singular and unique human being known as John Brown could be seen as a "prophet" in a DuBoisian critique and a "superior man" in Thoreau's eloquent eulogies, yet simultaneously be reviled in the vision of numerous historical critics as a madman, a devil, and a deluded and depressed psychotic, whose insanity was not merely figurative but hereditary.[19]

If Potter is right that the critical issue at stake in rethinking the legacy of John Brown is mired in the difficulty of interpretation, then Derrida's insistence that "readability" and the activity of assigning "intelligibility" are never neutral or philosophically nonviolent bears critically on our understanding of the intellectual and symbolic orders (as dimensions in which meaning is constructed) through which interpretation is generated. As such, perhaps every reading, every assertion of intelligibility, hides within itself a propensity for violation. Thus there is always a danger in casting an interpretive analysis in the guise of an objective discourse, which is often represented as truth and categorical knowledge.

This is certainly what Levinas indicates when he says that the claim to objectivity "is not a residue of finality." Instead, it is an assertion, one operative as a linguistic-symbolic value, whose meaning is "posited in a discourse, in a conversation [*entre-tien*] which proposes the world." Levinas adds that this "proposition is held between [*se tient entre*] two points which do not constitute a system, a cosmos, a totality" (*TI*, 96). And, as we have discovered in earlier chapters, the discourse that objectively "proposes the world" is already the language of power, in which the privilege of translation subsumes the alterity of the Other under the "rule of the same."

18. Derrida, "Force of Law," 36.
19. Henry David Thoreau, "A Plea for Captain John Brown," in *Collected Essays and Poems*, ed. Elizabeth Hall Witherell (New York: Literary Classics of the United States, 2001); W. E. B. DuBois, *John Brown* (New York: International Publishers, 1996).

One might argue, however, that one of the lingering aspects of John Brown's troubling legacy is its stubborn resistance to the discourses of objectivity. It may be this very resistance to conclusionary discourses that provokes the cultural hysteria that continues to surround Brown. This is one of the ways in which I will read the figure of John Brown. Eschewing the ruse of objectivity, I will delineate the disruptive content that lingers in the name "John Brown." In doing so, I will attempt to recover a trace of the face that signifies still—beyond death, and in excess of the competing narratives that have come to name his place in the national memory. I want to read John Brown as an enigma—as a challenge to the very terms through which ethical philosophy is articulated.

It is ethically conceivable that John Brown might be the Other—"this particular and *opposing* freedom"—who comes from the Levinasian "hitherside" of an existent and prescriptive justice that is itself foundationally unjust. It may be possible to regard John Brown's violence against the law of the republic as an eruption, an "ethical cry of revolt" that is participant in the higher summons that justice demands. When Levinas argues that "justice summons me to go beyond the straight line of justice," he admits the incalculable necessity of the particular individual, as a given I, whose being and presence is "necessary for justice" and who finds himself "responsible beyond every limit fixed by an objective law" (*TI*, 245). Such may be the enigmatic presence (and trace of the face) of John Brown. For if justice "does not result from the normal play of injustice," but must come "from outside, 'through the door,' [and] above the fray," then the realization of injustice depends upon that "someone" whose determination to "ask for an accounting" signifies as a symbolic presence—as the Other who "appears as a principle exterior to history" (*EN*, 30). As that "someone" who comes from outside the law to demand its accountability, John Brown becomes a great American criminal. In a democratic landscape where slavery is sanctioned by law, it is primarily through breaking that law that the "great criminal" unmasks the hidden disparity between the politics of law and the ethical imperative for justice. Whatever else one might say, John Brown surely counts as an Other standing "outside the safe conformities of conventional life," and one whose coming and *having-been-there* recalls to us the trace of a face as guilty and accused as it is enduringly accusative.[20]

---

20. Wyatt-Brown, "'Volcano,'" 17.

On November 2, 1859, John Brown was convicted and sentenced to execution by the state of Virginia. Just before his sentencing, he was permitted to address the court. According to Oates's account, "Brown drew himself up for a final burst of eloquence and delivered a five-minute discourse that was to awe an entire generation." He said:

> I see a book kissed which I suppose to be the Bible, or at least the New Testament, which teaches me that all things whatsoever I would that men should do to me, I should do to them. It teaches me further to remember them that are in bonds, as bound with them. I endeavored to act up to that instruction. I say I am yet too young to understand that God is any respecter of persons. I believe that to have interfered as I have done in behalf of His despised poor, is no wrong, but right. Now, if it is deemed necessary that I should forfeit my life for the furtherance of the ends of justice, and mingle my blood with the blood of millions in this slave country whose rights are disregarded by wicked, cruel, and unjust enactments, I say let it be done. (quoted in PLB, 327)

This is the culminating moment in John Brown's linguistic performance, and it testifies to his singular accomplishment as the "great criminal" before whom "the people" are moved to "shudder" in "admiration and awe," as Derrida has said. John Brown's eloquence in speech returns us to the ethical efficacy that resides in the dimension of voice and word, where speech disrupts the ontic certitude of vision to reveal the Other in his indisputable and exquisite exteriority. This is what Levinas confirms when he argues that "speech refuses vision, because the speaker does not deliver images of himself only, but is personally present in his speech, absolutely exterior to every image he would leave" (TI, 296). John Brown most fully achieves an ethically disruptive stance through language. Ralph Waldo Emerson would later celebrate the words Brown spoke in that Virginia courtroom as every bit as riveting and compelling as those delivered by Lincoln in his Gettysburg Address (PLB, 327).

In those extraordinary words, John Brown begins to exceed his representation in the competing narratives of cultural discourse. Not only in the significance of the words he chooses to speak, but in the act of saying them, the face of John Brown suddenly emerges as a presence irreducible to the "meaning the hearer would like to retain of it as a result acquired outside of the very relationship of discourse, as though this presence in speech were reducible to the *Sinngebung* of him who listens" (*TI*, 296). In speech and in word, John Brown becomes that signifying presence "whose format exceeds the measure of the I" (as those who would see him as criminal and insane), but whose difference "is not reabsorbed into my vision" (*TI*, 296). Here again is the irony that permeates the historical significance of John Brown: for a man so committed to action (and to acting), his relatively few words become his greatest weapon. They instigate an "ethical cry of revolt" that asserts the occasional necessity of force in the war for justice.

In this critical event of speech, John Brown contends "that to have interfered as I have done in behalf of His despised poor, is no wrong, but right." Not only does Brown claim the right of the citizen to strike against the state that is revealed as unjust, but he does so in the name of a higher law of justice that requires the intervention of the individual (and of force) to accomplish its command. In essence, Brown makes the distinction between differing orders of violence. His actions at Harpers Ferry might be understood as a "legitimate violence" whose real intelligibility "only the yet-to-come (*avenir*)" of a future republic and a new law can reveal.[21]

Derrida makes this same distinction when he argues that "all revolutionary discourses . . . justify the recourse to violence by alleging the founding, in progress or to come, of a new law. As this law to come will in return legitimate, retrospectively, the violence that may offend the sense of justice, its future anterior already justifies it." In the moment when he is declared guilty of murder and treasonous conspiracy, John Brown dares to suggest that the real meaning of his resort to violence at Harpers Ferry will find justification in the time beyond 1859, when the laws against slavery will supersede (and erase) the laws that presently legalize its existence. What constitutes a "revolutionary" situation for Derrida is precisely the kind of strike that John Brown enacts: he "exercises the conceded right to contest the order of existing law" in order to provoke a "revolutionary situation in which the task will be to found a new *droit*," or law.[22] Thus it is possible to see Brown's action as an initiating force, intended towards a foundational revision, where the invention of a new law brings the possibility of justice nearer to realization.

But in order to regard Brown's violence at Harpers Ferry in these terms, Derrida would insist that we investigate the primary relationships between

21. Derrida, "Force of Law," 36.
22. Ibid., 35.

violence and law, force and justice. To characterize John Brown's actions at Harpers Ferry as the irruption of a singular and peculiar event of violence, as Lincoln did, would be a failure to recognize the violence already at play in the inner workings of the law itself. Derrida makes a distinction "between two kinds of violence in law, in relation to law (*droit*)." The first of these is the "founding violence, the one that institutes and positions law."[23] This is the violence implicit in the law that legalizes the forced capture and enslavement of the African Other; this is the violence that has been in operation from the first moment in which the republic legally founded the European-American's "right" to brutalize and enslave (if not murder) the Other of African blood.

The second "violence in law" is the necessary violence, waged on the part of the state, "that conserves, the one that maintains, confirms, insures the permanence and enforceability of law."[24] Here we need only recall the institution of the 1852 Fugitive Slave Law and its specific order of violence in the service of maintaining the "permanence and enforceability" of slavery. As Douglass argued in his famous "What to the Slave is the Fourth of July?" address, in order to maintain the "enforceability" of slavery, the Fugitive Slave Law mandates that the "power to hold, hunt, and sell men, women and children as slaves remains no longer a mere state institution, but is now an institution of the whole United States."[25] One of Douglass's critical points is that the Fugitive Slave Law does not found the violence of slavery; it maintains and protects a violence already in effect through a prior institution of law, in which the right to enslave has been secured. The peculiarity of Brown's violence at Harpers Ferry is thus not that it is a violence waged in the absence of violence, but that it is a violence aimed against the violence of the law (and hence the authority of the state). It is an individualized violence, which the state must necessarily condemn. As Derrida argues, "Law has an 'interest in a monopoly of violence,'" and that interest "doesn't strive to protect any given just and legal ends . . . but law itself."[26]

Derrida's critique of the violence in law, the violence necessary to the maintenance of law, makes a clear distinction between law and justice. As

23. Ibid., 31.
24. Ibid.
25. Douglass, *Douglass Papers*, 2:375.
26. Derrida, "Force of Law," 33.

he writes, "Laws are not just *as* laws. One obeys them not because they are just but because they have authority." When John Brown attacks Harpers Ferry, his actions—indeed, his violence—pinpoint and reveal the existent violence that inheres in the law that authorizes slavery. In other words, Brown's violence is specifically disruptive, for it "interrupts the established *droit* to found" the possibility of a new law. In that respect, Harpers Ferry becomes a "revolutionary moment" that is itself "an instance of non-law." What Harpers Ferry accomplishes is a moment of suspense, of critical disruption, where the very foundation of the law is broken and thus "remains suspended in the void or over the abyss, suspended by a pure performative act that would not have to answer to or before anyone."[27]

This is Brown's very defense. "To have interfered as I have done," he argues, "is no wrong, but right." He places himself outside of the structure and order of law, where he is not answerable to or before the law as law itself, but to God and the "furtherance of the ends of justice." The state of Virginia may find him guilty of murder and treason, but Brown positions himself in terms of a justice, and thus the founding of a new law, that is yet-to-come—and whose arrival his actions will help to initiate. This is the core of the argument that Frederick Douglass makes in Brown's defense twenty years later. "Did John Brown fail?" Douglass inquires. His answer is formulated in terms of the newly founded law that enables the arrival of a greater state of justice, precipitated by John Brown's violence. To that troubling and pertinent question that plagues the American mind and memory, Douglass says, "Did John Brown fail? Ask Henry A. Wise in whose house less than two years after, a school for the emancipated slaves was taught. Did John Brown fail? Ask James M. Mason, the author of the inhuman slave bill, who was cooped up in Fort Warren, as a traitor less than two years from the time that he stood over the prostrate body of John Brown."[28]

Here, Douglass recovers an ethical component of John Brown's criminal presence and his moment of revolutionary violence: just two years later, the assault on Harpers Ferry would prove itself as a "pure performative act" whose real meaning could finally become intelligible through the arrival of a future-present, one inaugurated in the violence that John Brown waged against the authoritative injustice of the previous law. "If John Brown did not

---

27. Ibid., 12, 36.
28. Douglass, *Douglass Papers*, 5:35.

end the war that ended slavery," Douglass can now, in that future-present of 1881, confirm without doubt, "he did at least begin the war that ended slavery." As Douglass ultimately concludes, John Brown's attack at Harpers Ferry subsequently exceeds its cultural representation as a "misguided" and "peculiar" violence, fostered in the mind of a madman. Seen through the intelligibility that "only the yet-to-come" can produce—a "yet-to-come" that by 1881 has been violently instituted by a Civil War and its new law of emancipation—Douglass can reread the events at Harpers Ferry and retrospectively declare that John Brown "began the war that ended American slavery and made this a free Republic."[29]

If we apply Derrida's analysis of the relationship between a given irruption of violence and the "yet-to-come" of a new law that founds a closer approximation of justice, then we can argue that John Brown's failure at Harpers Ferry succeeds as a revolutionary event. As Derrida argues, a violence that is successfully revolutionary "will produce *après coup* what it was destined in advance to produce, namely, proper interpretative models." And these new models in interpretation—as acts of "reading" previously denied articulation or legitimacy—are able "to give sense, necessity, and above all legitimacy to the violence" that has retrospectively called into being a "new model" and paradigm, through which the ethical signification of this earlier and past violence must be reimagined and revised.[30] Perhaps this is the legacy of John Brown that Bertram Wyatt-Brown honors when he says that "as beneficiaries of that war against slavery, Americans of every race must honor Brown for his immense contribution to the eventual outcome."[31]

"Now, if it is deemed necessary that I should forfeit my life for the furtherance of the ends of justice, and mingle my blood with the blood of millions in this slave country whose rights are disregarded by wicked, cruel, and unjust enactments, I say let it be done" (quoted in *PLB*, 327). Such are John Brown's last words before the court that sentenced him to death. In Brown's testimony, the violence of Harpers Ferry is executed in the service of a justice whose "furtherance" will conceivably demand the "blood of millions." Here Brown raises the critical question for any interpretation that seeks to recover

29. Ibid.
30. Derrida, "Force of Law," 36.
31. Wyatt-Brown, "'Volcano,'" 11.

the presence of the ethical in his legacy: whether, and under what conditions, violence can be ethically justifiable. More specifically, what is the relationship between ethics, violence, and justice?

As we have seen, at the very essence of Levinasian ethics is the commandment of the face—the primordial "No!" that is the first word of ethical resistance: "you shall not commit murder." This is the resistance of the face, its "primordial expression"; it is this fundamental (and prior) resistance to which Levinas refers when he says that the "epiphany of the face is ethical" (*TI*, 199). Levinas argues that the ethical relationship is one founded in a nonviolence that "maintains the plurality of the same and the other," a nonviolence that is (also) "peace" (*TI*, 203). If one were to follow the Levinasian edict to its logical end, then any act that results in the Other's death would be ethically indefensible, for every face (regardless of its specific presentation in a given historical moment) issues the command that prohibits its particular murder.

That John Brown kills at Harpers Ferry is indisputable and true. Indeed, further complicating the issue of violence at Harpers Ferry is Brown's direct responsibility for the deaths of those who accompany him, those who, like Shields Greene, would resolve "to go [down] wid the ole man."[32] Harpers Ferry exacted seventeen lives: each a unique and irreplaceable Other whose death can neither be forgotten nor expunged. Still more condemnatory is the fact that John Brown is twice guilty; Harpers Ferry is not the first time that he kills in the name of justice. Three years earlier, in May 1856, Brown orchestrated a late-night attack on the homes of five proslavery activists at Pottawatomie Creek, Kansas. The five victims of Brown's raid were reportedly dragged from their cabins and hacked to death with broadswords. At the residence of James P. Doyle, where he and his two sons were murdered, Brown, "who must have watched the executions in a kind of trance," walked over "and shot Doyle in the forehead with a revolver, to make certain work of it. The first blood in the slavery struggle on Pottawatomie Creek had been spilled" (*PLB*, 135). In the straight line of ethics, John Brown is guilty of murder, and his hands are stained with the blood of the Other.

But the violence at Pottawatomie Creek and the violence at Harpers Ferry do not belong to the same order of violence. While the first is ethically indefensible, the latter poses a different kind of question. At Pottawatomie

32. Quoted ibid., 24.

Creek, Brown murders in the absence of justification: this is a violence executed against the face of a particular, targeted Other, whose murder is brutally enacted in order to argue the superior claim to justice of Brown's political stance. But the moment that Brown kills, the moment in which he asserts that his perception (and person) is more just than each of those particular Others he willingly murders, is the moment that constitutes his irredeemable guilt. At Pottawatomie, John Brown is guilty of a violence executed in the fanaticism of the vigilante, and this is a violence not only devoid of the command for justice, but one in which the command for justice has been viciously and irreparably betrayed. As Derrida has argued, the moment that any given individual announces the right to "say 'this is just'" and, worse, that "'I am just,'" he cannot do so "without immediately betraying justice, if not law (*droit*)."[33]

But it is not necessarily true that Brown's guilt at Pottawatomie deconstructs the meaning of his violence at Harpers Ferry. Had he only committed the Pottawatomie murders, he would be no more than a footnote in the narrative of abolitionist extremism, a man whose name and face we would neither remember nor desire to interrogate. As Derrida's critique should help to make clear, what happens at Harpers Ferry engages an order of violence that is foundational—one waged against the law of the state and not the face of the other person. As an irruptive event in the line of American history, Harpers Ferry generates an opening, an aporia, through which a truer possibility of justice is ushered into being, into possibility. Returning to the words of Derrida, we can argue that the violence of Harpers Ferry is a "legitimate violence," one that is ethically defensible.

In his later writings, Levinas agrees that "there is an element of violence in the state" and that this violence "can involve justice." But, as he writes, "That does not mean violence must not be avoided as much as possible; everything that replaces it in the life between states, everything that can be left to negotiation, to speech, is absolutely essential" (*EN*, 106). Levinas's qualification situates violence as a last resort, defensible only when negotiation and speech have failed. In other words, the resort to violence must not replace the efficacy of speech; when it does so, it violates the command of ethics. This is the violation that illegitimatizes John Brown's Pottawatomie Creek attack. In 1856, Brown usurps the possibility of speech and negotiation and

---

33. Derrida, "Force of Law," 10.

replaces it with the finality of the sword. More insidious yet is that, at Pottawatomie, John Brown refuses the ethical responsibility he has to those with whom he would disagree: he constructs justice as if it were a contest between two opposing wills. And even if that were the case, then Brown, ethically speaking, is responsible for his neighbors and their right to a defense. On this point, Levinas is absolutely clear: "If there were two of us in the world, there wouldn't be any problem: it is the other who goes before me. And to a certain extent . . . I am responsible for the other even when he bothers me, even when he persecutes me" (*EN*, 106).

But Levinas is equally clear that, from the standpoint of ethics, "One cannot say that there is no legitimate violence" (*EN*, 106). However, the realm in which violence may be legitimate is not the space between only two parties; it is solely in relation to justice, which is the realm of the third party, that the violence of resistance can become justifiable. As we saw in the last chapter, Levinas constructs justice in terms of the relationship to "the third"; it involves the domain of the social, and therefore necessarily the domain of the state, where law and politics prevail. "It is the third party who is the source of justice, and thereby of justified repression," Levinas contends. We must understand "legitimate violence" as a violence of intervention, because it is only the "violence suffered by the third party that justifies stopping the violence of the other with violence" (*OG*, 83).

At Harpers Ferry, John Brown utilizes force in the service of an interventionary strike against the indisputable injustice of the state. Importantly, the injustice against which Brown elects to strike is already a violence aimed against a third party; the command of that which is "just" here demands the recourse to force. This is because the "concept or the idea of the just, in the sense of justice, implies analytically and a priori that the just be '*suivi*,' followed up, enforced, and it is just—also in the sense of 'just right' to think this way." Derrida explicitly asserts that "justice demands, as justice, recourse to force. The necessity of force is implied, then, in the '*juste*' in 'justice.'"[34] In this respect, the annihilating violence and the suffering of slavery which subsume the Other of African blood justifies the interventionary violence of force at Harpers Ferry to disrupt (and eventually to stop) the state's violence against "the third," who is here the African-made-slave.

Were we to reinvent the question Douglass places before the American

---

34. Ibid., 10, 11.

mind in 1881, we must ask not whether John Brown failed at Harpers Ferry, but whether his recourse to violence was a legitimate violence. In 1852, Douglass demanded of the American people whether he must argue the humanity of the African or the wrongness of slavery itself. His answer was exquisitely simple: "Every man beneath the canopy of Heaven knows that slavery is wrong *for him*."[35] We know that slavery legitimized and legislated the persecution of the African, sanctioning her capture, torture, and her useless suffering and murder. Insofar as John Brown acts at Harpers Ferry in the name and in defense of the millions of persecuted African Others who constitute "the third party," then he does so in the service of justice and from a responsibility that is ethical. As Levinas charges, "One cannot allow that third parties be persecuted!" (*OG*, 84).

One cannot assume the challenge of rereading the legacy of John Brown without wrestling with the question of Brown's "madness" and the accumulated historical evidence of an insanity that one may deem hereditary, private, or some combination of both. In the more recent literature, historian Robert E. McGlone examines the "politics of insanity" that surround the figure of John Brown and assures us that there is ample evidence to support an argument for Brown's instability of mind (and person). Was John Brown crazy? It depends on who you ask.[36]

I will not argue for John Brown's sanity. In fact, I will concede the presence of a certain madness that informs Brown's decision to strike against the state at Harpers Ferry. For an individual to believe that the power of his own force (along with that of a small band of comrades) could disrupt the law of the republic and interrupt the perpetuation of slavery is, in terms of the logic of reason, "mad." Even at his trial, Brown was forced to confess that there were "admitted instances of insanity on his mother's side," and that two of his sons had exhibited similarly disturbing symptoms and/or behavior (*PLB*, 324).

But when Brown's defense counsel, Lawson Botts, raised the issue of Brown's insanity—in an obvious effort to prevent his certain execution—Brown adamantly rejected it. Had he chosen to save his life under the legally

---

35. Douglass, *Douglass Papers*, 2:370.

36. Robert E. McGlone, "John Brown, Henry Wise, and the Politics of Insanity," in *His Soul Goes Marching On*, ed. Finkelman, 213–52.

permitted pretext of a plea of insanity, he would be (at least partially) released from the call of responsibility and relieved of the burden of his guilt. Perhaps this is what John Brown seemingly already understood: that his guilt would lend justification to his actions at Harpers Ferry and would grant meaning to the deaths of those whose lives had been sacrificed. In other words, it is not that John Brown is more just than all the others, but that he is more guilty.

"'We are all guilty for everything and everyone, and I more than all the others.'" This is the famous sentence in Dostoevsky's *Brothers Karamazov* to which Levinas returns again and again (*EN*, 105). Its centrality in Levinas's later thinking concerns both the problem of evil and the "exceptional situation of the I," which Levinas has named the "asymmetry of intersubjectivity." Levinas contends that "to speak of justice" necessarily introduces the "idea of the struggle with evil," and that justice will demand that "I separate myself from the idea of nonresistance to evil." If, in order to create justice, it is "necessary to allow judges, [and] it is necessary to allow institutions and the state" (*EN*, 105), then the command of justice must also be a summons upon the individual. When the state is "evil," when the state emerges as the "executioner" whose institutional violence persecutes "the third party," then justice demands my intervention and "all the resources of a singular presence" (*TI*, 245).

This is the "exceptional situation of the I," because it is the command of justice that "indicts my arbitrary and partial freedom," that summons me "to go beyond the straight line of justice" as well as the "straight line of the law." This is Levinas's point when he unequivocally answers that "I am therefore necessary for justice" and that I am "responsible beyond every limit fixed by an objective law" (*TI*, 245). The "exceptional situation of the I" reveals itself, in the optics that is ethics, as the weight of a responsibility that the I has not chosen, but that nevertheless calls and commands this given and particular I to an awakening in which the I—as the irreplaceable subject—both hears and answers the Other's cry, and does not permit her to suffer and die alone: "The proximity of the neighbor is my responsibility for him: to approach is to be the guardian of one's brother; to be the guardian of one's brother is to be his hostage. This is immediacy. Responsibility does not come from fraternity, it is fraternity that gives responsibility for the other its name, prior to my freedom" (*OG*, 72).

Both his supporters and his critics have clearly recognized John Brown's sense of fraternity with the enslaved African Other. At the time of his trial, even many of those resolutely opposed to Brown's methods came to agree with the *New York Tribune*, which suggested that John Brown and his comrades "'dared and died for what they felt to be right, though in a manner which seems to us fatally wrong'" (quoted in *PLB*, 311). Despite the outrage towards Brown's actions at Harpers Ferry, it was difficult to ignore, as Salmon P. Chase put it, Brown's "'unselfish desire to set free the oppressed— the bravery—the humanity towards his prisoners which defeated his purposes!'" (quoted in *PLB*, 311). John Brown once said of his mission in the war against slavery that "I do not harbour the feelings of revenge. *I act from a principle. My aim and object is to restore human rights*" (quoted in *PLB*, 257). If we grant Brown's words credence, then it is possible to argue that one of the principles that informed his attack at Harpers Ferry was this impassioned "desire to set free the oppressed" and to act on a responsibility to (and for) "the third party," whose restoration of human rights demanded "all the resources of a singular presence," of an I called to be answerable for the unjust persecution of his African "neighbor."

"Each of us is guilty before everyone, for everyone and for everything, and I more than the others."[37] To Dostoevsky's difficult proposition, Levinas adds the dimension of an impossible "election." The ethical command through which justice approaches and shimmers on the horizon as a possibility, albeit in the "yet-to-come" of a future-present, discovers me in the very privilege of my freedom and the immediacy of my guilt. And neither the seemingly impenetrable force of the state nor the "mystical authority" of its law can absolve me of my guilt or my responsibility.

From the moment of his capture, John Brown repeatedly claimed that he had acted to fulfill the command of God. Asked whether he considered the Harpers Ferry attack a "religious movement," Brown answered that his decision to intervene on behalf of the "oppressed and wronged" was, in his view, the "greatest service man can render to God" (quoted in *PLB*, 305). He recognized that such a response would be subject to competing logics of interpretation, for he added that his decision to invade Harpers Ferry "was my own prompting and that of my Maker, or that of the Devil—whichever you please to ascribe it to. I acknowledge no master in human form" (quoted

---

37. Emmanuel Levinas, *Is It Righteous to Be? Interviews with Emmanuel Levinas*, ed. Jill Robbins (Stanford: Stanford University Press, 2001), 72.

in *PLB*, 304). In that moment, Brown anticipated the issues of interpretation that would ultimately determine his fate and significance in the narrative of nineteenth-century American history.

One of those models of interpretation ascribes Brown's sense of a religious calling—as an "instrument in the hands of Providence"—to the delusions produced by his insanity (quoted in *PLB*, 305). Yet it is also possible to read Brown's religious conviction in terms of an answering to a summons specifically ethical. The "exceptional situation of the I" that Levinas delineates is the burdensome responsibility of a subject, already "under the accusation of an other," who is called to the point of substitution, where the "I obeys a commandment before having heard it." This is the posture of the subject as hostage, commanded to be "faithful to an engagement that it never made" (*OG*, 68), or to an "engagement" that comes from the otherwise, from beyond the sphere in which individual freedom and choice reign as supreme.

To read Brown's convictions in this light is to see Brown's disruptive intervention at Harpers Ferry as a "cry of ethical revolt," an act of "bearing witness to [the] responsibility" for the Other that ultimately belongs to a "'category' different from knowledge" (*OG*, 80). This is that ethical notion of "election," and even Levinas admits that "this is a responsibility whose limits are impossible to fix, whose extreme urgency cannot be measured." This is a responsibility "astonishing in every way," because it exceeds the categories of knowledge. The responsibility that is ethical astonishes because it exceeds reason to show itself as "extending all the way to the obligation to answer for the freedom of the other, all the way to being a responsibility for his responsibility" (*OG*, 70).

"We are each guilty with respect to all, and I more so than all the others": the first guilt is the position of the subject, the I, participating in the privileges of a freedom that permits the Other's torture and execution.[38] In the republic of 1859, every free American subject stands guilty and accused. It is John Brown's "madness" that delivers him into the posture of an I willing to answer on behalf of the Other, an I willing to die in defense of that Other's native human rights.

I cannot answer for the validity or the truth of John Brown's religious conviction. Perhaps it is enough, as Oates has suggested, to grant that Brown "was a revolutionary who believed himself called by God to a special destiny

---

38. Ibid., 229.

(a notion that stemmed from his Calvinist beliefs)" (*PLB*, 333). It is clear, however, that the real significance of John Brown's presence in the war against slavery is achieved in the aftermath of Harpers Ferry: his words and his passion persistently resonate beyond the frame of a given historical moment. Numerous historians have concurred that "John Brown's significance lies less in the inadequacies of his life than in the manner of his death," and that it was in facing his death that Brown would fulfill the "role of the martyr with almost artistic perfection."[39] What is perhaps most enigmatically compelling in the legacy of John Brown is the fact that he was "guiltier" than all the rest. For if John Brown bears the guilt of his freedom (like all the rest), he also bears the guilt of a specific subject, an I, whose hands have been stained by the blood of the Other.

Levinas argues that "we are not what we are conscious of being, but are the role we play in a drama of which we are no longer the authors" (*EN*, 23). There is no question of John Brown's guilt, and yet, ironically, it is his guilt that signifies from beyond his death, that grants his death an enduring and symbolic meaning. Astonishingly, at the moment of death, as John Brown calmly and courageously mounts the scaffold, he becomes a different kind of guilty subject—one who "awaits the meaning of his being from outside" and who is suddenly transformed, so that "he is no longer the man confessing his sins, but the one acquiescing to accusations" (*EN*, 23). The crux of John Brown's role in the American drama of "liberty and justice" is to signify, through the face of the "great criminal," the potentially ethical efficacy of a subject (as this I) willing to die for the Other and unwilling to let that Other die alone. This is the peculiar insight that Brown seemed already to grasp when he reflected on the "just" event of his death: "I can trust God with both the time and the manner of my death, believing, as I now do, that for me at this time to seal my testimony for God and humanity with my blood will do vastly more towards advancing the cause I have earnestly endeavored to promote, than all I have done in my life before" (quoted in *PLB*, 336).

Both in his exemplary guilt and "in the manner of [his] death," John Brown disrupts the American discourse on freedom to dramatize the primacy of the command for justice and the "irrecusable obligation" that should weigh on the life and consciousness of the individual. In the figure of the

---

39. Charles Joyner, "'Guilty of Holiest Crime': The Passion of John Brown," in *His Soul Goes Marching On*, ed. Finkelman, 299; Wyatt-Brown, "'Volcano,'" 28.

"great criminal," he intervenes upon the American imagination as that "individual who takes upon himself, as in primitive times, the stigma of the lawmaker or prophet."[40] In that extraordinary moment in which John Brown meets his death, he stands before an American republic in the full glory of the accused. And this, in the language of Levinas, is a "marvelous accusative," for it is the posture of the subject revealed and naked in his guilt.

Here, then, is the trace of an ethical posture that emerges through the disruptive face of John Brown. In his last moments, as he looks around him and says, "This is a beautiful country" (quoted in PLB, 351), his dying dramatizes the significance of his "having-been-here." Before the gaze of the entire nation, John Brown's death signifies the urgency of the "here I am," the stance of an individual citizen willing to sacrifice his life in the name of the Other's right to liberty. John Brown's presence in dying becomes an act of saying: the "'Here I am,' said to the neighbor to whom I am given over," (OG, 75), a "Here I am" that is issued in response to the urgency that justice demands.

Recently John Brown has been getting more attention as a figure who fundamentally altered the American way of dealing with the injustice that occurs within the nation's system of law. While the country is founded on an act of violence (the Revolution) that set out to correct the injustice of what had come to seem to be foreign domination, the Constitution set out to create a rule of law that would guarantee justice without further violence. But one deep paradox of American history is that the violence of slavery was built into the Constitution and the nation's law. Abolitionists fought that violence and injustice with words; those words were often heated and occasionally encouraged violence (and there were certainly violent acts before Brown's, perpetrated against slaveowners and slavecatchers). But nothing put the issue of violence in support of ethics before the nation with the force of John Brown's raid. Perhaps the most challenging recent reading of John Brown's significance is Gregory Eiselein's exploration of what he calls Brown's "dangerous philanthropy." Eiselein writes that Brown's raid was a departure "from abolitionism-as-usual" in that it replaced incendiary talk with actual violence on behalf of the African Other. Thus "dangerous philanthropy" was born, a new kind of philanthropic act that "quickly became a significant, con-

---

40. Derrida, "Force of Law," 40.

tested, and revealing cultural symbol" and brought about a "profound change in humanitarianism."[41]

Brown's act, argues Eiselein, raised a key ethical question: "Should humanitarians countenance the use of nonhumanitarian means, like violence or war, to achieve humanitarian ends, such as the abolition of slavery?"[42] Eiselein demonstrates that the almost immediate response to Brown's actions—the "contradictory, ambivalent, uncertain appropriations of John Brown" by a wide cross-section of citizens in the North and South alike—were a sure sign of a "crisis in humanitarian thought." Brown himself had cast his action as a frustration with the abolitionist love of words: "Talking is a national institution; but it does no good for the slave." Elsewhere, speaking of antislavery leaders, he scoffed, "These men are all talk: what is needed is action—action!"[43] Eiselein demonstrates that many abolitionists, in a kind of moral panic, quickly turned Brown's violent and dangerous acts back into heated but safe words: Henry David Thoreau, John Greenleaf Whittier, Lydia Marie Child, and others wrote in praise of Brown's courage but deemphasized or even erased his violence. Slaves themselves, however, celebrated the violence of Harpers Ferry. Thus what Eiselein calls a "John Brown humanitarianism" began to undermine a long philanthropic tradition in which the rich and educated philanthropist stood in a superior position to his "helpless" objects of aid. Brown recruited and worked alongside the African Other, even depending on them to carry out his violent interruption of America's institutions. Brown's "eccentric" philanthropy, Eiselein says, "did not simply or permanently reverse the positions of the agent and patient, but instead made these positions fluid, creating a flexible and democratic helping praxis in which all philanthropic actors operate as both agents and patients."[44]

Eiselein's emphasis on how Brown broke down the old hierarchies of separation between the agent of change and the victim of injustice is an important one, because it directly relates to the Levinasian moment of "facing" the Other, of looking the Other in the face and in that moment *seeing a face*, not an object of pity. That is one of John Brown's most significant accom-

---

41. Gregory Eiselein, *Literature and Humanitarian Reform in the Civil War Era* (Bloomington: Indiana University Press, 1996), 18.
42. Ibid.
43. Quoted ibid., 23.
44. Ibid., 39–40.

plishments. But I question Eiselein's privileging of Brown's actions over words. It was not only Whittier and Child and their ilk who turned his actions back into words—it was Brown himself. His verbal performance at his trial turned his violent act from a random, strange, and futile gesture into a symbolic and charged moment in America's encounter with its own injustice. Brown's own words transformed him from a failed hero into America's greatest criminal, into the guilty American. His redefinition of his own guilt—and his embrace of that guilt—turned his violent act from a historical sidelight into a culturally significant moment. His greatest act was not leading the raid on Harpers Ferry, but rather interpreting, on the national stage of his trial, the meaning of what he had tried to do. His violent act was destined to fail, but his interpretation of that failure assured the eventual success of his attack on injustice.

In the final analysis, justice is always a "yet-to-come"; and from the perspective of ethics, the cause of justice necessitates that "human beings, who are incomparable, be compared" (EN, 104). To whom should one compare John Brown? Guilty of murder at Pottawatomie, responsible for nineteen deaths at Harpers Ferry, John Brown exists as an enigma in the American historical consciousness. He is consummately guilty: on that most can probably agree. Perhaps only in the "improbable field of ethics"[45] can John Brown emerge not as the more "just" of his fellow citizens, but as the one "guiltier than all the rest," the one whose guilt serves to remind us of the individual intervention that justice requires. Levinas argues that it is only "in terms of the relation to the Face or of me before the other that we can speak of the legitimacy or illegitimacy of the state" (EN, 105). Justice begins in the relationship to the face of the Other, in the obligation owed that Other whose persecution we cannot permit. The ethical meaning of John Brown stems from his unique willingness to stand against the state and to assert, with the full force of his person, the primacy of justice before the privilege of freedom.

---

45. This is a variation on one of the phrases that Levinas repeatedly utilizes to describe the space in which ethics prevails. It is not that ethics is logical or even natural. Ethics, Levinas repeatedly argues, transpires in the realm of obligation and election, which exceed the laws of reason (OG, 75).

Bibliography

Abensour, Miguel. "To Think Utopia Otherwise." Translated by Bettina Bergo. *Graduate Faculty Philosophy Journal* 20.2–21.1 (1998): 251–79.
Adams, John. "On the Feudal and the Canon Law." In *The Rising Glory of America, 1760–1820*. Edited by Gordon S. Wood. Boston: Northeastern University Press, 1990. 25–39.
Aldridge, A. Owen. *Thomas Paine's American Ideology*. Newark: University of Delaware Press, 1984.
Ankersmit, F. R. *Aesthetic Politics*. Stanford: Stanford University Press, 1996.
Arendt, Hannah. *The Human Condition*. Chicago: University of Chicago Press, 1958.
———. *On Revolution*. New York: Viking, 1965.
Aristotle. *The Politics*. Translated by Ernest Barker. Oxford, U.K.: Oxford University Press, 1958.
Bailyn, Bernard. *Faces of Revolution*. New York: Knopf, 1990.
Barthes, Roland. *Camera Lucida*. Translated by Richard Howard. New York: Hill and Wang, 1981.
———. *Image, Music, Text*. New York: Hill and Wang, 1977.
Baudrillard, Jean. *Simulacra and Simulation*. Translated by Sheila Faria Glaser. Ann Arbor: University of Michigan Press, 1994.
Beale, D. A. "Language, Poetry, and the Rights of Man." *Theoria* 75 (1990): 37–51.
Burke, Edmund. *A Philosophical Enquiry into the Origin of Our Ideas of the Sublime and Beautiful*. Edited by James T. Boulton. Notre Dame, Ind.: University of Notre Dame Press, 1986.
Cadava, Eduardo. *Words of Light*. Princeton, N.J.: Princeton University Press, 1997.
Canfield, Gae Whitney. *Sarah Winnemucca of the Northern Paiutes*. Norman: University of Oklahoma Press, 1983.
Cheyfitz, Eric. *The Poetics of Imperialism*. Oxford, U.K.: Oxford University Press, 1991.
Cixous, Hélène, and Catherine Clément. *Newly Born Woman*. Translated by Betsy Wing. Minneapolis: University of Minnesota Press, 1991.

Claeys, Gregory. *Thomas Paine: Social and Political Thought.* Boston: Unwin Hyman, 1989.

Commager, Henry Steele. *Jefferson, Nationalism, and the Enlightenment.* New York: Braziller, 1975.

Cornell, Drucilla. *The Philosophy of the Limit.* New York: Routledge, 1992.

Crèvecoeur, J. Hector St. John de. *Letters from an American Farmer.* New York: Dutton, 1957.

Derrida, Jacques. "Declarations of Independence." Translated by Thomas Keenan and Thomas Pepper. *New Political Science* 15 (1986): 7–15.

———. "Force of Law: The 'Mystical Foundation of Authority.'" Translated by Mary Quaintance. In *Deconstruction and the Possibility of Justice.* Edited by Drucilla Cornell, Michael Rosenfeld, and David Gray Carlson. New York: Routledge, 1992. 3–67.

———. *Memoires for Paul de Man.* Translated by Cecile Lindsay, Jonathan Culler, and Eduardo Cadava. New York: Columbia University Press, 1986.

———. "Racism's Last Word." Translated by Peggy Kamuf. *Critical Inquiry* 12 (1985): 290–9.

Dimock, Wai-chee. *Residues of Justice: Literature, Law, Philosophy.* Berkeley: University of California Press, 1996.

Douglass, Frederick. *The Frederick Douglass Papers.* Edited by John W. Blassingame. 5 vols. New Haven: Yale University Press, 1979.

———. "The Heroic Slave." In *Violence in the Black Imagination.* Edited by Ronald T. Takaki. New York: Putnam, 1972. 37–77.

———. *My Bondage and My Freedom.* New York: Dover, 1969.

———. *The Narrative of the Life of Frederick Douglass, an American Slave.* New York: Anchor, 1989.

Drinnon, Richard. *Facing West: The Metaphysics of Indian-Hating and Empire-Building.* Norman: University of Oklahoma Press, 1997.

Durfee, Harold A. "War, Politics, and Radical Pluralism." *Philosophy and Phenomenological Research* 35 (1975): 549–58.

Eaglestone, Robert. *Ethical Criticism: Reading after Levinas.* Edinburgh: Edinburgh University Press, 1997.

Edwards, Elizabeth. "Introduction." *Anthropology and Photography, 1860–1920.* Edited by Elizabeth Edwards. New Haven: Yale University Press, 1992. 3–17.

Eiselein, Gregory. *Literature and Humanitarian Reform in the Civil War Era.* Bloomington: Indiana University Press, 1996.

Engell, James. *The Creative Imagination.* Cambridge, Mass.: Harvard University Press, 1981.

Fabian, Johannes. *Time and the Other.* New York: Columbia University Press, 1983.

Fanon, Frantz. *The Wretched of the Earth.* New York: Grove, 1963.
Finkelman, Paul. "Jefferson and Slavery: Treason against the World." In *Jeffersonian Legacies.* Edited by Peter S. Onuf. Charlottesville: University Press of Virginia, 1993. 181–221.
———. "John Brown and His Raid." In *His Soul Goes Marching On: Responses to John Brown and the Harpers Ferry Raid.* Edited by Paul Finkelman. Charlottesville: University Press of Virginia, 1995. 3–9.
Fliegelman, Jay. *Declaring Independence.* Stanford: Stanford University Press, 1993.
Gates, Henry Louis, Jr. *Figures in Black: Words, Signs, and the Racial Self.* New York: Oxford University Press, 1987.
Gustafson, Thomas. *Representative Words: Politics, Literature, and the American Language.* New York: Cambridge University Press, 1992.
Hegel, Georg. *Phenomenology of Spirit.* Translated by A. V. Miller. Oxford, U.K.: Oxford University Press, 1976.
———. *The Philosophy of History.* Translated by J. Sibree. New York: Dover, 1956.
Holbo, Christine. "Imagination, Commerce, and the Politics of Associationism in Crèvecoeur's *Letters from an American Farmer*." *Early American Literature* 32 (1997): 20–65.
Honig, Bonnie. "Declarations of Independence: Arendt and Derrida on the Problem of Founding a Republic." In *Rhetorical Republic: Governing Representations in American Politics.* Edited by Frederick M. Dolan and Thomas L. Dumm. Amherst: University of Massachusetts Press, 1993. 201–25.
Hopkins, Sarah Winnemucca. *Life among the Piutes.* Reno: University of Nevada Press, 1994.
Jefferson, Thomas. *The Life and Selected Writings of Thomas Jefferson.* Edited by Adrienne Koch and William Peden. New York: Random House, 1972.
———. *Notes on the State of Virginia.* Edited by William Peden. New York: Norton, 1982.
———. *Writings.* Compiled by Merrill D. Peterson. New York: Literary Classics of the United States, 1984.
Jordan, Winthrop. *White over Black.* Chapel Hill: University of North Carolina Press, 1968.
Joyner, Charles. "'Guilty of Holiest Crime': The Passion of John Brown." In *His Soul Goes Marching On: Responses to John Brown and the Harpers Ferry Raid.* Edited by Paul Finkelman. Charlottesville: University Press of Virginia, 1995. 296–334.
Keane, John. *Tom Paine: A Political Life.* Boston: Little, Brown, 1995.
Lang, Beryl. *Act and Idea in the Nazi Genocide.* Chicago: University of Chicago Press, 1990.
Larkin, Edward. "'Could the Wolf Bleat Like the Lamb': Thomas Paine's Critique and the Early American Sphere." *Arizona Quarterly* 55 (1999): 1–37.

Levinas, Emmanuel. *Collected Philosophical Papers*. Translated by Alphonso Lingis. Dordrecht: M. Nijhoff, 1987.
———. *Entre Nous*. Translated by Michael B. Smith and Barbara Harshav. New York: Columbia University Press, 1998.
———. *Existence and Existents*. Translated by Alphonso Lingis. The Hague: M. Nijhoff, 1978.
———. *God, Death, and Time*. Translated by Bettina Bergo. Stanford: Stanford University Press, 2000.
———. *Of God Who Comes to Mind*. Translated by Bettina Bergo. Stanford: Stanford University Press, 1998.
———. *Otherwise than Being; or, Beyond Essence*. Translated by Alphonso Lingis. Boston: M. Nijhoff, 1981.
———. "The Proximity of the Other." In *Is It Righteous to Be? Interviews with Emmanuel Levinas*. Edited by Jill Robbins. Stanford: Stanford University Press, 2001. 211–8.
———. "Reality and Its Shadow." Translated by Alphonso Lingis. In *The Levinas Reader*. New York: Blackwell, 1989. 129–43.
———. "The Rights of Man and the Rights of the Other." Translated by Michael B. Smith. In *Outside the Subject*. Stanford: Stanford University Press, 1994. 116–25.
———. *Time and the Other*. Translated by Richard A. Cohen. Pittsburgh: Duquesne University Press, 1987.
———. *Totality and Infinity*. Translated by Alphonso Lingis. Pittsburgh: Duquesne University Press, 1969.
———. "Transcendence of Words." In *The Levinas Reader*. New York: Blackwell, 1989. 144–9.
Locke, John. *Second Treatise of Government*. Edited by C. B. Macpherson. Indianapolis: Hackett, 1980.
McGlone, Robert E. "John Brown, Henry Wise, and the Politics of Insanity." In *His Soul Goes Marching On: Responses to John Brown and the Harpers Ferry Raid*. Edited by Paul Finkelman. Charlottesville: University Press of Virginia, 1995. 213–52.
Momaday, N. Scott. *The Man Made of Words*. New York: St. Martin's Press, 1997.
———. *The Names*. Tucson: University of Arizona Press, 1976.
Oates, Stephen B. *To Purge This Land with Blood*. Amherst: University of Massachusetts Press, 1984.
Ong, Walter J. *The Presence of the Word*. New Haven: Yale University Press, 1967.
Paine, Thomas. *Collected Writings*. Edited by Eric Foner. New York: Library of America, 1995.
———. *The Complete Writings of Thomas Paine*. Compiled by Philip S. Foner. New York: Citadel, 1945.

Pearce, Roy Harvey. *Savagism and Civilization.* Berkeley: University of California Press, 1988.
Pelmas, Sarah. "Freedom's Performative Legacy." *Qui Parle* 7.1 (1993): 22–56.
Peperzak, Adriaan T. *Beyond: The Philosophy of Emmanuel Levinas.* Evanston, Ill.: Northwestern University Press, 1997.
———. *To the Other.* West Lafayette, Ind.: Purdue University Press, 1993.
Philbrick, Thomas. *St. John de Crèvecoeur.* New York: Twayne, 1970.
Plumstead, A. W. "Hector St. John de Crèvecoeur." In *American Literature, 1764–1789.* Edited by Everett Emerson. Madison: University of Wisconsin Press, 1977. 213–31.
Potter, David M. *The Impending Crisis: 1848–1861.* New York: Harper and Row, 1976.
Quarles, Benjamin, ed. *Blacks on John Brown.* Urbana: University of Illinois Press, 1972.
Randall, John H. *The Career of Philosophy.* Vol. 1. New York: Columbia University Press, 1962.
Rapaport, Herman. *Is There Truth in Art?* Ithaca, N.Y.: Cornell University Press, 1997.
Read, Alan. *Theatre and Everyday Life.* London: Routledge, 1993.
Rousseau, Jean-Jacques. "Discourse on the Origin and Foundation of Inequality among Mankind." In *The Social Contract and Discourse on the Origin of Inequality.* Edited by Lester G. Crocker. New York: Simon and Schuster, 1967. 149–246.
Schechner, Richard. *Performance Theory.* New York: Routledge, 1988.
Scherer, Joanna. "The Public Faces of Sarah Winnemucca." *Cultural Anthropology* 3 (1988): 178–204.
Slotkin, Richard. *Regeneration through Violence: The Mythology of the American Frontier, 1600–1860.* Middletown, Conn.: Wesleyan University Press, 1973.
Smith, Sidonie. "Performativity, Autobiographical Practice, Resistance." *a/b: Auto/Biography Studies* 10.1 (1995): 17–33.
Strauss, Leo. *Natural Right and History.* Chicago: University of Chicago Press, 1953.
Tagg, John. *The Burden of Representation.* Amherst: University of Massachusetts Press, 1988.
Thomas, Wynn. "Weather and Whitman." Lecture. Department of English. University of Iowa. February 24, 1998.
Tocqueville, Alexis de. *Democracy in America.* Translated by George Lawrence. New York: Harper, 1966.
Vizenor, Gerald. *Fugitive Poses.* Lincoln: University of Nebraska Press, 1998.
———. *Shadow Distance.* Hanover, N.H.: University Press of New England, 1994.
Wald, Priscilla. *Constituting Americans.* Durham, N.C.: Duke University Press, 1995.
Walker, Peter. *Moral Choices: Memory, Desire, and Imagination in Nineteenth-Century American Abolition.* Baton Rouge: Louisiana State University Press, 1978.

West, Cornel. *The Ethical Dimensions of Marxist Thought.* New York: Monthly Review, 1991.

Wills, Garry. *Inventing America: Jefferson's Declaration of Independence.* Garden City, N.Y.: Doubleday, 1978.

Wong, Hertha D. Sweet. "First-Person Plural: Subjectivity and Community in Native American Women's Autobiography." In *Women, Autobiography, Theory.* Edited by Sidonie Smith and Julia Watson. Madison: University of Wisconsin Press, 1998. 168–78.

Wood, Gordon S. *The Creation of the American Republic, 1776–1787.* Chapel Hill: University of North Carolina Press, 1969.

Wyatt-Brown, Bertram. "'A Volcano beneath a Mountain of Snow': John Brown and the Problem of Interpretation." In *His Soul Goes Marching On: Responses to John Brown and the Harpers Ferry Raid.* Edited by Paul Finkelman. Charlottesville: University Press of Virginia, 1995. 10–38.

Yarborough, Richard. "Race, Violence, and Manhood: The Masculine Ideal in Frederick Douglass's 'The Heroic Slave.'" In *Frederick Douglass: New Literary and Historical Essays.* Edited by Eric J. Sundquist. New York: Cambridge University Press, 1990. 166–88.

Index

Abensour, Miguel, 93
abolitionism, 15, 63–67, 95, 124–8, 130–2, 140, 142–3, 146, 148n, 157, 169, 172–6, 178, 179–80, 182–7, 189–91, 193, 195–7. *See also* Brown, John; Garrison, William Lloyd; slavery
accountability. *See* obligation, ethical
Adams, John, 21, 55–6, 96
African Americans, 1–2, 5, 7, 8, 9, 12, 15, 16, 30, 33–51, 63–4, 77–8, 87–8, 94–5, 102–5, 107, 113–5, 121, 123, 124–6, 128–48, 169–70, 172–5, 177–80, 182–7, 188, 190–1, 193, 196–7. *See also* African in the tree; Brown, John; Crèvecoeur, J. Hector St. John de; Douglass, Frederick; Jefferson, Thomas; Paine, Thomas
African in the tree (Crèvecoeur), 33–51
Aldridge, A. Owen, 60–1
alterity. *See* face of the Other
"American mind" (Jefferson), 1–2, 54, 55, 56, 95–6, 148, 149, 158, 175, 186, 190–1
Ankersmit, F. R., 83–4, 88
anschauung, 56, 63, 84, 86, 92, 108, 180, 192
anti-Semitism, 3, 8–9, 12, 167–8. *See also* Himmler, Heinrich
Arendt, Hannah, 72–3, 97, 98, 100, 116–8, 120
Aristotle, 70–2, 74, 99

"back settlers" (Crèvecoeur), 26–9, 51–2
Bailyn, Bernard, 57, 59–60, 96–7

Barthes, Roland, 167
Baudrillard, Jean, 88
Beale, D. A., 61
Being. *See* ontology
Bentham, Jeremy, 96
Botts, Lawson, 191
Brothers Karamazov, The (Dostoevsky), 192–4
Brown, John: and African American supporters, 172–3, 188, 197; death of, 172, 175, 187, 195–6; as "great criminal," 172–4, 176–8, 182–3, 193, 195–6, 198; at Harpers Ferry, 172–7, 179, 184–5, 187–8, 189, 190–2, 193–4, 198; alleged insanity of, 175, 176, 177, 181, 184, 187, 191–2, 194; trial of, 175, 177–8, 183, 191–2, 198; post-trial oratory of, 183–4, 186; religious convictions of, 183, 193–5; at Pottawatomie Creek, 188–90, 198; mentioned, 2, 16, 123
Buber, Martin, 61
Burke, Edmund, 37–42. *See also* "substitution"; sympathy

Cadava, Eduardo, 163
Camus, Albert, 3
Canfield, Gae Whitney, 149–50, 151
Certeau, Michel de, 129
Chase, Salmon P., 193
Cheyfitz, Eric, 24, 133, 143–4
Child, Lydia Marie, 197–8
Claeys, Gregory, 54

205

Commager, Henry Steele, 104
Conway, Moncure Daniel, 66
Cornell, Drucilla, 28, 32
Crèvecoeur, J. Hector St. John de: *Letters from an American Farmer*, 15, 17–53, 55–6, 98, 102, 110; life of, 17; and Native Americans, 27, 29, 30–4, 51–3, 55; and African Americans, 30, 33–51; mentioned, 2, 57. *See also* African in the tree; "back settlers"

Deane, Silas, 79, 82
Derrida, Jacques, 32, 113, 118–9, 122, 156, 172–3, 176, 178, 179, 181, 183, 184–7, 189–90, 195–6. *See also* "remains, the"; "yet-to-come, the"
Dimock, Wai-chee, 20, 33
Dostoevsky, Fyodor. *See The Brothers Karamazov*
Douglass, Frederick: and oratory, 15, 127–48, 169–70; "The Heroic Slave," 124–7, 130–2, 137, 146; *The Narrative of the Life . . .* , 130–4, 139–41, 146, 152, 157; *My Bondage and My Freedom*, 132, 140–2; and John Brown, 178–81, 186–7; mentioned, 2, 123, 151, 191
Doyle, James P., 188
Drinnon, Richard, 109
Du Bois, W. E. B., 181
Durfee, Harold A., 86–8

Eaglestone, Robert, 164
Eden, America as, 17–8, 23, 30, 35
Edwards, Elizabeth, 160
egology. *See* Same, the
Eiselein, Gregory, 196–8
Emerson, Ralph Waldo, 173, 183
Engell, James, 39, 40
Enlightenment rationalism, 19–20, 28, 42, 50, 52, 102, 104–6, 111, 115
ethics: and politics/history, 2, 8, 12–3, 60, 66–7, 69–79, 83–4, 86–90, 92, 93, 145, 182, 184–6, 190, 192, 198; as disruption, 4, 7, 10, 12, 15–6, 20, 32–4, 36–7, 47–9, 52–3, 57, 78, 81, 90, 92–3, 96, 107, 123, 124–30, 133, 136–7, 139, 146, 152, 165–6, 169, 176, 182, 186, 194–6. *See also* Levinas, Emmanuel

Fabian, Johannes, 111
face of the Other, 4, 5, 7, 10, 12, 13–4, 15, 20, 35, 37, 42, 44–9, 52, 62–3, 65, 68, 86–90, 96, 107–8, 119–20, 122–3, 125–6, 129, 132, 134, 136–7, 142, 144–7, 150, 155, 158, 160–1, 163–9, 171, 175–6, 182, 188, 189, 196, 197–8. *See also* Levinas, Emmanuel
Fanon, Franz, 98
Finkelman, Paul, 102–3, 174
Fliegelman, Jay, 119–21
Foner, Eric, 66n
Franklin, Benjamin, 18
freedom: versus justice, 1–2, 4–7, 10–5, 20–1, 33–4, 41–2, 47–50, 52–3, 56, 62, 74, 81, 84–5, 90, 95–6, 106, 113, 116, 121–3, 141, 148, 194, 198; and property, 21–5, 55–6, 57, 82, 96, 98, 105. *See also* ethics
"fugitive pose" (Vizenor), 124, 127n, 138, 165–6, 169–71

Garrison, William Lloyd, 132–4, 142–4, 146
Gates, Henry Louis, 128n, 132, 134, 141
Green, Rayna, 159
Gustafson, Thomas, 85–6

Hamilton, Alexander, 76
Hegel, Georg, 21–3, 71–2, 92, 99
Heidegger, Martin, 3
Himmler, Heinrich, 8, 12
Holbo, Christine, 19–20, 37–41, 45–6, 51
Honig, Bonnie, 116–9
Hopkins, Sarah Winnemucca: oratory of, 15–6, 127, 128, 148–52; as "betrayer" of race and culture, 128, 149–50, 159–60, 162, 168, 171; and eastern suffragists, 148n; life of, 149–50, 152, 154, 158; as Indian princess, 150–2, 157–60, 162, 170; *Life among the Piutes*, 151–4, 156; as trickster, 160–1,

170–1; mentioned, 2, 123. *See also* Paiutes; photography
Howe, Julia Ward, 173
Hutcheson, Frances, 101

Ishi, 153–4, 153n, 157–8

"Jack the Blaster" (Spence), 75–6, 85
Jefferson, Thomas: and African Americans, 1–2, 94–5, 102–5, 107, 113–5, 121, 123; Declaration of Independence, 1–2, 15, 94–102, 113, 116–22; *Notes on Virginia*, 15, 102–15; life of, 94–5, 103; and Native Americans, 102–3, 105, 107, 108–13, 108n, 114, 115, 120–1, 123; mentioned, 55, 56, 58, 63, 64, 169. *See also* "American mind"
Johnson, Nathan, 157
Jordan, Winthrop, 115
Joyner, Charles, 195
justice. *See* freedom

Keane, John, 75

Lang, Beryl, 8n, 16
Langston, Charles H., 172–3
Larkin, Edward, 79–82
Lee, Henry, 1n, 95, 96n
Lee, Robert E., 174
Levinas, Emmanuel: life of, 2–3; general philosophy of ethics of, 3–16; *Totality and Infinity*, 3–7, 9–15, 25–6, 28, 34, 37, 46, 48, 50, 52, 61, 86–8, 102, 133–6, 140, 142, 144–5, 155–6, 176, 181–4, 188, 192; *Otherwise than Being*, 8–9, 42–4, 48; and language, 14, 46, 65, 67–8, 87–8, 123, 134–6, 140, 145–6, 155–6, 176, 181, 183–4, 189; *Of God Who Comes to Mind*, 45, 63, 65, 69, 105–7, 121–2, 147, 190, 192, 194, 198n; "immemorial past," 61–3, 65, 67; *Entre Nous*, 64–5, 88–9, 92, 106–8, 110, 123, 136–7, 145–6, 189–90, 192, 195, 198; and art, 160–6. *See also* anti-Semitism; face of the Other; freedom; obligation, ethical; ontology; Same, the; "substitution"; "third party, the"; "yet-to-come, the"
Lincoln, Abraham, 102, 180–1, 183, 185
Locke, John, 21, 23–4
Logan, Chief, 111–3

Marcel, Gabriel, 3
Marx, Karl, 92, 114
Mason, James M., 177–8, 186
McGlone, Robert E., 191
Momaday, N. Scott, 125n, 132, 155–6
murder. *See* violence

names/naming, 98, 136, 152–7, 168–9. *See also* Douglass, Frederick; Hopkins, Sarah Winnemucca; Ishi; Momaday, N. Scott
Native Americans, 2, 5, 6, 7, 9, 12, 15, 16, 27, 29, 30–4, 51–3, 55, 78, 102–3, 105, 107, 108–13, 108n, 114, 115, 120–1, 123, 128–9, 133, 148–71. *See also* Crèvecoeur, J. Hector St. John de; Hopkins, Sarah Winnemucca; Ishi; Jefferson, Thomas; Logan, Chief; Momaday, N. Scott; Paiutes; Pocahontas; Vizenor, Gerald
natural-rights theory, 21, 62–3, 67, 69–72, 74–5, 77, 101, 133
Nazism (National Socialism). *See* anti-Semitism; Himmler, Heinrich
Neel, Eric, 36n
Newton, Isaac, 104

Oates, Stephen B., 173–8, 183, 188, 191, 194–5
obligation, ethical, 4, 6–7, 11–3, 14, 16, 35, 36n, 43–7, 49, 62–3, 65–7, 73, 80, 85–7, 89–93, 96, 132, 137, 146–8, 151, 161, 163–4, 166, 182, 190, 192–4, 198. *See also* ethics; face of the Other
Ong, Walter J., 137–9, 144
ontology, 3–7, 9–11, 13, 25–9, 32, 34, 37, 71, 72, 100, 105–6, 122, 138, 156, 183
optics. *See anschauung*
Other, the. *See* face of the Other

Paine, Thomas: *Common Sense*, 15, 53, 56, 57–61, 69, 92, 96; *Rights of Man*, 15, 54–5, 56, 60, 61–2, 64, 67, 68, 69, 74–5, 85, 92, 96; life of, 54–6, 67, 75, 79–82; and African Americans, 63–4, 77–8, 87–8; "African Slavery in America," 63–7; *The Age of Reason*, 67–9; "Dissertations on Government," 75–7; "Letter to George Washington," 79–84; and language, 85–6, 88, 92–3; mentioned, 2
Paiutes, 128, 149, 152, 154–7, 158, 160, 162–4
Pearce, Roy Harvey, 15, 27, 29, 31, 112
Pelmas, Sarah, 121
Peperzak, Adriaan T., 3–5, 8–9, 10–1, 14–5, 41, 44, 135–6, 146–7
performativity, 15–6, 18, 26, 56, 84, 97, 111–3, 116–22, 124–52, 157–9, 161, 167–70, 175–6, 183, 186
Peterson, Merrill, 114
Philbrick, Thomas, 19, 20, 23, 34
photography, 16, 151, 157–71. *See also* Hopkins, Sarah Winnemucca
Plato, 72
Plumstead, A. W., 17–8
Pocahontas, 149, 150, 159
Potter, David M., 174–6, 180–1
Price, Richard, 96

Randall, John H., 105
Rapaport, Herman, 164–9
Raynal, Abbé, 19, 56
Read, Alan, 129–30, 135–8, 148–9
"remains, the" (Derrida), 32–4, 32n, 113, 155, 158
representation, 33–4, 37, 47, 49, 53, 62, 83, 108n, 119, 128, 129, 136–7, 141, 145–6, 155, 160–1, 170, 183. *See also* performativity; photography
responsibility. *See* obligation, ethical
Rousseau, Jean-Jacques, 58
Rush, Benjamin, 54

Same, the, 4–7, 9–13, 18–20, 19n, 25–7, 34, 40–1, 43, 51–2, 86–7, 96, 100, 101, 105–7, 110–1, 120, 128, 134, 145–6, 181. *See also* face of the Other
Sartre, Jean-Paul, 3
"savage, the." *See* Native Americans
Schechner, Richard, 127, 135
Scherer, Joanna, 151, 158–62
Self, the. *See* Same, the
Sherman, William Tecumseh, 179
slavery, 22, 27, 38, 41, 46, 49–50, 63–7, 71–3, 77–8, 87, 94–5, 102, 113–4, 124–6, 129, 130–43, 146, 147–8, 152, 169, 170, 172–5, 177–80, 182–7, 190–1, 193, 196–7. *See also* abolitionism; African Americans; Brown, John; Douglass, Frederick
Slotkin, Richard, 30–1
Smith, Adam, 37
Smith, Sidonie, 134
Socrates, 6, 165
Spence, Thomas. *See* "Jack the Blaster"
Strauss, Leo, 70–4
"substitution": in Burke, 39, 41–2; in Levinas: 41–4, 87, 164, 167, 194
sympathy (Burke), 37–49

Tagg, John, 160–2
theatre. *See* performativity
"third party, the" (Levinas), 14, 64, 67, 86, 146–8, 190–3
Thomas, Wynn, 35n
Thoreau, Henry David, 181, 197
Tocqueville, Alexis de, 115–6

violence: ontological, 3–6, 10–1, 28, 30–2, 37, 86–7, 107, 110, 153n, 155–7, 162–5, 167, 172–3, 181, 185; murder, 8–9, 11–12, 13, 34–7, 40–2, 46–50, 63–6, 78, 88, 110–1, 122–3, 132, 145, 167, 168–9, 170, 177–8, 184–6, 188–9, 192, 194, 195, 198; legitimate, 15–6, 97, 130, 172–3, 178–80, 184, 186–91, 196–7. *See also* Brown, John; Derrida, Jacques; Levinas, Emmanuel
Vizenor, Gerald, 12, 108, 111, 113, 120–1, 127n,

153–8, 153n, 165–6, 170–1. *See also* "fugitive pose"

Wald, Priscilla, 129, 133
Walker, Peter, 140–4
Washington, George, 79–80, 82–3
Whitman, Walt, 35, 35n
Whittier, John Greenleaf, 197–8
Wills, Gary, 100–4
Wilson, James, 101

Winnemucca, Sarah. *See* Hopkins, Sarah Winnemucca
Wise, Henry A., 177, 186
Wong, Hertha D. Sweet, 152
Wood, Gordon S., 76–7, 82
Wyatt-Brown, Bertram, 178, 182, 187

Yarborough, Richard, 130–1
"yet-to-come, the," 56, 69, 184, 186–7, 193, 198

www.ingramcontent.com/pod-product-compliance
Lightning Source LLC
Chambersburg PA
CBHW060952230426
43665CB00015B/2162